W9-AGU-114

Recipes from Historic TEXAS

Recipes from Historic
TEXAS

A Restaurant Guide and Cookbook

LINDA & STEVE BAUER

Taylor Trade Publishing
Lanham • New York • Oxford

First Taylor Trade Publishing edition 2003

This Taylor Trade Publishing hardcover edition of *Recipes from Historic Texas* is an original publication. It is published by arrangement with the authors.

Published by Taylor Trade Publishing
A Member of the Rowman & Littlefield Publishing Group
4501 Forbes Boulevard, Suite 200
Lanham, Maryland 20706

Distributed by National Book Network

Interior design by Piper E. Furbush

Library of Congress Cataloging-in-Publication Data
Bauer, Linda.
Recipes from historic Texas : a restaurant guide and cookbook / Linda and Steve Bauer. — 1st Taylor Trade Publishing ed.
p. cm.
Includes index.
ISBN 1-58979-048-0 (cloth : alk. paper)
1. Cookery—Texas. 2. Restaurants—Texas—Guidebooks. I. Bauer, Steve, 1943– II. Title.
TX715 .B34923 2003
641.5'09764—dc21
2003005843

∞™ The paper used in this publication meets the minimum requirements of American National Standard for Information Sciences—Permanence of Paper for Printed Library Materials, ANSI/NISO Z39.48–1992.
Manufactured in the United States of America.

Dedication

This book is dedicated to our sons Michael and Christopher, who share our love of travel and good food. Your presence has made our journeys infinitely more fun.

We also want to thank all of the wonderful proprietors and staff at the restaurants featured in this book. Your creative cuisine and excellent service are surpassed only by your concern for your patrons.

STATE OF TEXAS
OFFICE OF THE GOVERNOR

Greetings:

Welcome to the wonderful world of dining in historic Texas.

America's most beautiful and unique restaurants make a home in our great state, home to the finest of culinary traditions and an industry of professionals focused on excellence.

Home to unique cuisine, renowned the world over for its distinctive flair, Texas' culinary delights reflect the diversity of the Lone Star State.

Eat and enjoy!

Sincerely,

Rick Perry

Rick Perry
Governor

Oklahoma
New Mexico
Arkansas
Mexico
Gulf of Mexico
Panhandle Plains
Prairies and Lakes
Piney Woods
Big Bend Country
Hill Country
Gulf Coast
South Texas Plains
TEXAS
The Lone Star State
Area: 266,807 Square Miles
Population: 20,851,820
State Flower: Bluebonnet
State Bird: Mockingbird
State Tree: Pecan
0
100
200
Miles
AMARILLO
LUBBOCK
EL PASO
FORT WORTH
DALLAS
AUSTIN
SAN ANTONIO
HOUSTON
GALVESTON
CORPUS CHRISTI

CONTENTS

INTRODUCTION

The lure of Texas is world renowned because it is the largest state in size in the contiguous United States. An area of 266,807 square miles encompasses beaches, forests, mountains and lakes. At 21 million, it boasts one of the highest populations in the country, and includes some of the largest cities in the nation such as Houston, Dallas, Fort Worth, Austin and San Antonio. Friendly Texans have a "howdy neighbor" attitude and it shines through at every opportunity.

The saying, "Texas: It's like a whole other country," is a true statement considering the vast expanses and travel opportunities available. In 1999, travel and tourism accounted for a whopping $36.7 billion of the state's economy. Where else could one tour some of the oldest missions in the New World, visit a working cattle ranch bigger than the state of Rhode Island, enjoy all types of professional sports, play on challenging golf courses, view the world's most prestigious piano competition and dine in the best restaurants? It's no accident when they say "dining out" is a regular pastime in Texas.

Only Texas has the armadillo as the state mammal, the bluebonnet as the state flower, the mockingbird as the state bird and the pecan as the state tree. This uniqueness, combined with great weather, many historic sites, diverse land formations and friendly people beckon snowbirds from the North to spend the winters in the Lone Star State and, perhaps, stay forever.

Texas has been blessed with Mexican, German, Polish and Czech immigrants, who built the state. The Lone Star State is uniquely comprised of 27 cultural and ethnic groups, all working together to provide a special form of southern hospitality. In fact, "Texas" is a derivation of "tejas," meaning friendship. This attitude is evident throughout the state and especially at the historic restaurants, where generations have lovingly passed down the properties. Owners want to share their stories with patrons and are eager to aid others in enjoying their often award-winning cuisine from barbecue and Tex-Mex family secrets to elegant dining.

Why not please your palate, nourish your mind and enjoy a bit of unique Texas history? From a sanitarium, to a winery, to a church, to a funeral home, the rich fabric of Texas has been preserved and is available to diners in some of the best restaurants in the country. *Recipes from Historic Texas* combines stories from the past with enticing recipes and information for travel, cooking and contacting the establishments. Elegant homes, warehouses, factories and mercantile stores have taken on a new life as restaurants, preserving their historic qualities and providing diners a bit of nostalgia with their meals.

In our eighteen years of writing international food and travel columns, we have been amazed at the way an excellent restaurant with a special atmosphere enhances any dining experience or vacation. The combination of a historic venue combined with interesting cuisine—whether it is ethnic,

Southwest, classic or family style—is a dining adventure of immense proportions. How exciting it is to visit a former stagecoach stop, bank, historic hotel, ranch or exclusive Victorian home and enjoy a delicious meal.

To Texans the bumper stickers are serious business that extol, "TEXAS—I wasn't born here, but got here as quick as I could!" Texans are proud of their colorful and important history. This volume is an effort to help visitors, locals and gourmands enjoy some of the finest food, and the most interesting restaurants in our country.

Simply choose an area in one of the seven regions and decide which historic restaurant to visit. Black-and-white, pen-and-ink drawings, or pictures of the property are included to depict the past. The restaurant is then described with a page or more of history. The location and method of contact is also offered and several recipes, which are on the menu, are included. After a visit, the diner may wish to recreate the dish at home. Our experience has shown that many people love to read cookbooks while others like travel guides. This book is a way to please both and allow singles, couples and families to learn a great deal of information about Texas history and enjoy the bounty of Texas-grown produce, livestock and chefs.

Most of the restaurants are in the moderate range, but they do vary. We attempted to include all ranges. If cost is a factor, please phone for prices.

Remember—Many of the restaurants in *Recipes from Historic Texas* are very popular, and it is important to CALL AHEAD FOR RESERVATIONS!! Bon Appetit!

1

Gulf Coast

The Texas Riviera. In this area Indians roamed the sandy beaches, coastal prairies and grassy dunes. With the Spaniards and French, colonizing, converting and exploring began. In the mid-19th century Captain Richard King built a ranch that would be the envy of cattle barons throughout the world. Galveston became known as the "Wall Street of the Southwest" due to cotton. The Great Texas Coastal Birding Trail attracts thousands of birders each year. The beaches, ports and water sports such as regattas, windsurfing, deep-sea fishing and swimming are all part of the fun. Major cities include Houston, Galveston, Corpus Christi, Beaumont, Brownsville and South Padre Island.

HOTEL GALVEZ

Galveston

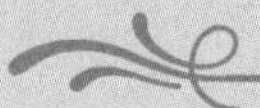
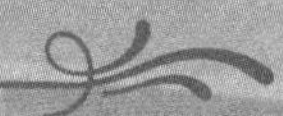

When Hotel Galvez opened in 1911, William H. Taft was president of the United States. Two dozen eggs cost 35¢ and the latest fashion for women was wash skirts. Today, Hotel Galvez stands proudly as "Queen of the Gulf," fully restored to its original glamour, while continuing to offer gracious hospitality, old-world charm and new-world conveniences.

After the devastation of the Great Storm of 1900, a group of prominent businessmen, dedicated to the economic recovery of Galveston Island, developed a public awareness campaign leading to the construction of Hotel Galvez. Galvestonians were in desperate need of a luxury, beachfront hotel to fill the void that was left when the Beach Hotel burned down in 1898.

At a cost of more than $1 million, the firm of Mauran & Russell of St. Louis, Missouri, designed and built the six-story Spanish Colonial Revival Hotel, which offered 275 elegant guest rooms, some with private baths. Named for Bernardo de Galvez, the Spanish colonial governor who first chartered the Texas Gulf Coast and for whom the city is named, the luxury hotel was billed by *Hotel Monthly* in 1912 as one of the "best arranged and most richly furnished seaside hotels in America." The public areas featured a barbershop, candy shop, drugstore, soda fountain and Gentleman's Bar & Grille. Roller chairs lined the front of the hotel for those wanting to take trips along the famous Seawall Boulevard.

In 1918 Hotel Galvez hosted more than 400 guests each day, while room rates started at $2 per night. In the 1920s the first bathing beauty contests in the nation were held at the hotel, with future movie stars Joan Blondell and Dorothy Lamour as participants. During the 1920s and 1930s Hotel Galvez became known as the "Playground of the Southwest," as hundreds of dignitaries and celebrities visited the hotel. Notable guests have included Presidents Franklin D. Roosevelt, Dwight D. Eisenhower, Lyndon B. Johnson and John F. Kennedy, as well as General Douglas MacArthur, Phil Harris, Alice Faye, Frank Sinatra, Jimmy Stewart and Howard Hughes.

On October 3, 1940, W. L. Moody, Jr. acquired Hotel Galvez. During World War II, the hotel served as a living and working facility for the U.S. Coast Guard. In 1950 Moody's hotel chain, The National Affiliated Hotels, added the motel to adjoin the main building on the east side.

After World War II prohibition caused Galvestonians to revert to rum running—allowing those who risked it to make tremendous fortunes, fostering investments in other illicit activities. Bordellos existed in a four-block area of the downtown section of Galveston, and casinos and dinner clubs arose, attracting people from all over the country. The Texas Rangers and State Attorney General outlawed gambling and its related activities in 1957.

In 1965 the owners spent more than $1 million to refurbish Hotel Galvez. In 1971, it was acquired by Harvey O. McCarthy, who jointly owned it with Dr. Leon Bromberg. Together they spent more than $1 million in modern improvements and renovations.

In 1978 well-known heart surgeon Denton Cooley purchased Hotel Galvez after a longstanding sentimental attachment to it. Not only had he stayed there as a child and a medical student, but also his parents had spent their wedding night at the hotel in 1916. Soon after he bought the hotel, Cooley sold half of his interest to Archie Bennett, Jr., president of the Mariner Corporation. In 1980 they spent the entire year and more than $12 million renovating the hotel, and it was then named to the National Register of Historic Places.

The most recent renovation was brought about through the efforts of Galveston preservationists and developers George and Cynthia Mitchell, who attained ownership of Hotel Galvez in March 1993. Since June 1, 1998, Wyndham International as Wyndham Historic Hotels has managed the hotel.

Today Hotel Galvez has undergone a full renovation, recapturing its original splendor with some dramatic new additions. Towering palms and lushly landscaped grounds surround a restored grand seawall entrance. Guests can relax by the tropical pool with swim-up bar. Each of the newly renovated 224 guest rooms and seven suites offer panoramic views of historic Galveston and ocean vistas. Bernardo's, located inside the Hotel Galvez, offers a wide variety of food choices on their menu.

Bernardo's in the Hotel Galvez, 2024 Seawall Blvd., Galveston, Texas, 77550, (409) 765-7721 x145, or visit Wyndham on the Internet at www.wyndham.com. Breakfast is served from 6:30 to 11 a.m. Monday through Saturday and Sundays from 6:30 to 10:30 a.m. Lunch is served from 11 a.m. to 2 p.m. daily, and dinner is served from 5:30 to 10 p.m. Monday through Friday and Saturdays from 5:30 to 11 p.m.

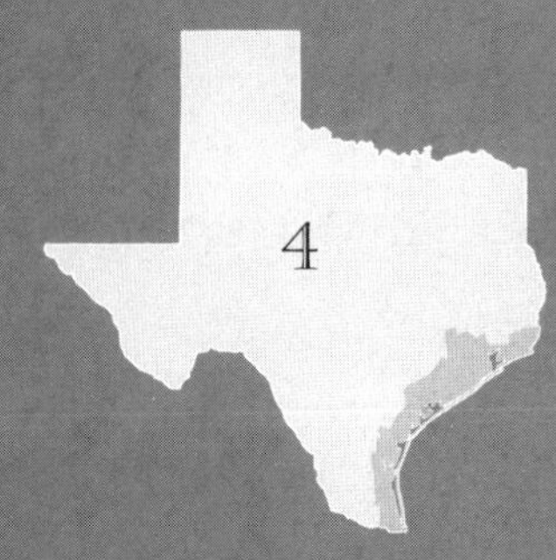

2–3 raw fresh baby artichokes

1–2 radishes

1/2 shallot

1/2 tablespoon flat leaf parsley, torn into small pieces

1 tablespoon fresh lemon juice

1 tablespoon extra virgin olive oil

dash kosher salt & fresh ground black pepper

1/8 ounce shaved Parmigiano-Reggiano

1 tablespoon balsamic vinegar

1 tablespoon extra virgin olive oil

3 red teardrop tomato quarters

3 yellow teardrop tomato quarters

1/8 ounce shaved Parmigiano-Reggiano (to sprinkle on top)

Shaved Artichoke Salad

with Parmigiano-Reggiano

Peel and trim the artichokes and reserve in water laced with lime juice until needed. When needed, using a mandolin, shave the artichokes very thinly into a small stainless steel bowl. Add the torn parsley leaves, lemon juice, olive oil, salt, pepper and 1/8 ounce Parmigiano-Reggiano. Toss gently to coat completely. Mound the artichoke mixture in the center of the plate. Combine the balsamic vinegar and olive oil to make a simple broken vinaigrette. Drizzle this around the artichoke salad onto the plate. Garnish the salad with the teardrop tomato quarters. Place the remaining Parmigiano-Reggiano on the artichoke salad.

YIELD

1 portion

Meyer Lemon Tart

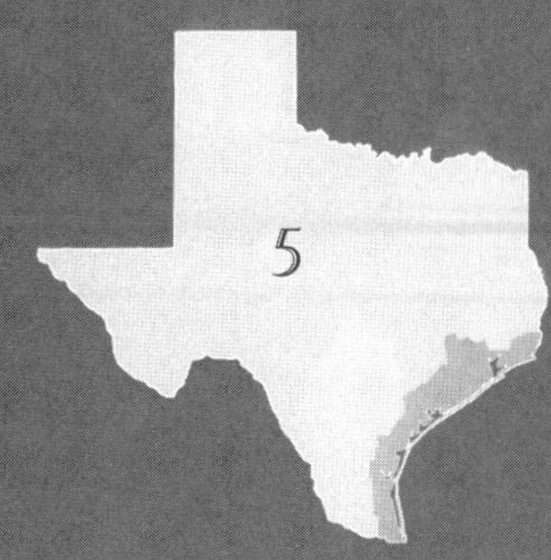

FOR THE CRUST:

1 3/4 cups unsalted butter cut into pieces at room temperature

1 1/2 cups powdered sugar, sifted

3 eggs

6 cups flour

1/4 + 1/8 teaspoon baking powder

additional butter, melted for pans

FOR THE FILLING:

1 cup unsalted butter, melted

12 Meyer lemons

12 eggs

3 3/4 cups granulated sugar

TO PREPARE THE CRUST:

In the mixer, combine the butter and sugar on low speed. Beat until smooth, about 3 minutes. Add the eggs and beat until creamy. Using a rubber spatula, fold in the flour and baking powder just until incorporated. Then beat on low speed until the dough is evenly mixed and clings together—2 to 3 minutes. Shape the dough into 3 balls, wrap tightly in plastic wrap and refrigerate for at least 2 hours. Bring to room temperature to use. Preheat oven to 400 degrees. Brush the bottoms and sides of the pans with the additional butter.

On a lightly floured surface, roll out the dough into a round 12-inch circle about 1/8-inch thick. Drape the dough over a rolling pin and transfer to the prepared tart pan. Unwrap the dough from the pin and press it gently into the pan. Roll the pin over the top of the pan to remove excess dough. Line the pan with waxed paper and add pie weights and bake until the pastry is half cooked—about 15 minutes. Remove from the oven and immediately remove the weights and waxed paper.

TO PREPARE THE FILLING:

Grate the zest from the lemons, cut the lemons in half and squeeze the juice through a strainer into a measuring cup. You should have about 1 1/2 cups of juice. Add the lemon juice and eggs to the zest and whisk until blended. Add

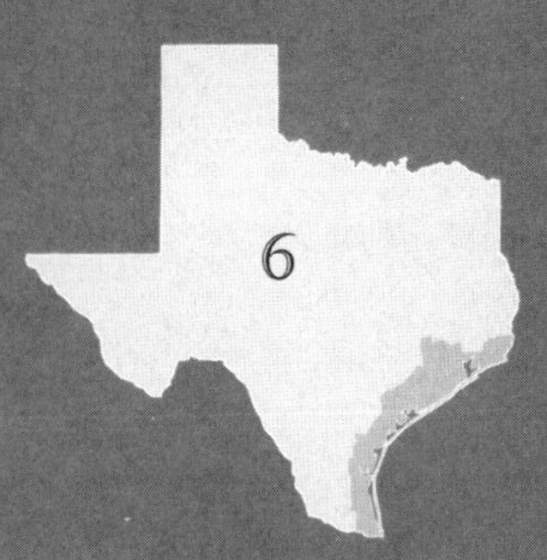

the sugar, and mix until well combined. Stir in the cup of melted butter.

ASSEMBLY:

Pour the filling mixture into the warm tart shells and return to the oven. Bake until the filling is set and the edges are golden brown—about 20 minutes.

When the tart is done, transfer it to a rack and remove the pan sides and cool completely. Serve at room temperature with raspberry coulis and garnish.

YIELD

Three 9-inch tarts or 12 4-inch individual tartlets

Grilled Asparagus with Gazpacho Vinaigrette

Trim, peel and blanch the asparagus, then toss with the olive oil. Season with kosher salt and freshly ground black pepper. Place the asparagus in the center of the plate. Ladle the gazpacho vinaigrette over the center of the asparagus spears. Garnish the plate by scattering the eggplant croutons, diced tomato, celery, red onion and parsley around the plate.

YIELD

1 portion

FOR THE GAZPACHO VINAIGRETTE:

Here you are essentially making a gazpacho. As needed you combine some of the gazpacho with additional lemon juice and extra virgin olive oil and then blend with a hand blender to froth it up. Cut the cucumber into smaller pieces and place in a food processor or blender with the peeled tomatoes, shallots, lemon juice, tomato juice, parsley, garlic and green onion. Pulse to puree. Remove from processor, taste and add salt, pepper and Tabasco to taste. To finish the vinaigrette take 1 cup of gazpacho and add the juice of one lemon and 1 cup of extra virgin olive oil and blend using a hand blender until thickened and frothy.

YIELD

6–8 portions

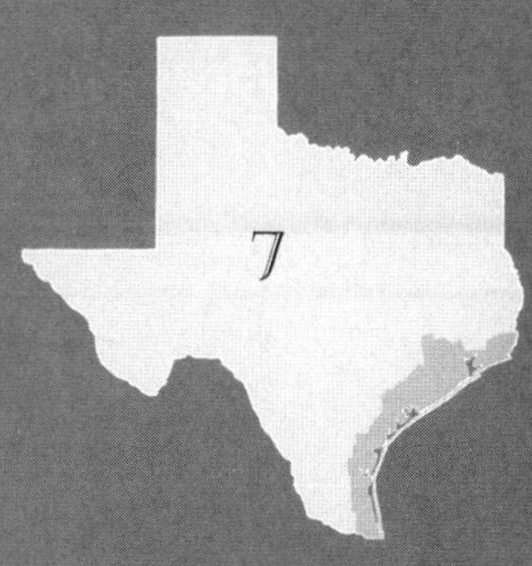

8 ounces asparagus, blanched, trimmed and peeled

1 teaspoon extra virgin olive oil

kosher salt and fresh ground black pepper, to taste

1 1/2 ounces gazpacho vinaigrette (recipe follows)

1 ounce eggplant croutons (recipe follows)

1/2 ounce cucumber, with Parisienne scoop

1/2 ounce diced, peeled and seeded tomato

1 teaspoon celery, very fine brunoise

1 teaspoon red onion, very fine brunoise

1/2 teaspoon flat leaf parsley, torn into small pieces

FOR THE GAZPACHO VINAIGRETTE:

6 Roma tomatoes, peeled

1 cucumber, peeled and seeded

3 shallots

4 lemons, juice strained of seeds

1 cup tomato juice

2 tablespoons flat leaf parsley, chopped

2 garlic cloves

1/2 cup green onion, green part

(continued on next page)

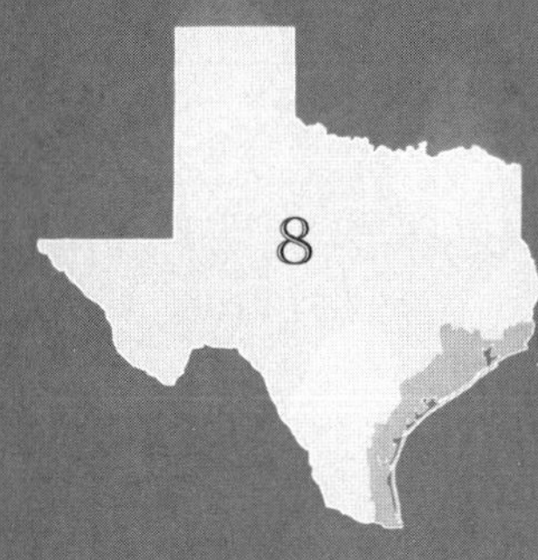

dash salt & fresh ground black pepper

1/2 tablespoon Tabasco

4 cups extra virgin olive oil

4 lemons juiced

FOR THE EGGPLANT CROUTONS:

2 cups eggplant croutons

1 cup milk

1 cup semolina

dash salt

FOR THE EGGPLANT CROUTONS:

Dredge the cubed eggplant (no skin) in the milk and then in the semolina. Deep fry at 375 degrees until lightly browned. Season immediately with salt.

YIELD

6–8 portions

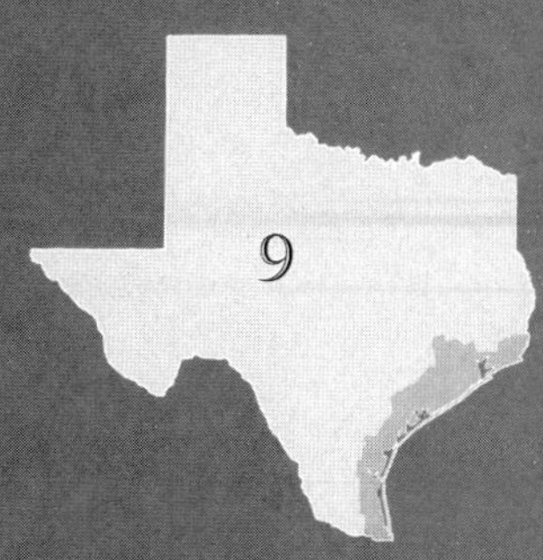

Fettuccine Primavera Full

Heat the olive oil in a hot sauté pan. Add the green onions, carrots, bell pepper, leeks and garlic. Sauté briefly until just tender. Add the peas, asparagus, pasta, chicken stock, mixed chopped herbs and parsley. Top with Parmigiano-Reggiano.

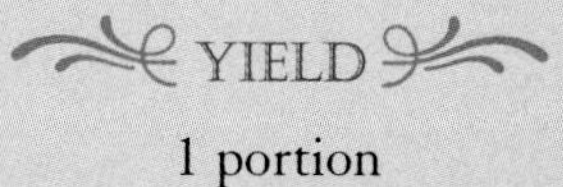

1 portion

- 1 tablespoon olive oil
- 2 ounces green onions, white part only, cut into 1 1/2 inch lengths
- 1/2 ounce carrots, very fine julienne
- 1/2 ounce red bell pepper, very fine julienne
- 1/2 ounce leeks, very fine julienne
- 1/2 teaspoon garlic, sliced very thinly
- 1 ounce fresh English peas
- 1 ounce asparagus tips and stems peeled and chopped
- 6 ounces fettuccine, cooked al dente
- 3/4 cup good chicken stock
- 1 tablespoon rosemary, chopped
- 1 tablespoon flat leaf parsley, chopped
- 1 tablespoon thyme, chopped
- dash salt and fresh ground black pepper
- 2 red teardrop tomatoes, split
- 2 yellow teardrop tomatoes, split
- 1/8 ounce shaved Parmigiano-Reggiano
- chopped fresh herbs to garnish

THE LANCASTER HOTEL

Houston

At the corner of Texas Avenue and Louisiana in the heart of Houston's Theater District, stands an elegantly understated building that, by current downtown standards, is small at only 12 stories high. An uninformed passerby might miss it entirely, or assume that behind the street-friendly, burgundy-canopied exterior is an exclusive private club. And that is just the impression Bill Sharman intended to create when he and his partners undertook restoration on The Auditorium Hotel in 1983.

Built in 1926, The Auditorium Hotel was a favorite stopover through the 1930s for well-known performing artists and entertainers. Some of the old hotel's most colorful and lively times were during World War II, when the hotel converted the basement into a USO entertainment center, similar to those in New York and Los Angeles. Servicemen were drawn to the area by the various live performance shows by visiting stars such as Helen Hayes, Fay Bainter and Gene Autry, who clomped down the stairs on his horse. After the war, the space was closed and now serves as the wine cellar for Clive's Bar & Grill next door.

When The Auditorium Hotel opened in 1926, it was touted as state-of-the-art for innovation and comfort, advertising itself in *The Houston Chronicle* as "Houston's newest hotel—200 rooms, 200 baths. Every room with ceiling fans, tub, shower and circulation ice water." The rates were $2 and $2.50 per single room.

By the time Sharman and his group came along in 1983, the grand old landmark had fallen on hard times. Their $8 million restoration, which created 96 rooms where there had been 200, saved the decaying hotel from the fate of many of its Texas Avenue peers—the wrecking ball. Renovations included The Bistro, a 65-seat restaurant that stole its chef from the well-known Café Anne. The hotel was designated a national landmark in 1984.

The Lancaster Hotel, 701 Texas Avenue, Houston, Texas 77002, (713) 228-9500. Or visit www.lancaster.com. The Bistro serves breakfast Monday through Friday from 6:30 a.m. to 11 a.m. and Saturday and Sunday from 7:30 a.m. to 1 p.m. Lunch is served daily from 11 a.m. to 5 p.m. and dinner is served daily from 5 to 11 p.m.

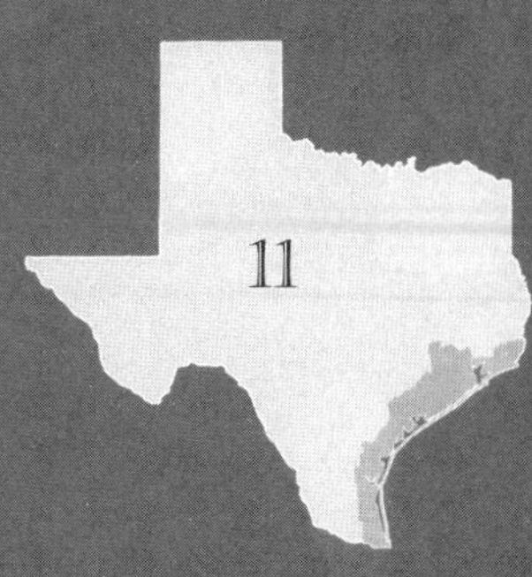

Lancaster Candied Walnuts

2 egg whites

1 pound walnut halves

1 1/2 tablespoons cold water

1 1/2 cups granulated sugar

1/2 teaspoon ground cloves

1/2 teaspoon allspice

1/2 teaspoon ground cinnamon

1 teaspoon salt

Lightly whisk egg whites in small bowl and set aside. In large saucepan, mix together water, sugar, spices and salt. Heat and stir until sugar dissolves. Cool slightly (until warm to the touch). Fold in egg whites. Add the walnuts and coat evenly with sugar mixture. Allow the coated nuts to drain slightly if there is too much coating. Spray baking sheet with a good coating of high-quality, non-stick spray. Spread walnut halves in a single layer and bake at 250 degrees for about an hour. Cool and store at room temperature in a sealed container.

These walnuts are great served alone at a cocktail party or as a Christmas or hostess gift. The Bistro uses them in their classic Spinach Salad.

YIELD

1 pound candied nuts

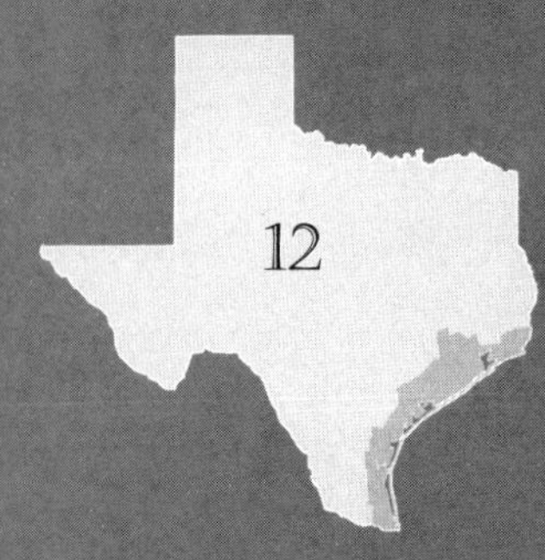

Roasted Corn and Leek Chowder

- 2 small leeks, white part only, rough chopped and washed
- 3 cups corn kernels, fresh or frozen
- 1/4 cup olive oil
- 3 slices bacon, rough chopped
- 1 teaspoon chopped garlic
- 1/2 teaspoon fresh thyme (or 1/4 teaspoon dried)
- 1 teaspoon fresh tarragon (or 1/2 teaspoon dried)
- dash salt and pepper
- 1/4 cup chicken or vegetable stock
- 1/4 cup butter, melted
- 1/4 cup flour
- 1/2 to 3/4 cup heavy cream
- 1 bunch chives, chopped

Preheat oven to 350 degrees. Place chopped leeks and corn kernels on baking sheet and toss with olive oil. Roast for 10 to 15 minutes until lightly browned. In medium saucepot over medium heat, sauté chopped bacon for 3 minutes. Add roasted corn and leeks, tarragon and thyme and season lightly with salt and pepper. Cover and sweat for 3 to 4 minutes. Add stock and bring to a boil.

In small bowl, combine melted butter and flour and whisk until smooth to make a roux. Add roux to boiling soup and whisk until smooth. Reduce heat to low and simmer gently for 10 to 12 minutes. Remove from heat. Handling hot soup carefully, process in blender in batches until almost smooth. Pour back into saucepot and add cream. Adjust seasoning with salt and pepper. Keep hot until ready to serve. Sprinkle top of soup with chopped chives when served.

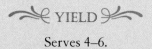

Serves 4–6.

MARK*S AMERICAN CUISINE

Houston

The building that currently houses the Mark*s restaurant was originally St. Matthews Church that opened in 1927. It remained so until World War II, after which the congregation of St. Matthews moved to a new building on Main Street where they are still located today.

During the war the vacant church was a broom factory. Sometime after the war the building served as the Alliance to the Blind. The building was closed for about 20 years, after which it was reported to have been reopened as a warehouse for tires.

In the early 1970s the building became a club/bar under a variety of names such as Gantry's, Pearl's Oyster Bar, and The Church. From 1985 to 1995 it was operated as a funky clothing shop called Dream Merchant. From 1995 to 1996 it was leased to a man who turned it into an Italian restaurant called Alfresco. After six months he decided to get out of the restaurant business and turned the property over to Mark Cox and his wife. They loved the 24-foot-high ceiling, the choir loft and the Gothic design, plus the new kitchen that had been built for the previous restaurant.

Mark*s opened in July of 1997. Mark Cox had spent years at Brennan's and was the Corporate Chef for the Vallone Restaurant Group. His following overwhelmed the 100 available seats, causing an extensive renovation of the deck area. Once this area was enclosed, they could accommodate 40 more guests for private parties or public overflow.

Mark*s received the International Wine Award for Excellence as well as being named a Distinguished Restaurant of North America recipient for 2001 and 2002 and the #1 spot for food in Houston by *Zagat Survey* for 2001 and 2002.

Mark*s, 1658 Westheimer, Houston, Texas 77006, (713) 523-3800, is open for lunch Monday through Friday from 11 a.m. until 2 p.m. They are open for dinner Monday through Thursday from 6 p.m. to 11 p.m., Friday from 5:30 p.m. to midnight, Saturday from 5 p.m. until midnight and Sunday from 5 p.m. until 10 p.m.

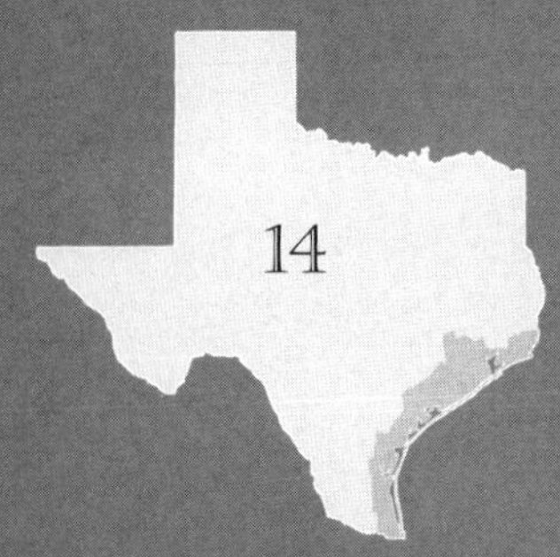

Sauté Curry Shrimp

with Cucumber Mango Salsa, Scallion Aioli

SCALLION AIOLI:

1/2 cup lemon juice

2 large egg yolks

1 tablespoon Dijon mustard

1 tablespoon water

2 bunches scallions (green part only) chopped fine

1 cup extra virgin olive oil

dash salt and pepper

CUCUMBER MANGO RELISH:

1 fresh mango, peeled, seeded and cut into medium pieces

2 tablespoons yellow onion, minced

1/4 cup red pepper, minced

1/4 cup cucumber, peeled, seeded, and minced

1/4 cup cilantro leaves, chopped

1 teaspoon Serrano pepper, minced

1 tablespoon fresh ginger, minced

5 tablespoons fresh lime juice

dash salt

SHRIMP:

1 pound 16–20 count shrimp, peeled, deveined and butterflied

1/2 teaspoon curry powder

dash salt and ground white pepper

4 tablespoons unsalted butter, softened

SCALLION AIOLI:

In a stainless steel bowl combine the lemon juice, one tablespoon water and the egg yolks. Place over a simmering saucepan of water, creating steam to lightly cook the egg yolk mixture. Stirring constantly, using a wire whisk, stir until the egg yolk/lemon juice mixture reaches 170 degrees as read on a small thermometer. This should take about 5 minutes. Transfer into a blender, combining the egg yolk mixture, mustard and scallions on high speed. Gradually, add olive oil in a steady stream and season with Tabasco.

Refrigerate until ready to use. Can be made two days ahead.

CUCUMBER MANGO RELISH:

Combine all ingredients in a small bowl. Season to taste. Reserve for service.

SHRIMP:

Sprinkle the shrimp with the curry powder and season with salt and pepper.

Over medium heat in a sauté pan, melt the butter. Sauté the shrimp until barely cooked—about 3 minutes. Remove from the heat. Serve atop the Cucumber Mango Relish. Drizzle with the Scallion Aioli sauce and serve.

Serves 4.

Cumin and Pumpkin Seed Dusted Snapper

with Tequila Lime Sauce

TEQUILA LIME SAUCE:

Combine all the ingredients except the lime zest and whisk lightly. Set aside.

SNAPPER:

To toast the pumpkin and cumin seeds, place together on a flat baking pan, spreading evenly. Bake in a 350-degree oven until the seeds begin to pop and become lightly golden brown. Allow to cool completely before crusting the snapper.

Season the snapper with salt and pepper on both sides. Press the presentation side only of the snapper into the flour, then lightly coat the flour-sided fillet with the prepared eggs. Proceed by pressing the coated side of the snapper into the toasted pumpkin seed mixture.

Using a 10-inch sauté skillet, heat half of the canola oil (4 tablespoons) until it is very warm. Place crusted side of the snapper into the sauté pan, and lightly sauté to a golden brown—about 1 1/2 to 2 minutes on both sides. Remove the fish from the pan and place into a baking dish. Repeat the process for the remaining two fillets. For serving, finish the snapper in a preheated 350-degree oven for 8–10 minutes. Remove from the oven and plate. Cover with the tequila lime sauce and sprinkle with lime zest.

Serves 4.

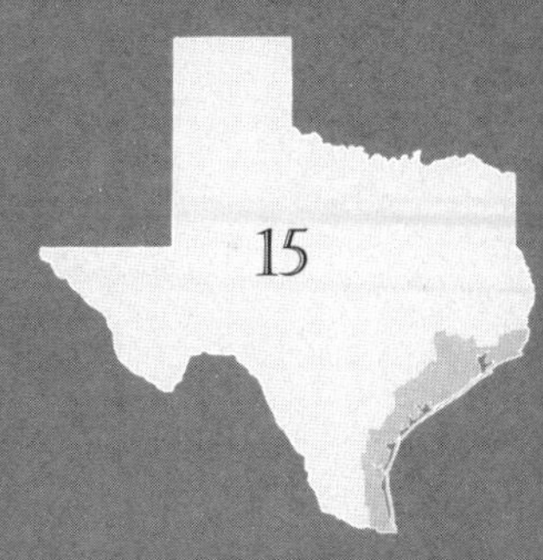

TEQUILA LIME SAUCE:

2 tablespoons lime juice

4 tablespoons tequila

2 tablespoons heavy cream

6 tablespoons unsalted butter, softened

1 tablespoon freshly grated lime zest

dash salt and pepper

SNAPPER:

4 fillets red snapper (5 ounces each)

dash salt and ground white pepper

1/2 cup all-purpose flour

2 eggs, lightly beaten

1 cup toasted petitas (unsalted pumpkin seeds)

2 tablespoons cumin seeds

8 tablespoons canola oil for sautéing

THE PIG STAND

Beaumont

If you have traveled the highways and byways of Texas for any period of time, you have probably run across a Pig Stand somewhere. It all started in Dallas when Jessie G. Kirby imagined a new approach to travel and eating. His thinking was prophetic; "People with cars are so lazy they don't want to get out of them to eat!" He convinced a Dallas physician, Ruben W. Jackson, to be a partner, and they erected a small, wood-framed sandwich stand next to the curb for convenient drive-up service; hence the term "curb service" was born.

It opened in September of 1921, and the original Pig Stand delighted everyone who owned a car with the novel idea of buying lunch and eating it in the comfort and privacy of your own automobile. The marriage between your private vehicle and "fast food" dining had begun. America's first drive-in restaurant was an instant hit.

Unfortunately, the Dallas location has been closed for some time now, as are more than 50 other locations from California to Florida. Of the seven remaining locations in Texas, the Beaumont Pig Stand offers a fascinating glimpse of the genesis of our current roadside culture.

Imagine yourself in a 1920s vintage auto. As you pull into the parking lot, a spirited, young waiter hops onto your running board to get a headstart on taking your order. In no time, you are referring to him as a "carhop" and the label sticks. He quickly returns with food and drink, turning your car into a picnic table on wheels.

The Calder Street Pig Stand is believed to be the nation's oldest circular drive-in, and it still offers curb service during weekdays at lunch. It also serves some very original dishes. Royce Hailey, who started in Dallas as a carhop at the Pig Stand, worked his way up to District Manager for several stores in Beaumont. One day he asked the Rainbow Bakery to slice their bread thicker. Unfortunately it would not fit in the toaster. One of the Pig Stand cooks suggested they butter both sides and cook it on the grill. Texas Toast was born, and is still a big hit today.

In Dallas, one of the cooks accidentally dropped a sliced onion into some breading batter. On a whim, he cooked it in hot oil and fried onion rings were added to the menu of every Pig Stand. Royce Hailey also created the chicken-fried steak sandwich in the 1940s in response to a national menu competition. He won first place and added to the legend of the Pig Stands.

Under Royce's leadership, the company also experimented with the first drive-through window and they were the first to use drive-in "rock 'n' roll" car canopies—metal awnings with bright neon lights and, of course, music.

Royce's son, Richard Hailey, is now the president of the company. He says they were "the first restaurant to use fluorescent lighting, back in the thirties, and were one of the first to use neon lights and air conditioning." The corporate motto, "America's Motor Lunch" was particularly appropriate. They were so successful that some of their customers today have been regulars for decades. Older couples often visit to sit in the same booth they used in high school many years ago.

Pig Stand #7 in San Antonio on Broadway was featured in scenes in *The Evening Star*, the sequel to Larry McMurtry's Academy Award-winning *Terms of Endearment*. Shirley MacLaine not only loved their milk shakes but her character in the movie was crazy about Pig Sandwiches. One of the booths there has a brass plate honoring the actors and the movie.

The Pig Stand #41, 1595 Calder Street, Beaumont, Texas 77704, (409) 813-1444, offers curb service under a "rock 'n' roll" canopy Monday through Friday from 11 a.m. to 3 p.m. Open every day from 6 a.m. to 9 p.m.

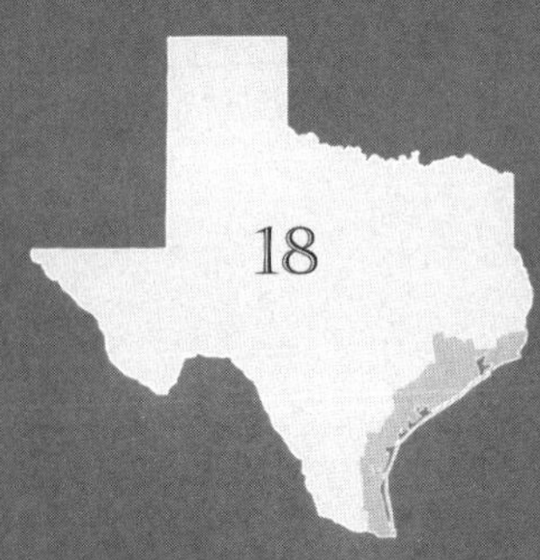

Cowboy Omelet

- 2 eggs, beaten
- 1/2 pattie hamburger, cooked and chopped
- 1 slice cheese, chopped or grated
- 1 slice onion, chopped
- 1/2 soufflé cup picante sauce
- 3 ounces hash browns or grits
- 1 tablespoon butter

Place butter on a hot grill or in a pan. Pour on the eggs. Put ingredients on one side of eggs then fold over to close. Serve on large plate and garnish with 1/2 orange slice and parsley sprig.

YIELD

Serves 1.

Pig Stand Special Dressing

- 1 quart light style mayonnaise (salad dressing)
- 1/2 ounce Spanish paprika
- large pinch cayenne pepper
- 1/4 ounce powdered garlic
- 1/2 lemon, juiced
- 1/2 ounce vegetable oil
- 6 ounces Pet evaporated milk

If heavy salad dressing (mayonnaise) is used, thin with Pet evaporated milk. Be sure the salad dressing is thin enough to flow easily. Cayenne pepper, garlic and paprika should be well sifted before being added to salad dressing. Add ingredients in order named. Whip until smooth.

Cole Slaw and Dressing

- 1 quart light style mayonnaise (salad dressing)
- 3/4 cup sugar
- 1/2 cup cider vinegar
- 1 teaspoon white pepper
- 1 teaspoon salt
- 2 quarts cole slaw

Blend and mix all ingredients.

YIELD

Serves 10–12.

TREEBEARDS

Houston

Treebeards is a familiar name to many diners in Houston and a few in Dallas. The original Treebeards was a 30-seat café located in the neglected Market Square between a peep show arcade and a rowdy bar. It opened in 1978 in what had been a pool hall. The menu featured many of the same Southern style dishes that they still serve today.

Fortunately, so many people did find them and enjoyed their food that they outgrew their original location and moved to their present site on Travis Street two years later. Known to historians as the Travis Building, it was built around 1870 and is regarded as the second oldest building in Houston.

The Travis Building was the property of Rebecca Baker when she married Joseph Meyer Sr., and it is still owned by their descendents. Over the past 100 years tenants have included a seed store, a tailor shop run by former Texas State Representative Rex Brown, a toy store, and several lounges including the Super Market, a pop psychedelic night club in the late 1960s. Treebeards has occupied the Travis Building since 1980.

The success of the Travis Building restaurant has allowed Treebeards to expand to four other locations in Houston and one in Dallas. The first expansion came when the clergy at Christ Church Cathedral asked them to run their restaurant in The Cloister (see separate listing for this historical facility). Renovations at the church temporarily closed this facility for a year, forcing the company to find a third location. They settled into a location in the fascinating tunnel system connecting many of the major office facilities in downtown Houston. Treebeards in the Tunnel at 1100 Louisiana opened in 1990, just as The Cloister reopened.

Further expansion took them to the Plaza of the Americas in downtown Dallas where they discovered many former patrons who had moved there before them. Numerous requests for takeout meals caused them to open Treebeards Take-Away at 700 Rusk (tunnel level). Visiting this location or the newest Take-Away at 1600 Smith will give you a good idea of which menu items are ordered most by regular customers as these two sites serve limited menus of only the most popular dishes.

Treebeards, 315 Travis Street, Houston, Texas 77002, (713) 228-2622, or visit www.treebeards.com. Open for lunch Monday through Friday 11 a.m. to 2 p.m.

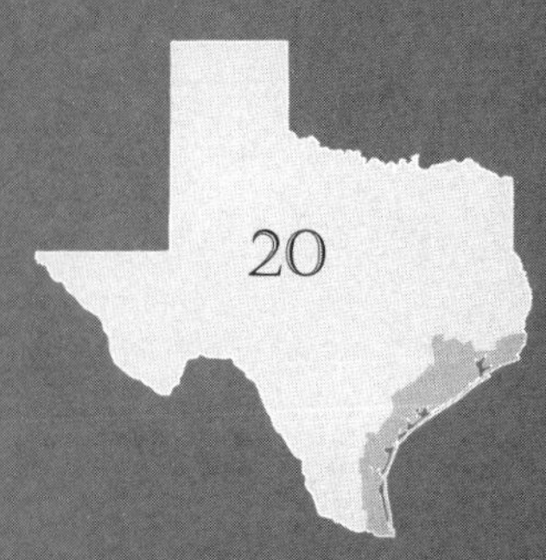

Rice Pudding

PUDDING:

2 cups milk

1/2 cup sugar

3 eggs, beaten

1 teaspoon vanilla

1/2 cup cooked rice

3 tablespoons raisins (dried or fresh fruit such as cranberries, cherries or raspberries can be substituted)

VANILLA SAUCE:

1/4 cup sugar

1 1/2 teaspoons cornstarch (dissolved in a small amount of milk)

1 egg, beaten

1 cup milk

1/2 teaspoon vanilla

1/2 teaspoons ground cinnamon

This is the original Rice Hotel recipe for rice pudding. It was a specialty at the historic Rice Hotel around the corner at Texas Avenue and Travis on the site of the first capital of Texas.

PUDDING:

Combine milk, sugar, eggs and vanilla. Set aside. Place a scant tablespoon of cooked rice and a teaspoon of raisins in the bottom of each of eight custard cups. Fill to 1/4 inch of top with custard mixture. Place cups in a large baking pan and add hot water to come halfway up sides of cups. Bake at 375 degrees for approximately 30 minutes or until the tops are golden and a sharp paring knife inserted in the center comes out clean. Do not overbake. Remove from hot water and cool.

VANILLA SAUCE:

Combine sugar, dissolved cornstarch mixture, and egg in a small bowl and set aside. Bring milk to a boil. Add the sugar mixture gradually and whisk over medium heat about one minute (the sauce will start to thicken). Add vanilla. Cool and spoon over the pudding. Top with ground cinnamon.

Serves 8.

Treebeards' Seafood Gumbo

Served at all Treebeards restaurants on Thursdays and Fridays, this gumbo is packed with four kinds of seafood in a dark, rich, roux base. Do not mistake dark roux for burned roux; dark roux is your flavor base for any good gumbo. Too light a roux will give your gumbo a floury taste.

- 3/4 teaspoon salt
- 3/4 teaspoon garlic powder
- 3/4 teaspoon ground thyme
- 1/2 teaspoon cayenne pepper
- 1/4 teaspoon black pepper
- 2 bay leaves
- 1 3/4 cups onions, chopped into 1/2-inch cubes
- 1 1/4 cups celery, chopped into 1/2-inch pieces
- 1 1/4 cups bell pepper, chopped into 1/2-inch cubes
- 1/2 cup + 3 tablespoons vegetable oil
- 1/2 cup + 3 tablespoons flour
- 4 teaspoons Worcestershire sauce
- 2 teaspoons fish sauce (available at Asian markets or in some groceries)
- 3 1/2 cups water mixed with 2 teaspoons shrimp base (available at Asian markets or in some groceries)
- 2 cups okra, sliced into 1/2-inch pieces
- 1 1/4 cups chopped tomatoes
- 1/3 cup chopped green onions (including tops)
- 2 tablespoons butter
- 1 pound Treebeards shrimp (recipe follows)

(*continued on next page*)

In small bowl, combine salt, garlic powder, thyme, cayenne and black pepper. Set aside.

In medium bowl, combine chopped onions, celery and bell pepper. Set aside.

In heavy-bottom, 5-quart Dutch oven over medium-high heat, heat oil to 260–280 degrees (you will see the oil ripple). Carefully add the flour. Whisk constantly until roux becomes thick, has lost its reddish tinges and becomes a dark brown color. Remove pot from heat and add vegetable mixture. Quickly stir to coat vegetables.

Return pot to stove and add spice mixture. Stir. Add bay leaf, Worcestershire sauce, fish sauce and shrimp-base broth. Bring to boil, reduce heat and simmer for 10 to 15 minutes. Add okra and tomatoes. Simmer 15 to 20 minutes. Add green onions, butter, shrimp, scallops/catfish mixture and crabmeat. Gently simmer 5 to 10 minutes, stirring only once so seafood will not break up into pieces.

Serve over hot rice.

Serves 6.

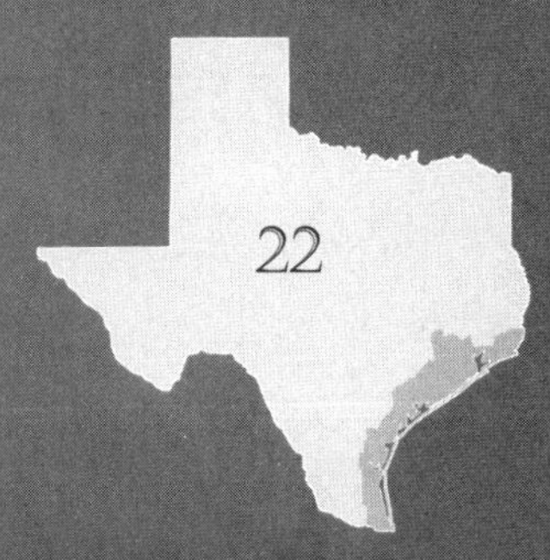

1 pound Treebeards' bay scallops/catfish mixture (recipe follows)

8 ounces crabmeat

SCALLOPS/CATFISH MIXTURE FOR GUMBO:

1/2 pound bay scallops

1/2 pound catfish fillet, cut into 3/4-inch cubes

1/4 teaspoon salt

1/4 teaspoon cayenne pepper

1/4 teaspoon garlic powder

1/4 teaspoon black pepper

1/2 cup vegetable oil

SCALLOPS/CATFISH MIXTURE FOR GUMBO:

Place scallops and catfish chunks in medium bowl. Combine spices and sprinkle over seafood. Gently stir to coat.

Heat oil in skillet over medium heat. When hot, add seafood and cook for 5 to 10 minutes or until fish and scallops are opaque. Do not overcook or stir too frequently or it will break into pieces. Drain off excess oil before adding to gumbo.

Treebeards' Shrimp

1/2 teaspoon garlic powder

1/2 teaspoon salt

1/2 teaspoon cayenne pepper

1/2 teaspoon black pepper

2 pounds shrimp, peeled and deveined

1/2 cup vegetable oil

6 tablespoons green onions, chopped, including tops

1 teaspoon fish sauce

Combine spices and sprinkle over cleaned shrimp and toss to coat. Set aside.

In large skillet over medium-high heat, heat oil. When hot, add chopped green onions and fish sauce. Add seasoned shrimp and cook, tossing constantly, until shrimp are pink and opaque and cooked through, being careful not to overcook.

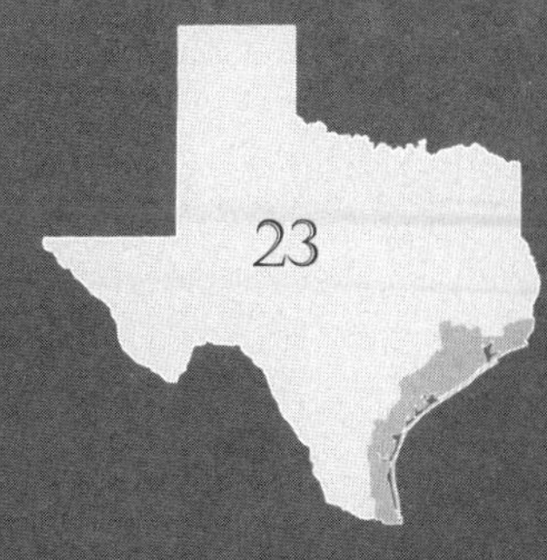

Treebeards' Cajun-Fried Chicken

2 1/2-pound frying chicken, cut up
1/2 teaspoon salt
1/2 teaspoon cayenne pepper
1/2 teaspoon black pepper
1/2 teaspoon garlic powder
3/4 cup flour
vegetable oil for frying

This is not your average fried chicken. As you would expect from Treebeards, the fried chicken is coated with a juicy crust. The secret to the crispiest crust is in the dipping and resting process. By coating the chicken and letting it rest for 30 minutes before recoating and frying, you get a crisp crust with the moistness sealed in.

Combine all seasonings and flour in a plastic bag. Dip chicken pieces in water and drop in bag, a couple of pieces at a time, and shake to coat evenly with seasoned flour. Remove chicken pieces from bag and refrigerate chicken pieces for 30 minutes or more. Return chicken pieces to bag and once again shake in seasoned flour.

In deep skillet over medium heat, heat 3/4 inches of oil. When hot, carefully add chicken pieces, being careful not to overcrowd, and fry chicken 15 to 20 minutes or until chicken is cooked through and golden brown on all sides. Turn chicken with a wooden spoon or tongs so chicken is not pierced while cooking.

Serves 4.

TREEBEARDS CATHEDRAL

Houston

One of the more unusual sites for a restaurant in Texas is The Cloister, located in Christ Church Cathedral. Built in 1845, Christ Church Cathedral is Houston's first congregation and is the only one still worshiping on its original site from the days when Houston was the capital of the Republic of Texas.

The church has its origins in Virginia. Colonel William Fairfax Gray moved his family to Texas in 1837 when his church in Virginia was already a hundred years old. Shortly after settling into his new community, Colonel Grey circulated a petition of support from local and national leaders of Texas. Among the signers were the republic's attorney general, the secretaries of treasury and state and navy, and the Texas ministers to the United States and Mexico.

The church was actually built by the Reverend Charles Gillett from Connecticut, who served as its first rector. In a little more than a decade, the congregation had already outgrown the first building, and plans were made to add a second building next door. The Civil War slowed construction and when the second building was finally completed in 1866 it was insufficient for the continuously growing congregation.

The Cloister was completed in 1876, but in attempting to attach the new building to the old, a wall collapsed forcing the rebuilding of the main building, which is the structure you see today. The first service was held in the present-day church in 1893. The first bishop of Texas, the Right Reverend Alexander Gregg, a Southern aristocrat, believed the best way to serve the Lord was for black and white people to worship under the same roof. Christ Church had black members before, during and after the Civil War. They have always been an integral part of the church community.

In 1981 the church clergy invited Treebeards to come in and run the restaurant in The Cloister. This provided Treebeards with the opportunity to expand from their location on Texas Street.

The Cloister, in Christ Church Cathedral, 1117 Texas Avenue, Houston, Texas 77002, (713) 228-8228, or visit www.treebeards.com. Open for lunch Monday through Friday from 11 a.m. to 2 p.m.

Treebeards' Cucumber Soup

One of our most refreshing menu items, chilled cucumber soup is light and creamy with a hint of fresh mint. For a soup that's lower in calories, use 2 cups plain yogurt and omit the sour cream.

Peel cucumbers lengthwise so that each cucumber is striped in appearance. Cut in half lengthwise and remove seeds. Cut into 1-inch pieces. In food processor with knife blade attachment, process cucumbers, onions, garlic, mint and dill until smooth.

In a large bowl, whisk together sour cream, yogurt, chicken broth, vinegar, olive oil, pepper and salt until smooth. Add pureed cucumber mixture and stir until blended.

Chill at least two hours before serving.

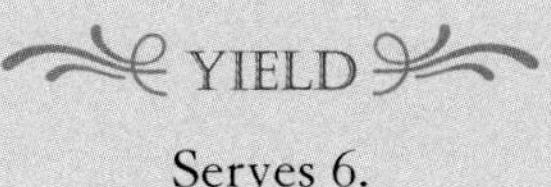

Serves 6.

3 1/2 medium cucumbers

1/4 cup chopped onions

1 clove garlic, small

3 tablespoons chopped fresh mint

2 tablespoons chopped fresh dill

1 cup sour cream

1 cup plain yogurt

1/2 cup chicken broth

2 teaspoons vinegar

1 1/2 teaspoons olive oil

1/2 teaspoon white pepper

3/4 teaspoon salt

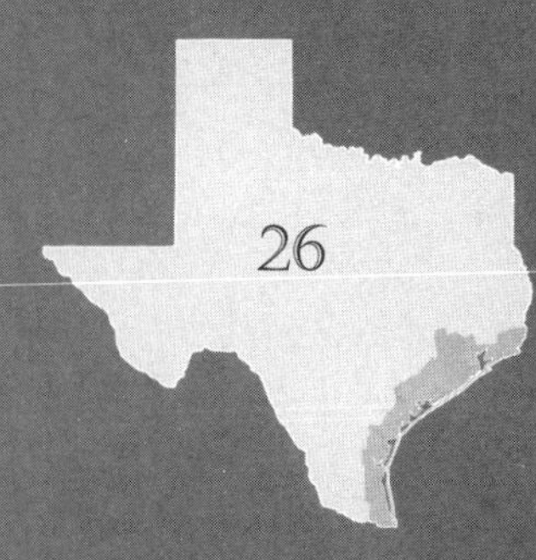

Coconut Beer Shrimp

1/2 pound shrimp, peeled and deveined, tails intact

3/4 cup beer

3/4 cup pancake mix

1/4 cup flour

1 cup flaked coconut

oil for frying

The unexpected sweet crunch that surrounds the shrimp makes for a real taste treat. A delicious, although unusual, combination.

Heat 3 to 4 inches of oil in a deep fryer or deep skillet to 375 degrees. In a small bowl with wire whisk, combine pancake mix and beer until smooth. Set aside.

Dredge shrimp in flour. Shake to remove excess flour. Dip shrimp in pancake and beer mixture. Let drip a few seconds to remove excess batter. Roll in coconut. Repeat with remaining shrimp.

Carefully lower shrimp into hot oil and fry until golden brown. For best results, fry in small batches of 5 or 6 shrimp at a time. Serve immediately.

YIELD

Serves 3–4.

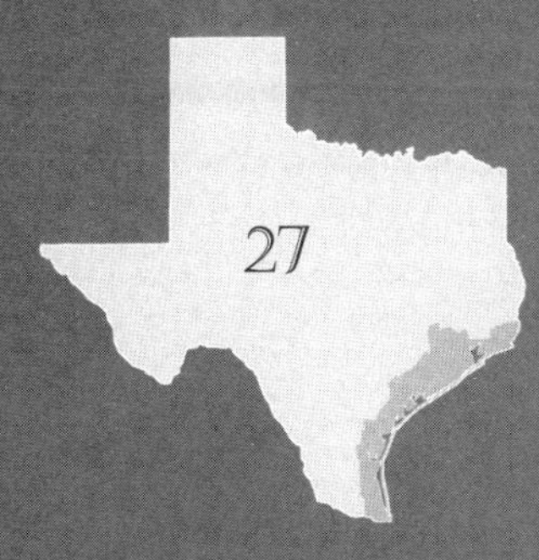

Treebeards' Jambalaya

Treebeards' jambalaya looks different from any other jambalaya we've ever tasted and perhaps that's why we like it so much. The vegetables are left crisp tender rather than being cooked down. Treebeards also serves their jambalaya over rice rather than cooking it with rice. We offer our jambalaya two ways: sausage and shrimp or sausage and chicken.

3/4 pound smoked sausage, cut into 1/2-inch slices

5 stalks celery, cut into 1/2-inch pieces

1 1/2 bell peppers, cut into 1/2-inch pieces

2 medium onions, cut into 1/2-inch pieces

1/2 teaspoon garlic powder

1/2 teaspoon thyme

1/4 teaspoon salt

28 ounces whole tomatoes

1/2 pound Treebeards' shrimp (see recipe under Treebeards, Houston)

In a five-quart Dutch oven over medium heat, sauté sausage pieces until they begin to brown—about 3 minutes. Reduce heat to simmer and add celery, bell pepper and onions. Toss lightly to coat with sausage drippings. Add garlic powder, thyme, cayenne pepper, bay leaves and salt. Stir. Place whole tomatoes in a medium bowl and, with hands, carefully squeeze tomatoes to break into pieces. Pour tomatoes into pot and stir.

Cover and simmer 25 minutes until vegetables start to soften. Just before serving, add shrimp or chicken and cook only until shrimp or chicken is heated through. Serve over hot rice.

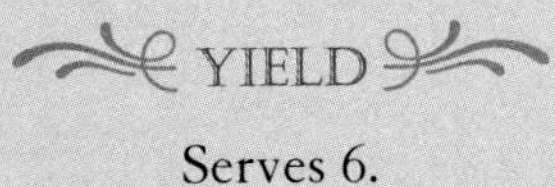

Serves 6.

THE TREMONT HOUSE

Galveston

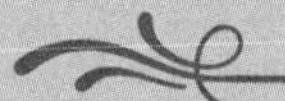

A glimpse into the century-old guest register of The Tremont House would reveal names like General Sam Houston, Ulysses S. Grant, Clara Barton, Edwin Booth and Buffalo Bill. From the earliest days of the original Tremont House, which was built in 1839, the hotel has attracted a fascinating array of guests from Texas, the United States and beyond.

Elegant Victorian ladies and gentlemen came to dance at grand balls; soldiers from three wars returned to homecoming banquets; General Sam Houston delivered his last public address; cotton merchants negotiated deals; Sioux Chiefs sampled southern meals; six presidents came to call; and refugees of the great storm of 1900 sought shelter—all at The Tremont House.

A 117-room luxury hotel in the heart of Galveston's Strand National Historic Landmark District, The Tremont House is the latest incarnation of the 1879 Leon & H. Blum Building, formerly a wholesale dry goods business and later, a newspaper publishing company. The neo-Renaissance building, which is four stories high and a full block long, features elegant architectural details such as a cornice crowned by an oculus, narrow windows crowned by voussoirs and a ground-floor arcade with open bays and stately masonry piers.

Constructed in 1879 by Leon, Hyman and Sylvain Blum, the massive brick structure was designed by Houston architect Eugene T. Heiner to house the Blum brothers' enormous wholesale dry goods business. From this building Blum also managed his million-acre real estate empire, which included land in every Texas county.

The Blums' wholesale business was founded in 1858, when the pioneer Texas businessmen operated as "importers of staples and fancy dry goods, hats, boots, shoes and notions." It became one of the largest wholesale houses in the Southwest, with a trade territory extending over Texas, Louisiana, New Mexico, the Indian Territory and Mexico. Annual transactions averaged $5 million and more. Leon Blum earned the name "The Merchant Prince" during the company's prosperous years. The Blum Building remained in family hands until after the turn of the century, when another dry goods wholesaler purchased it.

The original Tremont House, a sturdy, square, two-story brick building, opened on the corner of Post Office and Tremont Streets, and was the largest and finest hotel in the Republic of Texas for many years. It contained a bar, a billiard saloon and a dining room on the ground floor, with suites of rooms upstairs. Early guests included Texas President Anson Jones and foreign ministers for France and England.

In 1865, the original Tremont House was destroyed by a great fire that raged for days, sweeping through The Strand District and razing entire city blocks. The old landmark lay in ruins for more than five years. After the Civil War and with business booming again, a number of the city's prominent businessmen organized a company to build a new Tremont on the ashes of the old. The company engaged a Memphis architectural firm, Jones & Baldwin, who appointed Nicholas J. Clayton to oversee the plans, and the new Tremont Hotel opened in 1872.

The *Galveston Tribune* acquired the Blum Building in 1923 and the newspaper was published and printed there for the next 40 years. The Galveston Historical Foundation purchased the building and held it until 1981, when Galveston preservationists and developers George and Cynthia Mitchell purchased it as part of their project to redevelop Galveston's historic Strand District. The Mitchells began renovation of the building as a hotel in 1984. They wanted to recreate the atmosphere of Galveston's legendary 19th century hotel, The Tremont, which itself had been through two separate incarnations on two different sites.

Architects Ford, Powell & Carson, Inc., of San Antonio, worked within guidelines of the Texas Historical Commission, and directed a massive exterior restoration of the Blum Building, including work on the building's brick façade, which was plastered in the 1880s to create the appearance of stone.

The first-floor arcade openings were filled with wood and glass panels to match the proportion and style of the originals. A long-missing fourth floor with mansard roof was restored, with dormer windows to provide light for upper rooms. In addition, the building's crown was completely restored.

The interior now features a four-story, white stucco, skylighted atrium, with palm trees growing from grated openings at its base. Guest rooms on the perimeter of the atrium open through glazed French doors onto ironwork balconies. Interior bridges connect the upper level hallways. Birdcage elevators carry guests to the upper floors.

The Merchant Prince, an intimate restaurant named after Leon Blum, is situated on the ground floor, and an ebony marble stairway marks the front entry. The Toujouse Bar, adjacent to The Merchant Prince, is dominated by an ornate rosewood bar, hand-crafted in 1872. Guest rooms on the upper three floors incorporate 19th century charm with 20th century comfort. Decorated in crisp black and pristine white, most rooms have 14-foot ceilings and 11-foot windows. Custom-crafted furnishings include white enamel and brass beds with crisp white bed linens; airy lace curtains; specially woven black-and-white rugs on polished, hardwood floors; massive armoires and, in the adjoining baths, European towel warmers, personalized toiletries and tiles hand-painted in Italy.

Wyndham Historic Hotels handles the operations and management of The Tremont House for the Mitchells, who have retained ownership of the property. The Merchant Prince inside The Tremont House, located at 2300 Ship's Mechanic Row in Galveston, (409) 763-0300, serves breakfast and lunch Sunday through Thursday from 6 a.m. to 2 p.m. and dinner Sunday through Thursday from 5:30 to 10 p.m. and Fridays and Saturdays until 11 p.m.

Spicy Oriental Dumpling Soup

4 ounces diced fresh celery

4 ounces diced carrots

4 ounces diced yellow onions

1 pint water

1 1/2 cups tomato juice

1 ounce fresh lemon juice

1 tablespoon Worcestershire sauce

1/2 teaspoon Tabasco sauce

1 teaspoon Chinese garlic sauce

1/2 ounce fresh minced garlic

1/2 bay leaf

1 teaspoon chili powder

1/2 teaspoon ground black pepper

1/8 bunch fresh chopped cilantro

4 ounces diced red and green bell peppers

8 dumplings

Sauté vegetables in olive oil for 5 minutes, then add liquid and spices. Add dumplings. Bring to simmer for 10 minutes and thicken with cornstarch. Make sure when serving soup to pour 2 dumplings per dish.

Serves 4.

Tortilla Soup

- 10 ounces black beans
- 10 ounces diced cooked chicken
- 6 ounces frozen corn
- 1 1/2 ounces yellow onions, diced
- 6 ounces fresh tomatoes, diced
- 5 ounces fresh bacon cooked crisp, diced before cooking
- 3 cups chicken stock
- 1 clove fresh garlic, minced
- 1 1/2 teaspoons ground cumin
- 1 teaspoon chili powder
- 1 1/2 ounces green and red bell peppers, diced

Sauté vegetables in a saucepan and add bacon. Add the remaining ingredients and simmer for 10 minutes.

Serving Ideas: Garnish soup with nice slices of fresh avocado; shredded cheddar cheese; chopped, fresh cilantro and crisp, fried tortilla strips.

Serves 8.

Honey Walnut Mayonnaise

- 1 cup honey
- 1/2 cup mayonnaise
- 1/4 cup chopped walnuts
- 1 1/2 teaspoons cinnamon

Mix all ingredients very well and keep it in cool place.

Serving Ideas: Served on French bread with French fries, or use this sauce for Turkey Waldorf.

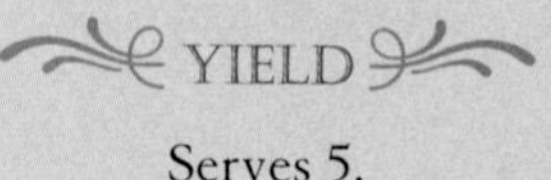

Serves 5.

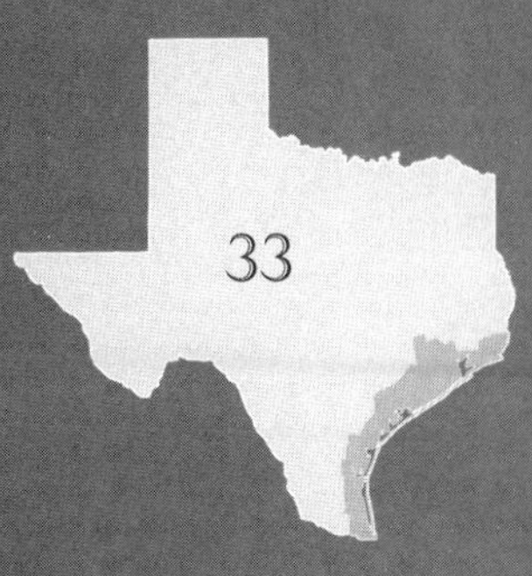

Smoked Turkey Waldorf Sandwich

- 5 ounces sliced turkey breast
- 1 French bread, sliced
- 2 ounces honey walnut mayonnaise
- 1 ounce sliced fresh apples
- 4 ounces French fries
- 1 fruit setup (green leaf, sliced orange and fresh strawberry)

Slice French bread and spread mayonnaise. Add turkey and apples and cut in half. Serving: 1

Honey Lemon Dijon Dressing

- 1 1/4 cups water
- 7 ounces Dijon mustard
- 5 ounces fresh lemon juice
- 1/2 cup olive oil
- 4 teaspoons salt
- 4 teaspoons black pepper
- 7 teaspoons fresh minced garlic
- 1 cup honey

Combine all the ingredients in a bowl and whisk until well blended.

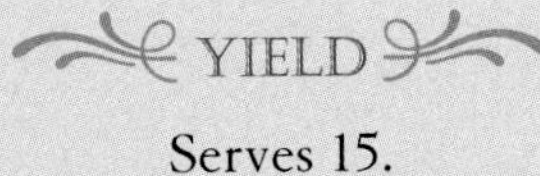

Serves 15.

- 10-ounce package couscous
- 1/2 yellow onion
- 1/2 green bell pepper, diced
- 1/2 can roasted red bell pepper, diced
- 1/2 pound raisins
- 1 bunch green onions
- 4 ounces chicken base
- 2 quarts water
- 1 1/2 teaspoons curry
- 4 teaspoons dried basil
- 1/4 cup butter
- 1/4 teaspoon allspice
- 1 1/2 teaspoons steak seasoning

Couscous

Sauté all vegetables with butter. Add water, chicken base, raisins and spices, and bring to simmer for 5 minutes. Then add couscous and cook for 5 more minutes.

Serving Idea: Served with chicken entrées.

YIELD

Serves 12.

THE WARWICK HOTEL

Houston

The Warwick was originally constructed in 1925 and opened on March 2, 1926. On that day in the *Houston Post* there was a five-page spread detailing the grand opening. The hotel was originally used as an apartment high-rise with some guest rooms. It operated successfully through the Depression, a world war and the 1950s.

Thirty-seven years later, it went on the auction block in 1962. Warwick Inc. announced that its intentions to sell the property were due to their decreasing interest in operating a hotel in Houston. Nearly 250 people attended the auction, many of whom were long-term Warwick residents concerned about the fate of the hotel. One of them was the Houston National Bank president who had moved in on opening day in 1926.

While the estimated value of the hotel was in excess of $5 million, Texas oilman John W. Mecom bought it for $1.5 million. His interest was more than just financial—he had actually lived in the hotel in 1927.

Mr. Mecom must have been able to see into the future to know what was necessary to perpetuate the life of this hotel into the next generation. He elected to spend $11 million in 1962 to fully restore the Warwick to its rightful place of excellence in Houston. He added a 12th floor that contained the Presidential Suite and the famous Warwick Club. He attached Houston's first observation elevator to the side of the building. It stopped only at the top and bottom floors, and provided unique transportation for Warwick Club Members.

A close examination of early photos will reveal that the old front of the hotel is now the back, and the back is now the front. In the new back, Mecom added a pool, a string of suites that wrap around it and additional meeting rooms below. The room below the pool is the La Fontaine Ballroom. It is uniquely shaped into a half circle, and the stage elevator Mecom installed can lift an entire band from the basement up to the middle floor.

The new front to the hotel was added with the upper floors containing guest rooms and the ground floor, a magnificent lobby. Mr. Mecom changed the outside color from the original terra cotta to white. A parking garage was also added across the street with a tunnel connecting to the hotel.

Treasures from Europe abound. The front lobby holds two large Satsuma urns from 19th century Japan. The hand-carved wood paneling located in the lobby and some other areas of the hotel once graced some of Europe's most famous chateaux and palaces. Much of this paneling, from the 17th and 18th century, came from the palatial homes of Prince Murat whose wife, Caroline, was a sister of Napoleon. Its pure style and precision carving are typical of the work of the Parisian artisans of the period.

At the rear of the lobby hangs an 8-foot by 20-foot Aubusson tapestry, woven in France more than 275 years ago. It depicts the story of Diana, Goddess of the Moon and the Hunt who, after having been surprised during her bath by the young Actaeon, turned him into a stag. The tapestry clearly shows the horns beginning to develop from the head. Unfortunately for the young Actaeon, having been turned into a stag, his own dogs tore him to pieces. The tapestry shows the dogs beginning to circle around him.

Opposite the tapestry is a painting of Napoleon. The original painting hangs in the Palace of Versailles, but Napoleon was so taken with the portrait that he had the artist paint several copies to be given out as court favorites. The Empress Eugenie gave this particular painting to her lady-in-waiting, the Duchess of Cadore.

Superbly carved oak doors from Madame Coty's Palace in France provide an appropriately imposing entrance to the Presidential Suite on the 12th floor. Glittering Baccarat crystal chandeliers cast highlights on the delicately carved antique Louis XV panels. The panel designs are excellent examples of French workmanship. Carvings, as deep as 6 inches, reveal the clarity of concept and purity of design typical of French love of elegance and beautiful décor. Old French oil lamps (now electric) provide light in the living and reception rooms. The arch over the fireplace was originally commissioned as a window frame for a French palace. The carved marble Louis XVI mantelpiece came from the Coty Townhouse.

The Hunt Room, for formal dining, offers the finest prime steaks, ribs and chops in a comfortable setting located conveniently off the lobby. The front of the Hunt Room is decorated with dark walnut paneling, also dating from an original tavern in France to which gentlemen would retreat after a day of fox hunting.

Guests and visitors may also enjoy award-winning food and beverages in The Terrace on Main, a sophisticated café and bar. The Terrace is open seven days a week and serves breakfast, lunch and a light dinner. Sunday Brunch is served on the top floor overlooking the breathtaking Houston skyline.

The Hunt Room at The Warwick Hotel, 5701 Main Street, Houston, Texas 77005, (713) 526-1991. Open for dinner only Monday through Saturday from 6 until 10 p.m. Closed Sunday. Casual attire is welcome.

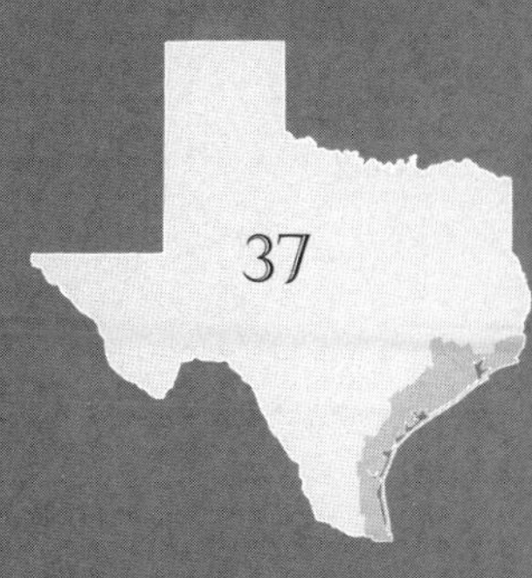

Smoked Salmon Tartare
with Plantain Chips, Cucumbers and Ginger Vinaigrette

SMOKED SALMON TARTARE:

- 3/4-pound smoked salmon, well chilled
- 1 tablespoon cilantro, finely chopped
- 1 tablespoon basil, finely chopped
- 1 teaspoon white sesame seeds
- 1 teaspoon black sesame seeds
- 1/4 cup green onions, thinly sliced into rounds
- 1 tablespoon red onion, finely diced
- 1/4 cup ginger vinaigrette (recipe follows)
- dash salt and freshly ground black pepper

GINGER VINAIGRETTE:

- 6 ounces fresh ginger
- 3 tablespoons fresh lime juice
- 3 tablespoons champagne vinegar
- dash Tabasco
- 2 drops sesame oil
- 1 teaspoon white sesame seeds
- 1 teaspoon black sesame seeds
- 1 tablespoon shallot, minced
- 1 clove garlic, minced and mashed to a paste with a sprinkle of salt
- 2 teaspoons Dijon mustard
- 1/2 cup extra virgin olive oil

SMOKED SALMON TARTARE:

Using a very sharp, thin-bladed knife, slice the smoked salmon into 1/4-inch cubes. Gently mix the salmon, cilantro, basil, sesame seeds, green onion and red onion together. Just before serving, add the ginger vinaigrette to the smoked salmon mixture. Season with salt and pepper to taste.

GINGER VINAIGRETTE:

Using the medium holes of a cheese grater, grate the ginger. Wrap the grated ginger in a thin kitchen towel or cheesecloth and squeeze to extract the juices from the ginger into a medium bowl. Whisk in the rest of the ingredients into the bowl, except the oils. Gradually whisk in the oils until the vinaigrette has emulsified. Season with salt and pepper to taste.

ASSEMBLY:

Pour enough oil into a medium pot to measure 1 inch. Heat the oil to 375 degrees. Carefully lower the plantain slices into the hot oil. Fry the plantains for approximately 1 minute. Remove the plantains with tongs and drain on a plate with paper towels.

Using a mandolin or a very sharp knife, slice the cucumbers into paper-thin slices. Place the ring mold in the center of a chilled large plate. Using the outside edge of the mold as a guide, make a ring of overlapping cucumber

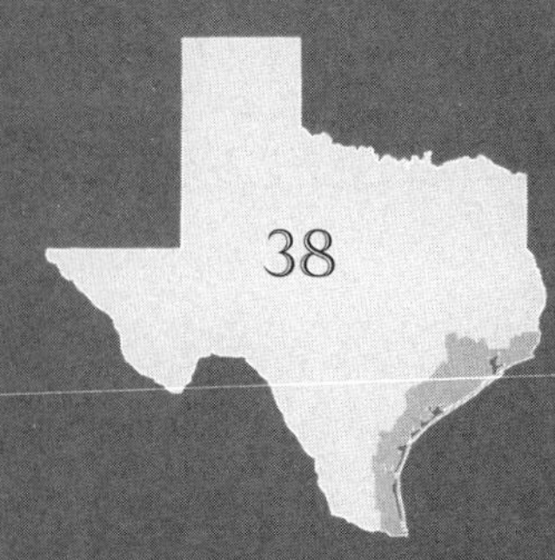

1/2 cup canola oil

dash salt and freshly ground black pepper

ASSEMBLY:

2 green plantains, peeled and very thinly sliced lengthwise

vegetable or canola oil, for deep-frying

1 large English hothouse cucumber

cilantro springs, to garnish

1 2 1/2-inch metal ring mold

4 dinner plates, chilled

slices around the mold. Leaving the mold in place, spoon the smoked salmon tartare into the mold, pressing down lightly. Stand 2 or 3 plantain chips in the top of the tartare. Carefully remove the ring mold from the plate and repeat the process with the remaining chilled plates. Drizzle the remaining ginger vinaigrette around the edges of the cucumbers and garnish with cilantro sprigs.

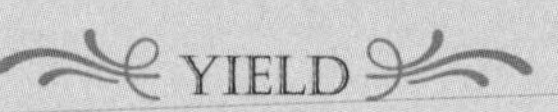

Serves 4.

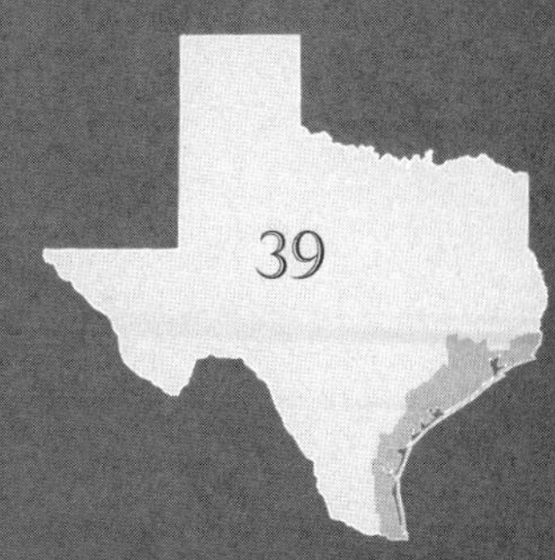

Ahi Tuna

with Caponata, Red Zinfandel Sauce, Kalamata Olive Oil, and Tarragon Oil

RED WINE SAUCE:

In a medium saucepan, bring the wine, vinegar, stock, shallots, garlic, bay leaf, peppercorns and thyme to a boil. Reduce heat and simmer, uncovered, until reduced to about 1 1/2 cups—approximately 30 to 40 minutes. Remove saucepan from the heat and one piece at a time, whisk in the butter. Season with salt and pepper and strain through a fine mesh sieve. Keep sauce warm over low heat.

TARRAGON OIL:

Add 3 cups water to a small saucepan and bring to a boil. Add the tarragon and blanch for 10 seconds. Remove the tarragon and shock in ice water. Drain off tarragon and pat dry. In a blender, combine the tarragon and oil and process until the tarragon is completely pureed—about three minutes. Scrape the tarragon oil into a small bowl and set aside for a few hours. Before using, strain the tarragon oil through a fine wire sieve into a small squirt bottle.

KALAMATA OLIVE OIL:

Puree olives and olive oil in a blender for two minutes. Pour into a small bowl and set aside.

CAPONATA:

In a colander, toss the eggplant with the kosher salt. Let the eggplant sit out for about 1 hour to release some of the

RED WINE SAUCE:

3 cups (750-ml bottle) red zinfandel

1/4 cup red wine vinegar

2 cups veal stock

2 tablespoons shallot, finely chopped

1 clove garlic, minced

1 bay leaf

7 black peppercorns

1 sprig thyme

1/2 cup butter, cut into small pieces

salt and freshly ground black pepper

TARRAGON OIL:

1/4 cup tarragon leaves

1/4 cup grape seed oil

KALAMATA OLIVE OIL:

1/4 cup Kalamata olives, pitted

1/4 cup extra virgin olive oil

CAPONATA:

2 cups eggplant, cut into 1/4-inch cubes

1 tablespoon kosher salt, plus extra to taste

2 cups celery, cut into 1/4-inch cubes

1/3 cup olive oil

2 cups yellow onion, cut into 1/4-inch cubes

(continued on next page)

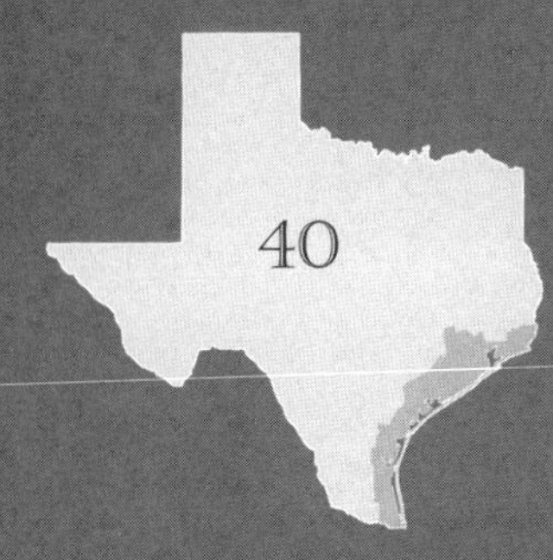

1/2 cup red wine vinegar

2 tablespoons sugar

2 cups Roma tomatoes, peeled, seeded and cut into 1/4-inch cubes

2 red bell peppers, roasted, peeled, seeded and cut into 1/4-inch cubes

1/4 cup Kalamata olives, chopped

2 tablespoons capers, rinsed and chopped

3 anchovies, rinsed and finely chopped

2 tablespoons tarragon leaves, chopped

TUNA AND ASSEMBLY:

6 5-oz. yellow fin tuna loin fillets (sushi quality), all skin and blood removed

extra virgin olive oil

kosher salt and freshly ground black pepper

6 preheated dinner plates

6 sprigs tarragon

bitterness from the eggplant. In a medium saucepan of boiling salted water, cook the celery for 3 minutes. Remove the celery and shock in ice water. Drain the celery and set aside in a bowl. Rinse the eggplant quickly under water to remove the salt. Squeeze the eggplant to remove excess liquid. In a large sauté pan, heat 1/4 cup of the oil over medium heat and sauté the eggplant until lightly browned—about 6 minutes. Using a slotted spoon, remove the eggplant and add to the bowl with the celery. Season with salt and pepper. In the same large sauté pan, heat the remaining oil over medium heat. Add the onion and sauté until softened but not browned—about 5 minutes. Add the vinegar and sugar and cook until the vinegar has almost completely cooked away. Add the tomatoes and cook over medium low heat for 10 minutes, stirring often. Add the onion-tomato mixture to the bowl with the eggplant. Add the remaining ingredients to the eggplant mixture and stir to combine. Season with salt and pepper to taste. Cool to room temperature.

TUNA AND ASSEMBLY:

Heat a large sauté pan over high heat. Rub the tuna fillets all over with the olive oil. Season the tuna with the kosher salt and black pepper. When the pan is very hot, add 2 tablespoons olive oil and sear the tuna fillets for approximately 30 seconds on each side (the tuna will remain rare on the inside). Remove the fish from the pan and cover loosely with aluminum foil. Using a 2 1/2-inch ring mold, spoon equal portions of the caponata onto the center of each preheated plate. Using a very sharp knife, slice the tuna crosswise into 1/4-inch-thick slices. Arrange the

tuna slices in an overlapping fan around the caponata. Spoon a few tablespoons of red zinfandel sauce around the tuna. Drizzle a few drops of tarragon oil and Kalamata olive oil around the plates. Place a tarragon sprig outside of the caponata and serve.

CHEF'S NOTES:

1. Ask your fishmonger to cut the tuna fillets in the shape of a square. This will aid in uniform cooking of the tuna and also aids in plate presentation.

2. Use only sushi-quality tuna for this recipe, since you will be serving the dish rare.

3. The chef prefers to serve the caponata at room temperature, but feel free to serve it hot.

4. The caponata can be made up to two days in advance, covered and refrigerated.

5. Be sure to slowly add the butter to incorporate it into the red wine reduction. If you add the butter too quickly, the sauce will break.

6. The flavored oils can be made up to two days in advance, covered and refrigerated. Bring to room temperature before service.

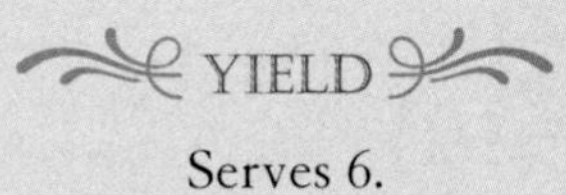

Serves 6.

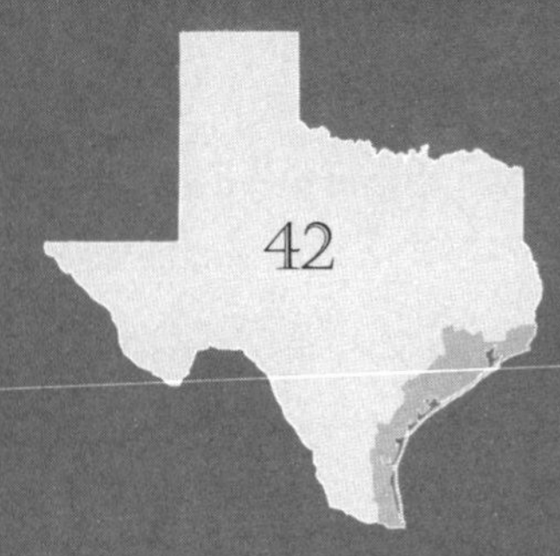

Jumbo Lump Crab Cakes

with Roasted Corn Flan, Chipotle Crème Fraiche, and Tobiko Caviar

CRAB CAKES:

- 1 pound jumbo lump crabmeat (cleaned)
- 2 tablespoons red pepper, finely diced
- 2 tablespoons green pepper, finely diced
- 2 tablespoons green onion, thinly sliced into rounds
- 1 tablespoon red onion, finely diced
- 2 teaspoons jalapeno pepper, finely diced
- 1 teaspoon garlic, minced
- 1 large egg
- 1/2 cup mayonnaise
- 2 teaspoons Dijon mustard
- 1 teaspoon dill
- 2 teaspoons Tony Chachere's Creole seasoning
- dash Worcestershire sauce
- dash Tabasco sauce
- 1/3 cup Japanese bread crumbs (panko), plus extra for dusting the cakes
- dash salt and freshly ground pepper
- 2 tablespoons vegetable or canola oil

CRAB CAKES:

Preheat oven to 400 degrees. In a small sauté pan, sauté the peppers and onions over medium heat until lightly browned—about 5 minutes. Add the garlic and stir until fragrant, about 1 minute. Transfer the sautéed vegetables to a medium bowl, and mix in all of the remaining ingredients, except the crabmeat. Carefully incorporate the crab into the vegetable mixture, being careful not to break up the large lumps of crabmeat.

Season the crabmeat with salt and freshly ground black pepper. Wrap the bowl with plastic wrap and refrigerate for 30 minutes. Remove the bowl from the refrigerator and form the crab mixture into 4 equal crab cakes and lay them on a sheet pan lined with parchment paper. Dust the crab cakes on all sides with the additional breadcrumbs. In a medium sauté pan, heat the oil over medium-high heat. Sauté the crab cakes until golden brown—about 2 minutes on each side.

Place pan in preheated oven and cook for an additional 5 minutes. Remove the cakes from the oven and drain on a paper towel-lined plate.

Serves 4.

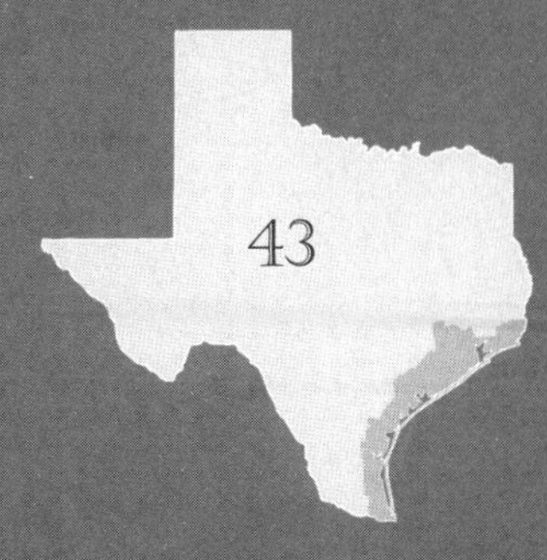

ROASTED CORN FLAN

Preheat oven to 300 degrees. Position rack in the center of the oven. Lightly butter the insides of the ramekins. In a blender, blend all of the ingredients until smooth. Set aside the blended ingredients for 1 hour. After 1 hour, skim the air bubbles off of the top. Season with salt and pepper to taste.

Place the ramekins in a baking dish large enough to hold all of them. Pour the roasted corn cream into the ramekins. Place the baking dish in the oven. Pour hot water into the baking dish to halfway cover the ramekins. Cover the pan with aluminum foil and bake until the custards are set—about 1 hour (the centers will still seem a little loose).

CHIPOTLE CRÈME FRAICHE:

Combine all ingredients and season with salt and pepper to taste. Transfer to the refrigerator and chill.

ASSEMBLY:

To assemble, unmold a hot, roasted corn flan onto the center of each preheated plate. Top the flan with 1 crab cake and place 1 tablespoon of the chipotle crème fraiche on top of each crab cake. Place 1/2 tablespoon of tobiko caviar on top of the crème fraiche. Sprinkle the chopped chives around the plates and serve.

Serves 4.

ROASTED CORN FLAN:

4 6-ounce ceramic ramekins

2 tablespoons unsalted butter, for the ramekins

1 1/4 cup heavy cream

3 large eggs

2 cups roasted corn kernels

1 teaspoon garlic, minced

1 tablespoon cilantro, chopped

2 teaspoons maple syrup

dash salt and freshly ground pepper

CHIPOTLE CRÈME FRAICHE:

1 cup crème fraiche

2 teaspoons canned chipotle chilies, seeded, stemmed, and pureed

1 teaspoon cilantro, chopped

1 teaspoon lime juice

dash salt and freshly ground pepper

ASSEMBLY:

2 tablespoons tobiko caviar (flying fish roe)

2 tablespoons chives, finely diced

4 tablespoons chipotle crème fraiche (recipe above)

4 preheated dinner plates

2

Piney Woods

East Texas. Caddo Indians over a thousand years ago settled the area, and their burial grounds are a legacy that predates the Spanish and French explorers. Nacogdoches set the stage for independence in Texas, displaying an early rebel spirit among the forests. This incredible area of woodlands, lakes and rivers is in sharp contrast to the west. Fishing, canoeing and riverboat trips with four national forests of ferns, cypresses, pines and wild orchids are cherished. Jefferson was once a wealthy riverboat landing. Wood and oil are part of the rich history in the quest for black gold. Cities such as The Woodlands, Huntsville, Tyler, Longview, Kilgore and Texarkana are part of Piney Woods.

BELLE-JIM HOTEL

Jasper

The original owner of this land will never be known because the courthouse burned in 1849, destroying all the old records. We do know that Mrs. Mamie Patten hired William Cook in 1910 to build a 17-room, two-story frame hotel on the site. She was already a widow and was eager to find a better way to raise her two daughters and two sons than in the much smaller "Brick Hotel" that she operated nearby. She had been serving as the postmistress of the Jasper Post Office for several years and continued to operate a Western Union office even after the hotel was built.

Mamie had a substantial following of traveling salesmen who had stayed with her before, and of course they moved with her to the new hotel. It was this group of loyal customers who dubbed the building the Belle-Jim after Mamie's two daughters. It was the homelike family setting that made the hotel so attractive and caused its continuing success. Regular customers not only came to stay in their favorite rooms, but also to enjoy the personal attention Mamie showed them. Special foods were often prepared with individual guests in mind, and anyone under the weather was given personal nursing care by Mrs. Patten herself.

Not only did Mamie supervise the kitchen, but she also did some of the cooking herself, in addition to making daily inspections of every room and bath. The Belle-Jim was her pride and joy and she took as good care of it as she did her own children. Patrons were so impressed with her and the hotel that many showed up every January for what became an annual banquet. Mamie did not consider it any coincidence that these January parties allowed the salesmen to book their future travel plans with the Belle-Jim for the new year. This celebration was continued by her daughter, Jim, for many years after Mamie passed away.

The Belle-Jim Hotel offered the finest dining room service in the area. Guests came from far and near to enjoy the food, the hospitality and the devoted attention from the staff. Christmas was a time for the famous "Belle-Jim Cake," served to all patrons with rave reviews. After dinner, people would gather in the beautiful sitting room adjoining the lobby for cigars and drinks. The Belle-Jim was noted for its large rooms and high ceilings, and its comfortable furniture and bedding.

Before Mamie died, she turned the hotel operation over to her daughter, Jim. The hotel and the Western Union operation continued for many years under Jim's ownership. In the early 1970s, Jim was notified that she had one of the two oldest Western Union offices in the United States that had been continuously operated by one family.

Jim passed away in 1974 and the hotel fell into disrepair after being used for a time as law offices. The Belle-Jim received a facelift in 1991, and today the current owners, David and Pat Stiles, offer a unique Bed and Breakfast experience in a turn-of-the-century atmosphere.

The Belle-Jim Hotel, 160 N. Austin, Jasper, Texas 75951, (409) 384-6923 offers breakfast to guests from 7:30 to 9:30 a.m. The restaurant is open to the public Monday through Friday from 11:00 a.m. to 1:30 p.m. for lunch. A private dining room is available for special occasions.

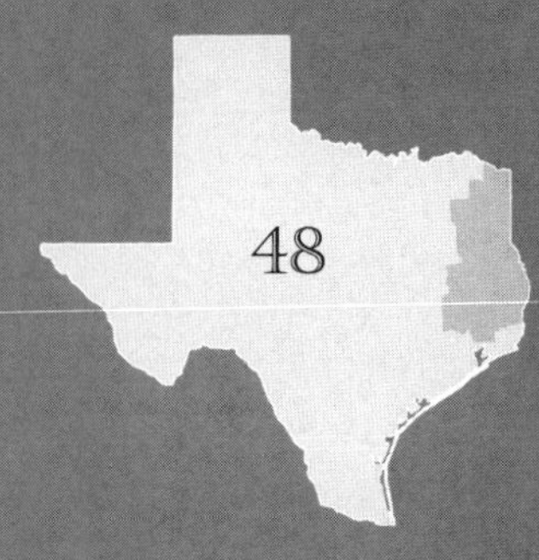

Cream of Corn Soup

14 ounces cream of mushroom soup

14 ounces milk

14 ounces corn

1 tablespoon real mayonnaise

Mix and heat thoroughly.

YIELD

Serves 6–8.

Broccoli Salad

1 bunch broccoli flowerets

2 tablespoons bacon bits (real bacon)

1 small purple onion, minced

2 tablespoons sunflower seeds

DRESSING:

1 cup real mayonnaise

1/4 cup sugar

2 tablespoons tarragon vinegar

DRESSING:

Mix ingredients and pour it over broccoli.

YIELD

Serves 4.

THE CARSON HOUSE INN & GRILLE AND MRS. B'S COTTAGE

Pittsburg

The Carson House was built in 1878 by Pierce Ligon and was purchased by William Henry Carson in 1887. It is the oldest house still standing in Pittsburg. William Carson was in the lumber business, and he held an interest in a circus and a rail line that ran between Texas and Mexico.

In 1898, Mr. Carson discovered a tract of land containing curly pine trees, a diseased tree with a very unique grain pattern. These trees are now thought to be extinct. He purchased the land and milled the wood. In 1900, the first cut of the lumber was used to decorate the inside of this house. The Carson House has more than one mile of curly pine that was painstakingly stripped and refinished during the restoration in 1990.

Alice Carson Parker, daughter of William and Sophia Carson, reports that her parents had seven children, six of whom were born in the house. Six of their nine grandchildren were also born in their house. Sophia and one of her daughters also died in the house. In 1910 or 1911 the chimney in the fireplace in the front room caught fire. There was a great deal of water damage and Alice found charred wood in a closet when she added some new wallpaper.

Early electrical wiring of houses was done inside the walls and without circuit breakers. William Carson was so worried about rats that chewed through wire coatings and caused fires that he had trouble sleeping at night. He had the house completely rewired in 1911–1912 with all wires exposed on the ceilings and attached with clay insulators. Similar clay insulators were put in holes in the walls to allow the wires to pass to the next room.

The windows had pulleys and ropes to raise and lower them. Occasionally, one of the ropes would break, sending a window crashing down. Sophia was so concerned that one of her children would be hurt that she had William remove the ropes and place curly pine sticks to prop up each open window.

Operating as both a restaurant and inn since 1991, the Carson House today offers food and beverages and six beautifully appointed guest rooms for overnight accommodations. One of the suites is located in the rail car on the back of the property and is especially appropriate for those special occasions often celebrated by couples. There are five guest rooms upstairs in the main house. You are encouraged to tour the property while you are there. The staff will be happy to show you around.

Mrs. B's Cottage was added in September 1999. This beautiful two-bedroom house was built in the 1920s and has been operated as a guesthouse since 1994. It is great for overnight and long-term visits.

The Carson House Inn & Grille & Mrs. B's Cottage, 302 Mt. Pleasant Street, Pittsburg, Texas 75686. Call (903) 856-2468 or (888) 302-1878, or visit www.carsonhouse.com. The restaurant is open for lunch Monday through Friday from 11 a.m. until 2 p.m. They are open for dinner Monday through Saturday from 5 until 10 p.m. They are normally closed on Sundays; however, they have a special Sunday brunch for Mother's Day and Easter Sunday. They are also open for brunch on Thanksgiving.

Carson House Artichoke Dip for Parties

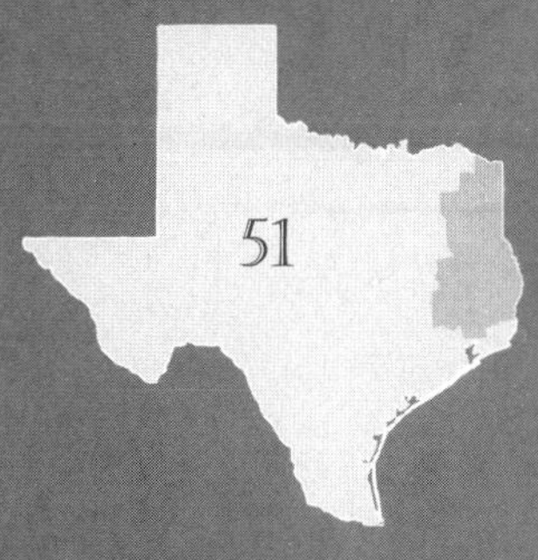

3 cans artichokes (8 ounces each)

1/4 cup creamy Italian dressing

1 1/2 cups fresh Parmesan, shredded

1 1/4 cups mayonnaise

1 1/2 cups Swiss cheese, grated

1 cup green onions, sliced 1/4 inch

1/2 can green chilies, diced

2 jalapeno peppers, seeded, minced fine

1 cup dry Parmesan cheese, grated

Combine all ingredients. Place into ceramic bowl that is microwave safe. Wrap the bowl and refrigerate.

When ready to serve guests, microwave the bowl two minutes at a time. Remove, stir and replace in microwave. Repeat until dip is warm but not hot. Place French bread slices in oven for 1 minute. You may choose to coat bread with oil, additional Parmesan cheese and chopped parsley.

Garnish the dip with sliced green onions and serve immediately.

Serves 12.

Berry Berry Salad

with Mandarin Organic Balsamic Vinaigrette

MANDARIN ORGANIC BALSAMIC VINAIGRETTE:

2 tablespoons honey

2 tablespoons olive oil

2 tablespoons balsamic vinegar

1 1/2 teaspoons ground ginger

1 1/2 teaspoons salt

3/4 teaspoon pepper

2 cups mandarin orange slices

CANDIED ALMONDS:

2 ounces butter

1/2 cup dark brown sugar

1 cup sliced almonds

SALAD:

For service, chill 8 salad plates. On each plate place 1 ounce Mesculin salad mix, 2 ounces fresh sliced strawberries, 1 ounce mandarin oranges and 1 ounce candied almonds(recipe follows). Drizzle 1 1/2 ounces of dressing (recipe follows) on each and serve immediately.

MANDARIN ORGANIC BALSAMIC VINAIGRETTE:

Combine all ingredients in a blender. Date, label and refrigerate.

CANDIED ALMONDS:

Melt 2 ounces of butter and 1/2 cup dark brown sugar in a nonstick pan. Add 1 cup sliced almonds. Cook over medium heat until golden brown. Drain excess liquid and let cool.

Sweet Potato Casserole

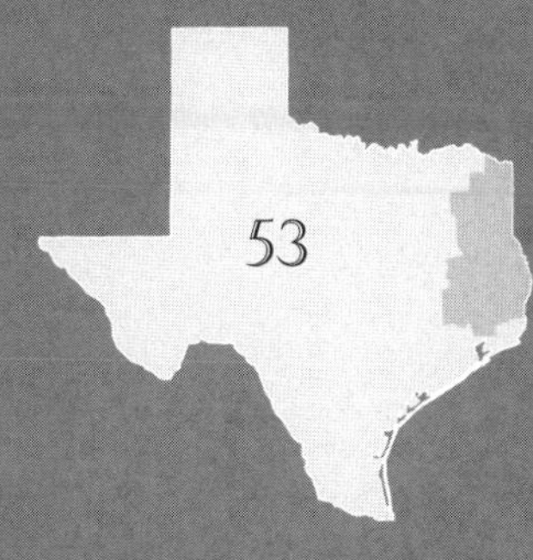

1 cup sweet potatoes, boiled

1/4 cup brown sugar

1/2 cup milk

2 1/2 ounces butter

1 egg

1/2 teaspoon nutmeg

TOPPING:

1/2 cup corn flakes, crushed

2 1/2 ounces margarine, whipped

1/4 cup coconut, grated

1/4 cup brown sugar

1/4 cup pecan pieces

1 teaspoon vanilla

Mash sweet potatoes. Mix in the remaining ingredients. Bake in a 2-quart casserole at 350 degrees until set—approximately 40 minutes.

TOPPING:

Mix all ingredients together. Spread over potatoes. Place in oven under broiler until topping browns.

Serves 5.

ESPECIALLY FOR YOU

Kaufman

The historic First National Bank Building was built in 1908 on the square in Kaufman. It is now a gift shop and is filled with displays of exquisite items offered by Nancy Murphy. Nestled in the rear of the bank building is Especially For You, a time-forgotten tea room offering special old-fashioned service, an array of soups, muffins, sandwiches, special hot lunches, desserts, gourmet coffees and its famous lemonade tea and honey mustard dressing.

The tea room has a Victorian style décor with Nancy's family linens gracing the windows of this historic bank building. It may be reserved for special events such as Victorian birthday parties, bridge parties, showers and special dinners hosted by Nancy.

Especially For You, 100 West Grove, Kaufman, Texas 75142, (972) 932-4274. The tea room is open Monday through Saturday from 11 a.m. until 2 p.m. They are closed Sundays. They have a seating capacity of 25 people and you must call ahead for reservations.

Baked Potato Soup

Place first four ingredients in a saucepan with 2 teaspoons of chicken bouillon. Bring to a boil, stirring constantly. Sauté the onions and celery until tender. Place the potatoes, water, celery and onions in a 2 1/2 quart saucepan and simmer until the potatoes are tender. Do not drain. Add the mustard and pepper to the white sauce. Put both mixtures together and bring to a full boil, stirring constantly.

When serving, put shredded cheese, green onions and diced bacon on top of each serving.

Serves 4.

1/2 cup Watkins cream soup base

1/2 cup flour

1 cup milk

1 1/2 cups water

2 teaspoons of chicken bouillon

1 cup potatoes, diced

3/4 cup onion, chopped

1/3 cup celery, diced

1 1/2 cups water

1/4 teaspoon dry mustard

dash pepper

shredded cheese, green onions and diced bacon (for garnish)

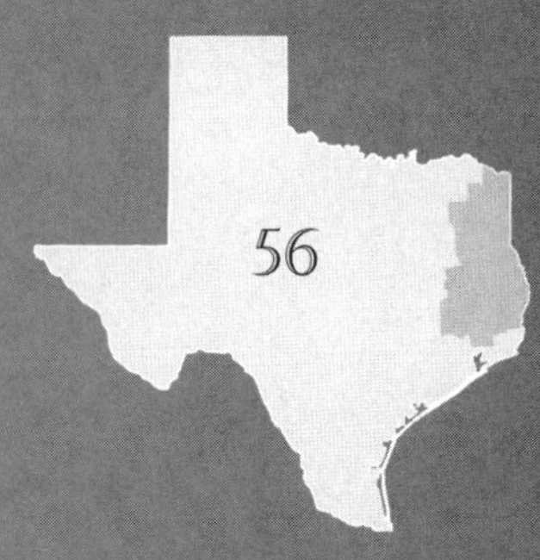

Nancy's Soup

- 2 cups chicken, cooked and diced
- 2 cups chicken broth
- 14 1/2 ounces stewed tomatoes
- 14 1/2 ounces cream of chicken soup
- 10 3/4 ounces home-style chunky chicken soup with vegetables
- 2 cups mixed vegetables
- 1/2 cup onions, chopped
- 1 1/2 cups celery, chopped
- 1/2 cup butter
- 1/2 teaspoon dry basil
- 1/2 teaspoon dry tarragon
- 1 clove garlic, mashed
- pinch salt and pepper

Sauté onions and celery in the butter until tender. Combine all ingredients and cook over low heat for 1 hour. This can also be put into a double boiler over low heat for several hours.

YIELD

Serves 6–8.

Dill Dip

- 1 package Danielle's dill dip
- 1 cup Hellman's mayonnaise
- 1 cup sour cream

Combine all ingredients and refrigerate for 2 hours.

YIELD

2 1/2 cups of dip

THE HOMESTEAD

Huntsville

HISTORY OF THE FRONT TWO CABINS

In 1826, Joseph Vehlein, a German merchant living in Mexico City, was given a contract with the Mexican government to settle 300 families in East Texas. Two years later Lemuel M. Collard traveled to Texas to study the advantages of settlement in the Vehlein Colony, but before he was able to acquire a land grant, the Mexican Congress enacted a law forbidding further settlement of Americans on most Impresario lands, including Vehlein's.

A convention was held at San Felipe de Austin in 1832 asking the Mexican government to repeal the law of 1830 and allow the further settlement of East Texas. The resolution was ignored by the Mexican government and another convention was held when Santa Anna became president in 1833. Lemuel, who had been joined by his brother in 1832, was apparently not discouraged by the political uncertainties, for in 1833, his father, mother and other members of the Collard family emigrated to Texas.

Finally, in 1834, the obstructions to settlement of the Impresario colonies had been removed and on November 21st of that year Lemuel, who by that time was married to Elizabeth Lindley, applied for a league of land (4,428 acres) just north of the present-day community of New Waverly. The next year, having satisfied all of the requirements for permanent settlement, Collard received clear title to his land.

It is probable that Collard built the west room of the present "Homestead" structure in the fall of 1834. He and his wife did not yet have any of their 13 children so had little need for a large house. The main room, constructed of hewn, square-notched pine logs, was apparently divided into a parlor and sleeping area. An L-shaped stairway led to a loft that would later serve as the children's sleeping quarters.

The first chimney was probably a "cat chimney" fashioned of mud and sticks. The floor and shingles were of rived boards. Cracks between the logs were covered with wooden "chinking" both inside and out and whitewashed. Mud was added as additional insulation on the east wall. The ten-foot-wide porch along the front was balanced by a shed room of the same dimensions, which served as the kitchen at the rear of the house.

By the next year, the Collards had probably begun the transformation of the rustic log cabin into a graceful clapboard-sided home. A ten-foot-wide central hall or "dogtrot" was added, as well as a second log room, the East Room of the current Homestead, with shed. The wood chinking on the exterior of the original "cabin" was removed and replaced with clapboard siding. The "cat chimney" was torn down and two brick chimneys were built.

In 1846 the Collards sold the house and 200 acres to H. C. Hoskins for $300.00. Other owners included various members of the Ripkowski family (1871–1933), Elliot Campbell (1933–1964) and H. T. Abbey (1964–1980). In 1979, the Abbeys, who had built a new brick home beside the old Collard House, began tearing the old house down to reuse the lumber. To their surprise they found hand-hewn logs instead of two-by-four studs. They hadn't realized that their former home was built of logs, for in 1904 the house had been extensively remodeled. The house then looked like any other turn-of-the-century rural East Texas farmhouse. In the 1920s the old Collard house had been enlarged with the addition of a kitchen wing and the clapboards were replaced with "modern" 117 siding. Mr. Abbey stopped demolishing the house and contacted the Walker County Historical Commission in an attempt to learn something about the origins of the old house as well as to locate someone who would be interested in moving and restoring it.

In 1980, Walker County preservationist George Russell purchased the Collard House and moved it to its present location across from Sam Houston Park. After nearly four years of exacting work, the old log home of Lemuel Collard was adaptively restored. It has been the home of "The Homestead on 19th" restaurant since the fall of 1995, 161 years after the original construction of the old Collard cabin.

HISTORY OF THE BACK CABIN

In 1837, James C. DeWitt founded the town of Cincinnati on the west bank of the Trinity River. DeWitt, who had fought in the Battle of San Jacinto, sold the first town lot to Jonathan S. Collard for thirty dollars. Jonathan was the elder brother of Lemuel Collard, builder of the front cabin. Cincinnati soon became a prosperous steamboat port and stagecoach stop. James Crowther Dunlap was attracted by the business opportunities offered by the growing community and established a saloon, store, hotel and freight service to Huntsville.

In the fall of 1853 a yellow-fever epidemic struck the town, killing nearly half the population. Legend has it that the rest of the populace fled, leaving Cincinnati a deserted ghost town. Although the "yellow jack" epidemic dealt the town a serious blow, the town was inhabited at least until 1889.

James Dunlap continued to run his store, saloon and hotel until the coming of the railroad in 1872, which spelled doom for the steamboat trade along the Trinity River. The Dunlaps moved across the Trinity River to a plantation in the Kittrell Community. The Dunlap plantation boasted a large main house and fourteen double-pen, dogtrot, log-out buildings. After the abandonment of the plantation operations, the log houses and cribs disappeared one by one.

By the 1970s all that remained was the plantation house and one log pen. After the plantation house burned a few years ago, the little log cabin served as the only reminder of the prosperous legacy of James Crowther Dunlap. Even that reminder was threatened by time and the elements. In 1983 the Dunlap heirs decided to sell the cabin to someone who would restore it. The cabin was purchased by preservationist George Russell, who numbered the logs and dismantled it. The cabin was then re-erected log by log, board by board, on its present site on 19th Street.

The process of disassembly and restoration permitted a thorough investigation of the architectural evolution of the cabin. The cabin was originally built as a two-pen dogtrot structure, sometime in the 1870s. An eight-foot-wide porch graced the front and there were two rooms on the back porch. The floor plan was thus almost identical to the Collard house. Logs were split and dressed with a plane to give smooth walls on the inside. Floor and ceiling joists were also made of pine logs but rafters were rough-sawn two-by-fours. Chimneys were made of "mud cats." There was no upstairs room.

At first the logs of this pen were not chinked, indicating that this side of the original house was used only during mild weather or for storage. Around the turn of the century the spaces between the logs were chinked with wood, board and batten siding was applied over the exterior walls and the attractive wooden fireplace mantel was built.

The Homestead, 1215 19th Street, Huntsville, Texas, 77340. Call (936) 291-7366, or visit www.thehomesteadon19th.com. Open Tuesday through Saturday for cocktails at 5:00 p.m. and dinner at 5:30 p.m., closing at 8:30 p.m., 9:30 p.m. on Fridays and Saturdays. Sunday brunch is served only on the first Sunday of every month from 11:30 a.m. to 1:30 p.m. Private luncheons are available by prior arrangements.

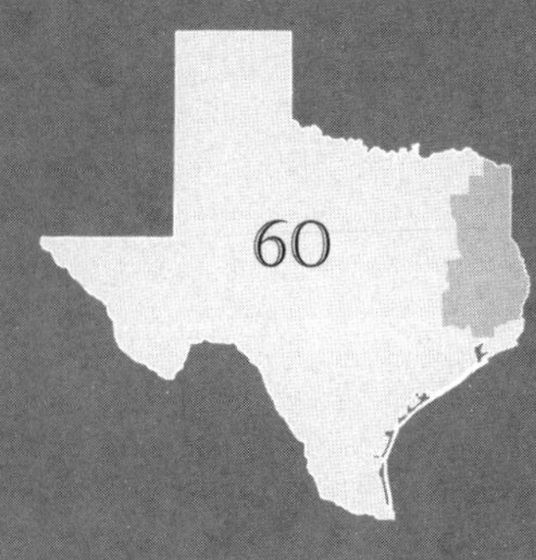

- 2 cups heavy cream
- 4 egg yolks
- 2 whole eggs
- 1 cup sugar
- 1 tablespoon fresh lemon zest, very fine
- 1 tablespoon lemon extract
- 1/2 tablespoon vanilla extract
- 1/2 cup fresh lemon juice
- 1 tablespoon corn starch
- 1/2 cup corn meal, for topping
- 1 1/2 cups cherries, pitted

Cherry Lemon Custard

There are numerous ways to prepare fresh cherries, from a classic pie to cherries jubilee—that is, if you can keep your family (or yourself) from eating them all. The following recipe is a really nice, homespun dish full of old-fashioned goodness; and although this rich custard is served warm, it actually tastes quite light and refreshing, with bright, fresh, lemon flavor wrapped around every juicy sweet cherry.

Pick cherries that are dark, firm, shiny, with stems intact and not blemished. Rinse well and dry before removing the pits. There are a number of different devices sold for this purpose. Use a fondue fork or a very small cocktail fork to pierce the cherry, grab the pit and push it through the other side. Be careful not to crush the cherry in the process.

Mix all of the ingredients for the custard (except the corn meal) in a bowl. Start with the eggs, zest, extracts and sugar with just a little of the lemon juice, and mix until very smooth. Use a little more of the lemon juice to dissolve the corn starch, then add it, along with the rest of the lemon juice and cream, to the bowl and mix well. Pour this into a shallow casserole pan or baking dish and drop in the cherries all around to disperse them evenly.

Place the dish into a larger baking pan that will allow you to fill it with hot water to at least half-way up the casserole pan. Place on the middle shelf of a preheated, 375-degree oven. Bake undisturbed for about 25 minutes. At that point it should just be starting to "set." Being careful not to shake the custard, pull the pan out so that you can sprinkle the corn meal evenly to cover the entire top of the custard. Turn the heat up to 400 degrees and continue baking until the custard is fully set (it will have risen slightly in the center and be noticeably firm) and nicely browned on top—another 10 to 20 minutes. Allow to cool for at least 10 minutes before serving. Hold warm for up to two hours if necessary.

It is not recommended to make this dish a day ahead; it is meant to be enjoyed from the oven. When serving the custard, make every effort to preserve the cornmeal topping, keeping it on top where it belongs—offering a pleasant little bit of crunchy texture that complements the silky smooth custard and incredible fresh flavors of lemon and cherry.

YIELD

Serves 4–6.

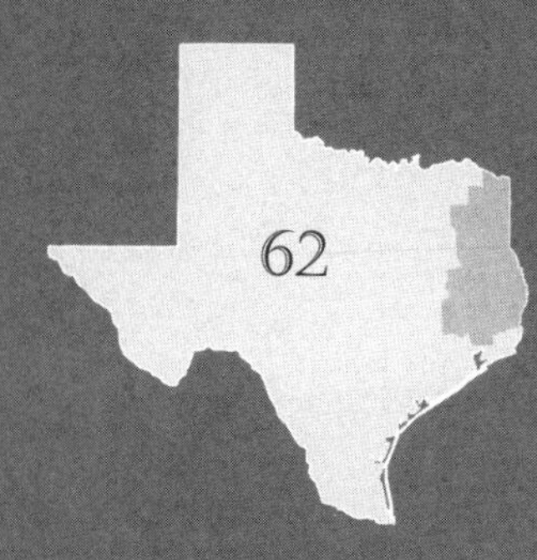

Peach Chutney

- 2 pounds peaches (5 medium or 4 large)
- 3/4 cup diced onion
- 1/4 cup salad oil
- 1/2 cup sugar
- 1/4 cup concentrated orange juice—not diluted
- 1/4 teaspoon ground black pepper
- 1/4 teaspoon allspice
- 1/4 teaspoon ginger
- 1/4 teaspoon cinnamon
- 1 bay leaf

The other day a friend asked how to make a peach chutney. First of all, a chutney can be defined as a relish that invariably features one or more fruit, cut small and cooked somewhat, usually along with diced onion and some spices. Crisp fruits, such as apple and pear, are excellent for chutneys, as are firm, less watery fruits such as mango, peach, papaya and pineapple. However, almost any fruit can be used.

Although not commonly offered in the United States, chutneys are popular worldwide. Originating from Indian and Oriental cuisines and distributed by the British during their reign over the high seas, chutneys are most often served as a condiment to any number of meats or meat dishes. Chutneys are often a little pungent, sometimes a little tart and always a little sweet and fruity. They are marvelous with game, roasts of all kinds and pates. The concept has not escaped inclusion in American fare either—good ol' Thanksgiving Day cranberry sauce (especially if it is made with onion) is essentially a chutney.

When my friend asked about the chutney, at first I thought that this was not a good time to be talking peaches—we were a couple of months away from peach season. Then I realized that for chutneys this is a great time for peaches—or should I say that for peaches, this is a great time to make chutney. Peaches that are too firm, too dry or not very sweet are great for making chutney.

First peel and destone the peaches, then dice the meat to a 1/4- to 1/2-inch dice. For appearances' sake, try to make the cuts as uniform as possible. Dice the onion no more than 1/4 inch. Heat a heavy bottomed saucepan or small skillet. Add the salad oil and, when heated, add the diced onion. Adjust heat to med-low and cook the onions until starting to brown, stirring and tossing frequently. This should take about 10 minutes. Next add the peaches, sugar, spices and concentrated orange juice. Stir to mix and allow to simmer on low for about 20 minutes. If the liquid reduces too quickly and it becomes too thick, just add a little water.

The chutney can be served warm, at room temperature or chilled. It is best, in fact, a couple of days after it is made. It will keep, well sealed, in the refrigerator for weeks and can be preserved (canned) to great effect.

YIELD

Approximately 3 cups.

MANSION ON THE HILL

Tyler

The Mansion on the Hill began as a physical symbol of the great oil boom in Texas around the turn of the 20th century. A farming family in New London discovered oil on their 100-acre spread, and their lives were forever changed.

Melissa Pool, the daughter of the family, took advantage of their newfound wealth to travel Europe extensively. She visited numerous cities and absorbed the many facets of their diverse cultures. When she finally returned to Tyler, she arranged for the construction of a family mansion in the style she felt represented the best of Europe.

Melissa, along with George and Herbert Heaton, designed the Mansion in 1936. Built with what she called a "European flair," they incorporated beautiful landscaping and various types of magnificent plants and flowers in the style she had observed on her travels. The Mansion was a showcase during its time.

As the years passed, the Mansion underwent many changes. Melissa and her family called the Mansion home, but it was also a popular location for film producers. Several small movies were filmed with the Mansion as the background.

In 1970 a local businessman bought the Mansion and used it for a residence for several years. In 1993, Giuseppe and Laura Cassini bought the property and began plans to convert it into a restaurant. In February of 1994, the Mansion on the Hill Restaurant and Club opened to "bring a little taste of international culture and cuisine to Tyler."

Born in Rome, Italy, Chef Giuseppe brings over 40 years of experience to Tyler. He attended hotel training school in Italy and Switzerland, and traveled to other European cities to learn all aspects of the business. He has since traveled the world gaining experience working as a chef for exclusive restaurants in both Europe and the USA.

With the marriage of a European-trained chef and a Mansion designed after the best of European styling, Tyler offers a truly unique dining experience. Menu selections are continental in style, including prime cuts of beef, Black Angus fillets, veal, seafood, live lobster, chicken and pasta. The restaurant is available for corporate gatherings, private parties and special events. Catering is also available.

The Mansion on the Hill, Highway 64 East and corner of Old Anderson Highway, Tyler, Texas 75711. Call (903) 533-1628 or visit www.mansiononthehill.com. The restaurant is open Monday through Saturday from 5 until 9 p.m. They are closed Sunday.

Fillet of Sea Bass "Mansion"

4 sea bass fillets (8 ounces each)
1/4 pound fresh crabmeat
4 ounces sun-dried tomatoes
2 red bell peppers
4 cloves garlic
2 teaspoons fresh basil
4 ounces white wine
1/4 cup heavy cream
1/2 cup butter
pinch thyme
salt and pepper

Place sea bass fillets in a pan. Season with salt and pepper to taste. Brush fillets with 1/4 cup liquefied butter. Place the fish in a nonstick pan or flat grill platter and sear each side well. Bake at 350 degrees for about 10 minutes.

SAUCE AND ASSEMBLY:

Roast the bell peppers in an open fire until the skin is brown. Wrap the peppers in plastic wrap and let them cool down. Nick the skin off.

Pour a cup of water in a small saucepan. Add the package of sun-dried tomatoes and cook for about 10 minutes. Lower the heat and simmer for about 20 minutes. Remove from the heat and let it cool down. Place the cooked sun-dried tomatoes, bell peppers, basil, thyme, crabmeat, salt and pepper in a food processor and mix well.

Melt 1/4 cup butter in a skillet. Add the chopped garlic and sauté until golden brown. Add the white wine to the mixed ingredients and finish it off with the heavy cream. Pour over the fish and serve.

Serves 4.

O'DELLS

Winona

The brick building that houses O'Dells was constructed in approximately 1927. It has survived many changes over the years due to the wide variety of businesses that have resided there. At times this facility was a soda fountain, drug store, pharmacy, constable's office, feed store and laundromat, to name a few.

The restaurant was established in 1996 not only to satisfy a need, but also a desire for hand-prepared food, pleasant ambiance and a generally enjoyable dining experience. O'Dells is named after the grandmother of the owner, Harry L. Jones III. She resided in Canada and maintained a passion for the culinary arts. O'Dell was from the "Gibson Girl" era and an eccentric for the time she lived in. It seemed appropriate to the owner to honor her memory and carry forward the same eccentricity and passion for this restaurant.

O'Dells serves basically an Italian fare along with a few American dishes. The restaurant was created with heart and energy and often is popular enough that they recommend you call ahead for reservations. In the spirit of many Texas establishments, you are encouraged to bring your own alcoholic refreshments.

O'Dells, 119 South Main Street (Texas Highway 155), Winona, Texas 75792, (903) 877-4488. They are open Wednesday through Sunday from 3 p.m. until 9 p.m. O'Dells is closed Monday and Tuesday.

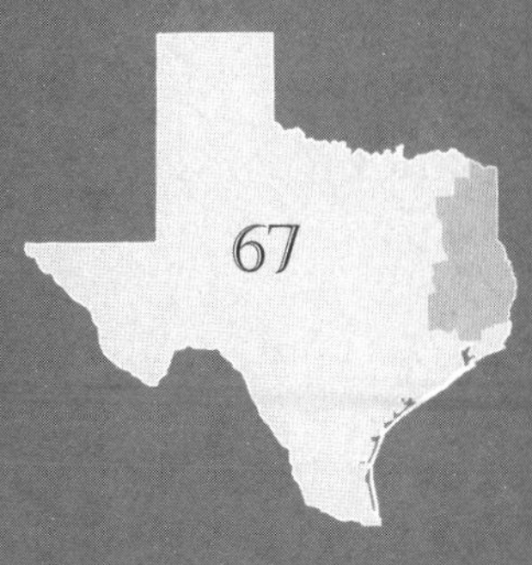

Anna's Chocolate Cake

Preheat oven to 350 degrees. Butter and flour a 9" × 13" pan. Heat butter, water and cocoa over low heat until butter is melted. Let cool. Add flour and sugar and mix well. Add remaining ingredients, mixing after each addition. Pour into prepared pan and bake for 30 minutes.

CHOCOLATE FROSTING:

Heat butter, cocoa and buttermilk over low heat until butter is melted. (It looks like a mess.) Add powdered sugar and beat well. While cake is still warm, spread with frosting.

1 cup butter

1 cup water

1/4 cup cocoa

2 cups flour

2 cups sugar

2 eggs

1/2 cup buttermilk

1 teaspoon soda

1 teaspoon vanilla

CHOCOLATE FROSTING:

1 stick butter

1/4 cup cocoa

1/4 cup buttermilk

2 cups powdered sugar

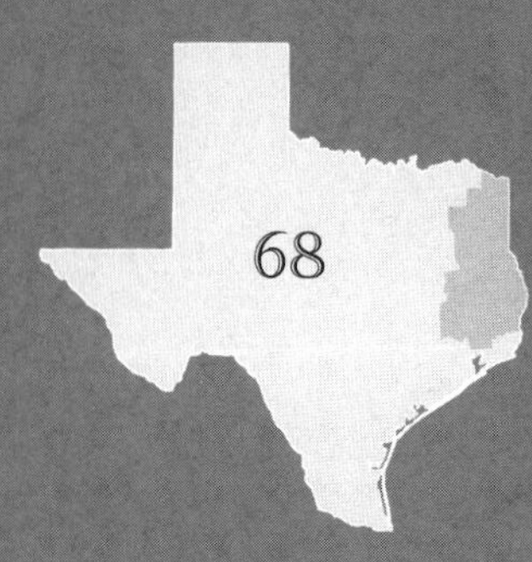

Garlic Butter Spread

1/2 pound margarine or butter

1 1/2 ounces fresh garlic

3/4 ounce garlic powder

1 1/4 ounces parsley

pinch salt

Soften margarine until it can be used in a blender or large mixer. As it is mixing, slowly add remaining ingredients. Mix well. Place into containers with lids and refrigerate (the longer the better). This spread is to be placed on slices of homemade bread and baked at 500 degrees for 3–5 minutes, depending on thickness of the bread.

Spinach and Artichoke Hearts

8 ounces cream cheese

1/2 cup butter

1 lemon

20 ounces spinach, cooked, well drained and well seasoned

14 ounces artichoke hearts, sliced

nutmeg to taste

Soften cream cheese and butter in top of a double boiler. Add spinach that has been seasoned with lemon and nutmeg. Place artichoke slices in greased casserole and pour spinach mixture over the top. Bake at 350 degrees for 15 minutes.

WOODBINE HOTEL

Madisonville

The history of the Woodbine Hotel began in 1904, when it first opened as the Shapira Hotel. Russian immigrants Jako and Sarah Shapira settled in Madisonville in the 1870s and ran a boarding house that burned to the ground in 1903. They rebuilt a structure that is now the Woodbine Hotel. Jake died after stepping on a nail during construction, leaving Sarah to operate the hotel until 1922.

Clara Wills purchased the hotel in 1929 and changed the name to the Wills Hotel. After 45 years of operation, the Willses closed the hotel to guests in 1974 and moved out in 1978. Randy Parten purchased the hotel in 1979 and began a two-year, $1.2 million total restoration. The building was entered into the National Register of Historic Places in 1980. It became a Texas Historic Landmark in 1982. Parten then donated the hotel to the Woodbine Foundation in 1997 and the foundation operated the hotel as a non-profit organization dedicated to charitable, educational and religious organizations.

In October 1999, Reinhard and Susan Warmuth purchased the Woodbine. They had both been in the hotel business for over 20 years but, due to their jobs, they were never together in the same city. They searched all over Texas for a property that met their exacting requirements and settled on the Woodbine as the ideal place to operate a bed and breakfast. Convenient to Houston, Dallas and Austin, the hotel offers guests a peaceful, quiet getaway from the hustle and bustle of everyday life.

The Woodbine Hotel, 209 North Madison, Madisonville, Texas 77864. Call (936) 348-3333. Or see www.woodbinehoteltexas.com. Open Tuesday through Friday for lunch from 11:30 a.m. until 2 p.m., dinner Tuesday through Saturday 6 p.m. until 9 p.m. and Sunday brunch 11 a.m. until 2 p.m.

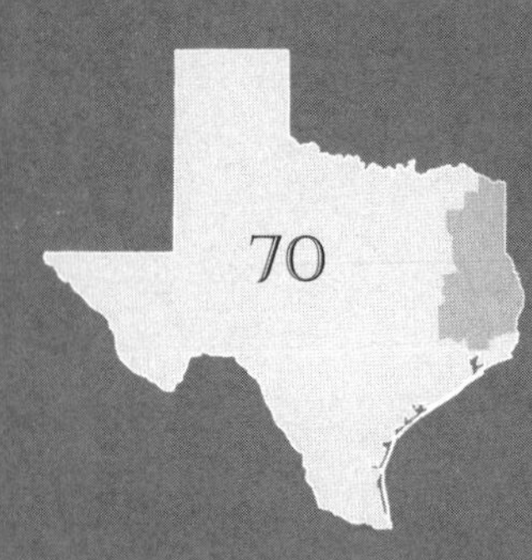

Southern Pecan Pie

1 1/4 cup sugar

1/2 cup dark corn syrup

1/4 cup butter

2 ounces bourbon (the better the bourbon, the better the pie)

3 eggs, beaten

1 cup whole pecans, shelled

1/4 cup chopped pecans

WHIPPED CREAM:

3/4 cup heavy whipping cream

2 tablespoons powdered sugar

1 ounce Triple Sec or orange flavored liqueur

PIE CRUST:

1 cup flour

1/2 teaspoon salt

1/3 cup shortening

3 3/4 tablespoons cold water

Preheat oven to 400 degrees.

PIE CRUST:

Combine flour and salt in a mixing bowl. Cut in shortening with a pastry cutter until flour mixture resembles coarse sand. Add water one tablespoon at a time and mix with a fork until dough forms into a ball. Do not overmix or crust will be tough.

Roll dough out on floured surface, place in a 10" pie shell. Trim edge of crust one inch away from shell. Roll edge under towards shell until it sits on top of pie shell edge. Then crimp piecrust however you like to decorate it.

Rolling the edges makes the edge thicker and prevents it from crumbling or getting too well done before the pie is finished.

Set pie shell aside.

PIE FILLING:

Combine sugar, corn syrup, butter and bourbon in saucepan. Bring to boil. Remove from heat and let cool to room temperature. Gradually add the beaten eggs.

ASSEMBLY:

Add chopped pecans to bottom of pie crust. Cover with whole pecans. Slowly pour pie filling over pecans. Bake 10 minutes at 400 degrees, and then bake from 20 to 25 minutes at 350 degrees or until done. Watch carefully;

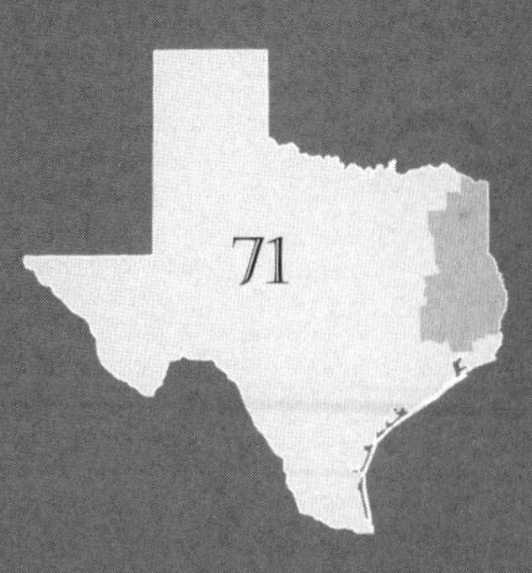

don't let the pie get too dark. Let cool, cut and serve with a dollop of fresh whipped cream (recipe follows).

WHIPPED CREAM:

Just before serving, whip the cream and sugar to soft peaks. (Be careful you don't make butter.) Slowly add liqueur while continuing to whip. Spoon whipped cream on top of pie servings.

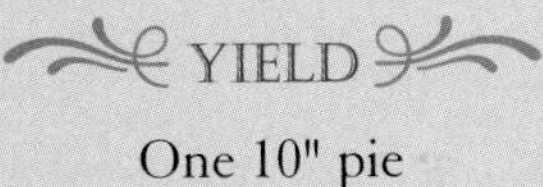

One 10" pie

2 pounds salmon fillet

1 zucchini

1 yellow squash

1 red bell pepper

1 box phyllo dough (freezer section of grocery, follow directions for thawing)

salt and pepper to taste

1 bunch fresh basil (6 ounces)

2 ounces olive oil

1 bunch green onions, chopped

1 mango

1/2 honeydew melon

1/2 cantaloupe

6 ounces olive oil

3 lemons, juiced

salt and pepper, to taste

1 pound spring mix or other assorted lettuces

1 bunch asparagus, blanched

1 jicama

salad dressing

Salmon Roll in Phyllo Dough

SALMON ROLL:

Preheat oven to 350 degrees. Cut salmon fillets into strips. Season with salt and pepper. Julienne zucchini, yellow squash, red bell pepper and fresh basil. Lay out 3 sheets of phyllo dough on top of each other on a clean, dry surface. Brush lightly with olive oil. Place salmon, vegetables and basil on top of sheets. Roll sheets forming long roll. Place on baking sheet. Bake in oven until golden brown. Remove from oven.

FRUIT SALSA:

Peel and seed honeydew and cantaloupe melons and mango. Dice all fruit into small dice and place in bowl. Combine with chopped green onions, olive oil and lemon juice. Add salt and pepper to taste.

PRESENTATION:

Peel jicama (large, bulbous root vegetable with a thin brown skin and white, crunchy flesh with a sweet, nutty flavor) and make a thin julienne. Trim asparagus and blanch.

ARRANGE ON PLATE:

Divide fruit salsa equally among six plates and place at bottom of plate. Slice salmon roll into 12 equal-sized pieces. Place two slices upright on salsa on each plate. Arrange asparagus above salsa/salmon on the plate. Top asparagus with spring greens and your favorite dressing. Sprinkle jicama juliennes over top of salad and salmon. Serve and enjoy.

Serves 6.

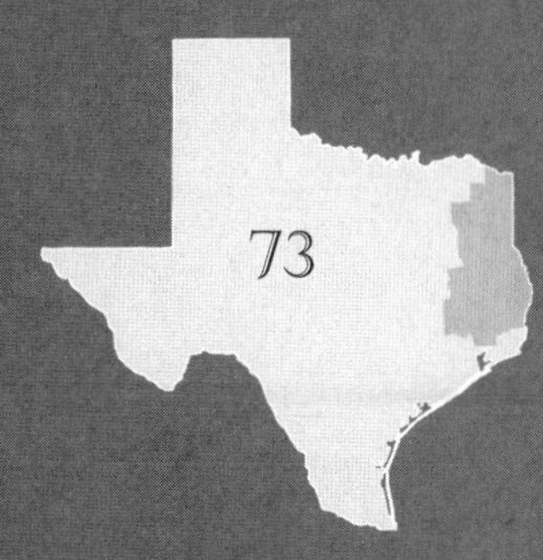

Five Cheese Soup
in Baked Acorn Squash Bowls with Roasted Red Bell Pepper Coulis

SQUASH SOUP BOWL:

Wash squash, cut in half. Remove seeds. Slice thin layer off bottom of each half so squash will sit flat and stable on a plate. Season with salt and pepper. Bake in 350 degree oven for 20–30 minutes until done. Remove from oven, let rest.

ROASTED RED BELL PEPPER COULIS (GARNISH):

Roast red bell peppers on a grill or under broiler until skin turns dark or black. Remove from grill and place in a bowl. Tightly wrap bowl with plastic wrap and let stand for approximately 15 minutes. Peel skin from pepper, cut in half and discard seeds. Put pepper flesh in blender, add olive oil, salt and pepper. Puree until smooth. Pour coulis into squeeze bottle. May be refrigerated up to 4 weeks. To spice up coulis, add flesh of 2 or 3 roasted jalapenos.

FIVE CHEESE SOUP:

Melt 6 ounces of butter in heavy saucepan over low flame and add flour slowly, stirring constantly. Cook until mixture just begins to turn beige, forming a "white roux." Add chicken stock slowly, again stirring constantly to not form lumps. When completely blended, let simmer 15 to 20 minutes.

In sauté pan, melt remaining 2 ounces of butter. Sauté chopped red onions, celery and herbs until onions are translucent. Stir in half-and-half. Bring to a boil. Remove

SOUP BOWL:

3 medium acorn squash

salt and pepper to taste

COULIS:

2 medium red bell peppers

1 ounce olive oil

salt and pepper to taste

FIVE CHEESE SOUP:

1/2 quart chicken stock

1/2 cup all-purpose flour

8 ounces butter

1 medium red onion, finely chopped

2–3 stalks celery, finely chopped

2 teaspoons fresh thyme, finely chopped

2 teaspoons fresh oregano, finely chopped

1/2 quart half-and-half

1 pound total:
- shredded sharp cheddar
- shredded Swiss
- shredded pepper Jack
- shredded Monterey Jack
- shredded Parmesan
- salt and pepper to taste

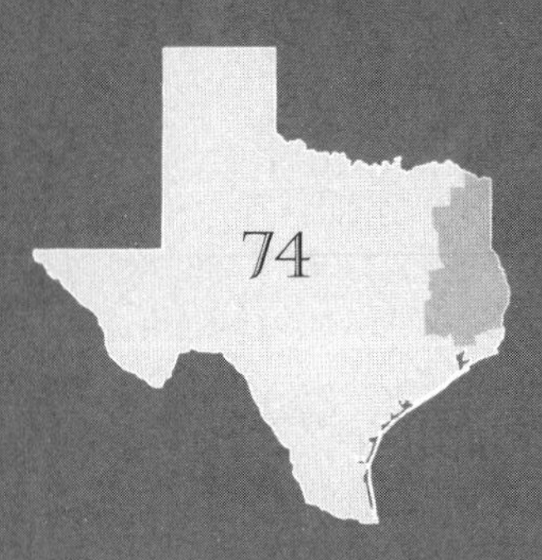

from heat. Stir in shredded cheeses. While constantly stirring, return to heat and bring back to simmer. Add white sauce to cheese mixture, mixing thoroughly. Return to simmer and hold.

ASSEMBLY:

Place acorn squash on dinner plate. Ladle hot soup into "bowl." Squirt red bell pepper coulis on top and serve immediately.

YIELD

Serves 6–8.

WUNSCHE BROTHERS CAFÉ & SALOON

Spring

The town was named, as legend has it, for the season of the year. The story claims that in the mid-1800s the men building the railroad right-of-way and laying the track between Palestine and Houston had experienced one of the worst winters in history. The railroad men fought ice, sleet, snow, freezing rain and below-freezing temperatures. They located a new camp just south of Spring Creek as they moved the railhead forward and when William Pierpont came in spring 1838, the camp became a town. The men rejoiced at the beautiful weather and called the new location "Camp Spring." Later the word "camp" was dropped and the town became officially known as Spring, Texas.

Jane and Carl Wunsche settled this land in 1846. The farm was left to two of their sons, Dell and Charlie who, together with brother William and his son Willie, built the Wunsche Brothers Saloon and Hotel in 1902 to satisfy the needs of railroad employees in the area. Lumber was cut in their own sawmill from old-stand longleaf pines that were four-to-six feet in diameter.

Spring was a Houston and Great Northern Railroad boomtown by 1902. Before long hotels, saloons, residences and general stores cropped up in this switchyard and stop on the Galveston–Houston–Palestine line. The town thrived until 1923 when the railyard was moved to Houston. By 1926 most of the town's wood buildings were salvaged for barn construction and firewood. The Wunsche Brothers Cafe & Saloon was the first two-story building erected in Spring and remains today the oldest survivor of the past. It is frequently given credit for the current prosperity of Old Town Spring.

Wunsche Brothers Café and Saloon, 103 Midway, Spring, Texas 77373. Monday it is open from 11 a.m. to 3 p.m. and Tuesday through Thursday from 11 a.m. to 9 p.m. Friday and Saturday the hours are 11 a.m. to 10 p.m. Sunday it is open from 11 a.m. to 8 p.m. For more information call (281) 350-1902 or visit www.wunschebroscafe.com.

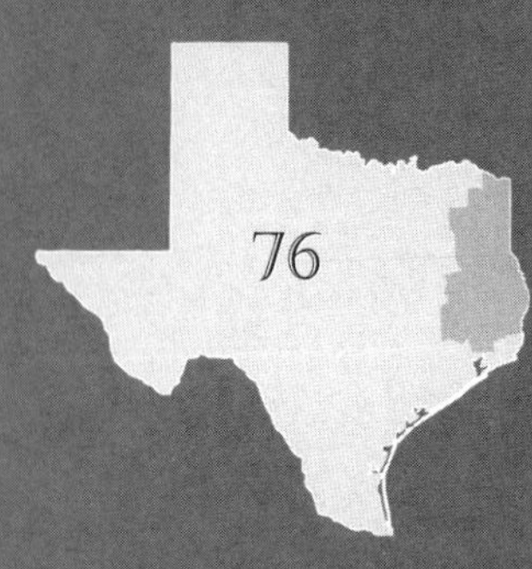

Sausage Sauerkraut Balls

Hands down, this is our most talked about food. People come here from all over the country and tell us they've heard about our sauerkraut balls. I love to hear a customer say, "Oh, I don't like sauerkraut." They are the very ones that end up raving about these and coming back for more.

—Brenda Greene Mitchell

1 pound bulk sausage

1 1/2 cups grated mild cheddar cheese

3 eggs

1 cup sauerkraut, drained and squeezed dry

1 small onion, chopped

dried bread crumbs

beer batter (recipe follows)

Mix all ingredients by hand. (Try not to break sauerkraut strands.) Shape into 1–1 1/2-inch balls and roll in bread crumbs. Refrigerate until ready to deep-fry. When ready to fry, dip in beer batter and deep-fry in 375-degree oil until golden brown. Serve with sour cream chive dip.

YIELD

Makes about 30 balls.

Beer Batter

2 cups all-purpose flour

1 teaspoon baking powder

1 tablespoon salt

1 1/2 cups beer

1 1/2 teaspoons garlic powder

oil for deep-frying

Combine flour, salt, garlic powder and baking powder in bowl. Add beer and whisk until smooth. Cover and chill 30 minutes. Whisk again; then let stand in refrigerator until ready to use. Batter can be prepared one day ahead, if desired.

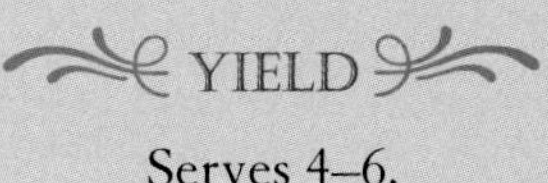

Cut zucchini vertically into long strips. Dip zucchini strips in flour, then in beer batter. Deep-fry in hot oil until golden brown.

YIELD

Serves 4–6.

3 zucchini

flour

beer batter (see above)

oil for deep-frying

3

Prairies and Lakes

Town and country. Gonzales boasts that it is where the first shot of the Texas Revolution was fired. Charming Brenham has a monastery where nuns raise miniature horses and Glen Rose has a wonderful wildlife ranch. This area has plenty of nightlife, parks and professional sports in the metropolitan areas of Dallas and Fort Worth. Chic and classy Dallas is a contrast to historical and art-museum-filled Fort Worth. Other cities such as Bryan-College Station, Granbury and Round Top are also proudly part of the Prairies and Lakes region.

A SCOOP IN TIME

Grapevine

Housed in a historic building in the heart of Grapevine, A Scoop In Time occupies one of the oldest buildings in town. Originally built in the early 1900s, it first served as a feed store. Later, it was the Lucas General Store downstairs, while the upstairs served as Lucas Funeral Home. A police officer killed by Bonnie and Clyde was laid out in this facility. This was the first building in Tarrant County to have an elevator installed, although the elevator has since been removed.

When Lucas built a new funeral home, the upstairs was used to build and store caskets. To hide the caskets from Main Street, the front windows were boarded up with a mural painted across the three windows. The picture wore off but the windows remained boarded up until 2000, when the current owners renovated the building and opened them up. A picture of the General Store as it stood in 1910 now hangs in the restaurant as a gift from the Lucas granddaughter.

When the Lucas family sold the building, the phone company had been housed upstairs for several years. United Supermarket filmed a television commercial at A Scoop In Time in 2000. The building had deteriorated to the point that it was on Grapevine's endangered list when Darla Batchler and Sharon O'Neil bought it and began renovations, creating a combination restaurant and ice cream parlor. Careful to maintain as much of its original character as possible, they may be responsible for the climate in which "unusual happenings" occasionally occur. Some of the upstairs tenants believe the building has ghosts.

A Scoop In Time, 412 South Main Street, Grapevine, Texas 76051, (817) 421-6393, is open from 11 a.m. to 5:30 p.m. Monday through Saturday and 1 p.m. to 5 p.m. on Sunday. In the summer they stay open until 9:00 p.m. on weekdays.

Grilled Pimento Cheese Sandwich

2 slices 5-grain wheat bread
butter
pimento cheese
mayonnaise

Butter one side of each slice and place the butter side down on griddle.

Pile one slice with pimento cheese. Let the bread brown. Spread mayonnaise on the other slice of bread and put the sandwich together.

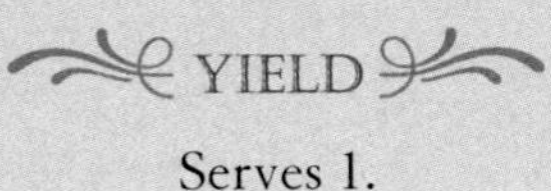

Serves 1.

Tomato Basil Soup

1/2 cup margarine
2 tablespoons basil
4 teaspoons Tones chicken base
7 cups crushed tomato puree
46 ounces tomato juice
9 1/2 ounces evaporated milk
2 tablespoons grated parmesan cheese

Sauté basil and chicken base in margarine for several minutes. Add tomato puree. Simmer five minutes. Add tomato juice and milk. Heat through. Add parmesan.

Serves 10.

BACK DOOR CAFÉ

Smithville

The building that is now occupied by the Back Door Café was originally constructed in 1889. Records indicate that two businesses occupied the floor space at that time: a barbershop and a butcher. Apparently people needed to eat more than they needed a haircut because a cobbler replaced the barber while the meat shop continued. A few years later, the meat shop grew into a grocery store.

Around 1915 the building became a pool hall for a short time while the floor space was combined with the shop next door. Within three years the property had changed again. Falkenberg Drug Store operated for a time until the name was changed to Falkenberg & Czichos Drugs and Jewelry. As a typical drug store of the era, they maintained a soda fountain, which was a popular gathering spot for the area's children.

The facility later became the City Drug Store but the entire operation closed when the local bank failed in 1932. A doctor maintained an office in part of the building, and a couple of years later he shared the premises with a dry cleaning business.

Over the next few years, the building housed several businesses including the May Day Ash Clothing Store, a thrift shop and an upholstery shop. The first eating establishment appeared here in 1977 as the Koz-Mo Restaurant expanded from next door in 1977. They stayed in business until 1987. For two years it was the Good Times Activity Center and then the building was vacant for several years until the owners, Lou and Cherrell Rose, cleaned it up for occupancy. Chef Rob Remlinger then renovated the interior and opened the Back Door Café in 1995.

You may have already seen Smithville at the movies. Twentieth Century Fox filmed Sandra Bullock, Harry Connick, Jr. and Gena Rowlands in *Hope Floats* in Smithville. The home used in many scenes is at 201 E. Eighth, but it is a private residence. Local travel guides can direct you to more than a dozen sites filmed in the movie, but they ask everyone to respect the privacy of the property owners.

Among the many local attractions in Smithville is the Jack Daniel's Chocolate Cream Pie at the Back Door. All the food at the Back Door Café is handmade in their own kitchen. Daily luncheons are buffet style, including a salad bar and two entrées. The evening menu includes a choice of entrées prepared especially for that night.

Back Door Café, 117 Main Street, Smithville, Texas 78957. Call (512) 237-3128. They are open every day for lunch (except Tuesdays) from 11 a.m. until 2 p.m. Sunday's offering is a special brunch at the same time. Dinner is available Thursday, Friday and Saturday from 5:30 until 9:30 p.m.

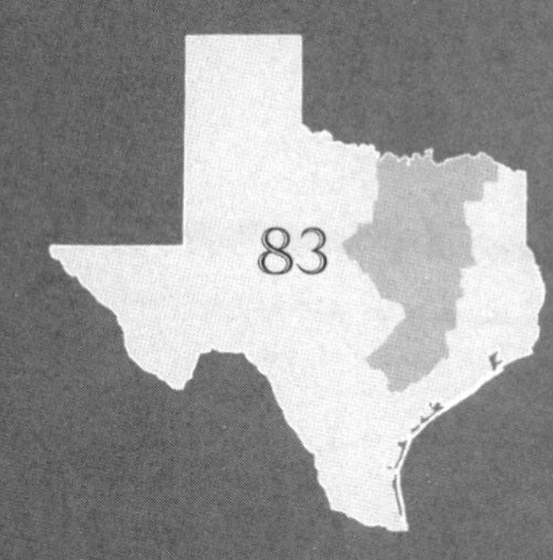

Smoked Chicken with Spicy Linguine

Heat oil in a sauté pan. Add tomatoes, peppers, chicken and garlic. Toss. When heated add black beans, cilantro (saving some for garnish) and pasta with a little water. Toss until hot. Salt and pepper to taste. Garnish with chopped cilantro.

YIELD

Serves 1.

1 breast Julienne mesquite chicken, smoked (8 ounces)

1 serving southwest-flavored linguine, cooked

1/3 cup black beans, cooked

1/2 bunch cilantro, chopped

1 teaspoon garlic, chopped

2 Roma tomatoes cut lengthwise into strips

1/2 bell pepper cut lengthwise into strips

salt and pepper to taste

light olive oil

1 cup sour cream

3 tablespoons brown sugar

2 teaspoons cinnamon

1 1/2 ounces Grand Marnier liquor

Romanoff Sauce

In a mixing bowl, add liquor to brown sugar. Whisk until there are no lumps of sugar. Add sour cream and cinnamon and mix.

Note: This sauce is best served over fresh strawberries.

YIELD

Yields 10 ounces.

Success

It's only food. Don't stress, just make it great. And don't be afraid to substitute for ingredients you don't have.

THE BRAZOS BELLE

Burton

Built in 1875, the building now known as "The Belle" has seen many changes. A deed dated May 5, 1875 stated that Lewis Dirr and his wife sold lot 5, block 45 with improvements and appurtenances to S. R. Kindra for one buggy and harness valued at $200, one pair of mules valued at $300, one set of wagon harness valued at $15, one gold watch valued at $125 and two promissory notes of $125 each. Adjacent pieces of property were simultaneously purchased and developed into commercial facilities, and the history of all three has been interconnected from the beginning.

Over the next 125 plus years these buildings housed doctors' offices, a dry goods store, The Humpty Dumpty Grocery, a mercantile business under the name Steiner and Dallmeyer, a ceramics shop, a drugstore, a cotton marketing center and a part-time post office. This was the location of the first telephone in Burton. In 1969, Raymond Winklemann purchased the buildings and remodeled the main structure into a beer parlor and dance hall known as The Brazos Belle. Another part of the complex was turned into an antique shop known as The Plantation House.

The history of Burton is closely related to nearby Union Hill. Both towns developed in the area called Kerr Settlement. The famous La Bahia Road went past the area nearby and was used as early as 1690 by the Spanish government. The same part was referred to as the Opelousas Trail in the 1800s when it was used for cattle drives. Even the indigenous Indian tribes frequented the area because of the natural springs.

In 1831, Hu h and Lucy Kerr moved to Texas with nine children. Their home was known as Kerr Settlement, and the area attracted numerous other settlers until the town population exceeded 1,000 residents in 10 short years. When the Houston/Texas Central Railroad developed a route in the area that missed Union Hill by two miles, most residents abandoned the area and moved to the area called Burton after the previous owners, John and Elizabeth Burton.

In 1989, French chef Andre Delacroix and his American wife Sandy bought the property and converted it into a restaurant. They offer "French and American food," primarily because patrons like it that way. But they follow their principles by only using fresh ingredients based on what is in season. The chef refuses to fry, bread or dip your dinner in grease. A testament to their success is not only the number of repeat patrons eating there, but also the traffic congestion at Burton's only stop sign. Due to the popularity of this unique restaurant, plan to come early, as they do not take reservations. They also don't accept credit cards.

The Brazos Belle Inn, 600 North Main Street, Burton, Texas 77835. Call (979) 289-2677, or visit www.brazosbellerestaurant.com. Open Fridays and Saturdays from 5:30 until 9:00 p.m. and Sunday from 11:30 a.m. until 2 p.m.

Grilled Salmon
with Fresh Tomato-Caper Sauce

4 fresh salmon fillets (6 ounces), boneless with all skin and "pin-bones" removed

MARINADE:

1/4 cup olive oil

1 6-inch section fresh lemongrass, finely chopped (stalk, not leaves)

1 teaspoon fresh thyme leaves

1 garlic clove, finely minced

cracked black pepper to taste

FRESH TOMATO-CAPER SAUCE:

3 tablespoons olive oil

1 teaspoon garlic, finely minced

1 tablespoon capers

black pepper to taste

2 Roma tomatoes, seeded, peeled and diced

Sauté garlic in oil until tender; do not brown. Add the capers and black pepper to taste. Sauté one minute longer, then add the diced Roma tomatoes. Bring to a boil, then remove from heat. Let cool to room temperature. Sauce can be prepared in advance and stored in refrigerator for several days.

Marinate the fillets for a minimum of 2 hours in the refrigerator in a flat glass container. Sear the marinated fillets in a very hot heavy skillet for approximately 3 minutes on each side. No additional oil should be added to the skillet; the marinade coating of each fillet is adequate for cooking. Top each fillet with Tomato-Caper Sauce and serve immediately.

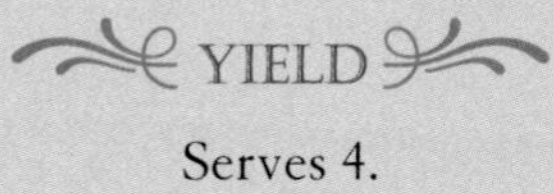

Serves 4.

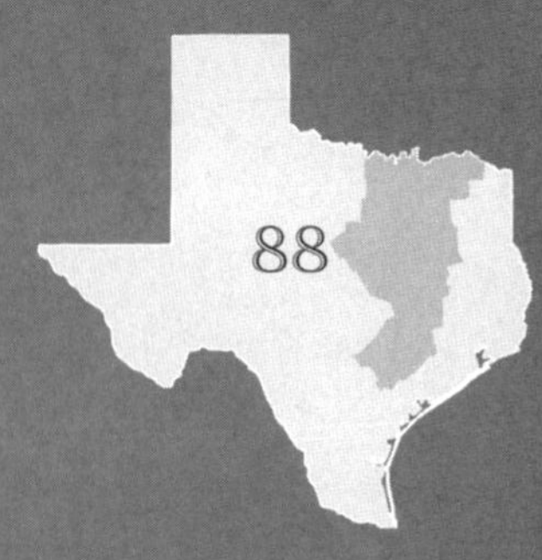

Brazos Belle Rack of Lamb

1 Frenched rack of lamb, 8 bone

4 teaspoons Dijon mustard

1 teaspoon rosemary leaves, finely chopped

MARINADE:

1 cup canola oil

1 garlic clove, finely minced

1 tablespoon fresh parsley, finely chopped

1 tablespoon four spice (contains black pepper, nutmeg, cinnamon and cloves)

1 tablespoon fresh thyme, finely chopped

black pepper to taste

Combine ingredients for marinade and blend well in blender. Marinate meat overnight.

Preheat oven to 425 degrees. In a very hot skillet, sear the meat on all sides. No additional oil should be added to the skillet, as the marinade coating is adequate for cooking. Remove from the skillet. Rub on a generous coating of Dijon mustard and finely chopped rosemary leaves. Place roast on open flat pan to finish cooking (approximately 10 minutes). Serve immediately. Delicious served with couscous and ratatouille.

YIELD

Serves 4.

Mousse au Chocolat

- 6-ounce chocolate pieces, semisweet
- 1/4 cup strong black coffee
- 1 tablespoon butter
- 1 tablespoon rum, or
- 1 tablespoon vanilla extract
- 4 eggs, separated
- whipped cream

In medium, heavy saucepan, melt chocolate in the coffee, over low heat. Cook, stirring constantly until chocolate is thick and creamy but still slips easily from the spoon (not too thick!). Remove from heat and beat in egg yolks, one at a time to thicken mixture. Beat in butter and rum (or vanilla). Cool slightly. Meanwhile, whip egg whites until stiff. Gently fold egg whites into the still "hot to the touch" chocolate. Pour into four mousse or parfait glasses. Cover and refrigerate at least six hours for flavors to blend. Serves cold, topped with whipped cream.

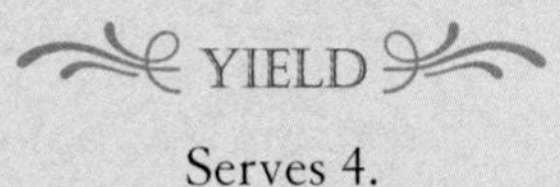

Serves 4.

Note: Chocolate mousse can be prepared two days ahead and kept refrigerated.

THE BURTON CAFÉ

Burton

In the late 1930s Bill and Margie Fischer were running a café in the landmark O. K. Saloon on Washington Street in downtown Burton. When the saloon burnt down in the summer of 1937, the Fischers leased a new building across the street and started what has ever since been The Burton Café.

Hugh Derrick and Ron Blackburn, the second renters, added a meat market to the café. More renters followed until 1970 when Mildred and Lee Roy Boehnemann, the operators since 1959, bought the building from the original owners, the Whitener family. In 1966 the wall that had separated the white and black dining areas was removed.

There is a reason why the restrooms in The Burton Café are called "In Houses." In 1983, when James and Rosalie Powell bought the café, outhouses that had been built by the WPA still graced the property—although hidden by rosebushes. The Powells built the "In Houses" when the new Burton sewer plant made it possible in 1984.

Yes, J. R. ate here. In 1983, Larry Hagman and six friends came to check out an oil well nearby and ate lunch at The Burton Café. Some Burton residents still have the mock hundred dollar bills he passed out with his own picture on them. You can see his autographed photo on the wall and may end up sitting in his chair. It is marked.

In 1984, *Texas Monthly* magazine declared The Burton Café one of the eight best country cafés in Texas. Houstonians Steve and Cindy Miller bought the café from Rosie Powell in 1991 and are continuing the tradition of a true hometown restaurant, although they have made the building more attractive and diversified the menu—in a limited fashion.

Milo Hamilton, radio announcer for the Houston Astros, recently stopped here to have a hamburger and a piece of Grace Boehnemann's delicious coconut crème pie. On his next broadcast, he said that everybody who travels on Highway 290 should turn off and stop at The Burton Café—if only for a piece of Grace's wonderful pie.

The Burton Café, 12513 Washington, Burton, Texas 77835, (979) 289-3849. Open from 7 a.m. to 8 p.m. Monday, Thursday and Friday; from 7 a.m. until 2 p.m. on Tuesday and Wednesday and 7 a.m. to 9 p.m. on Saturday.

Pecan Pie

1 cup sugar
1 cup light corn oil
1/3 cup melted butter or Oleo
dash salt
1/2 teaspoon vanilla
4 eggs
1 1/4 cup pecans, chopped
1 9-inch pie shell, unbaked

Cream together first 5 ingredients, then whisk in the eggs until well blended. Put the chopped pecans into the unbaked pie shell and pour the sugar mixture over the pecans. Bake at 350 degrees for approximately one hour.

YIELD

Yields one 9" pie.

Buttermilk Pie

1 1/2 cups sugar
1 tablespoon flour
1 tablespoon cornstarch
dash salt
4 eggs
1/4 cup melted butter
1 cup buttermilk
1/2 teaspoon vanilla
1/4 cup coconut
1 9-inch unbaked pie shell

Combine first four ingredients. Whisk in eggs, butter, buttermilk and vanilla. Sprinkle coconut in bottom of unbaked pie shell and pour liquid mixture over top. Bake at 350 degrees for one hour until lightly browned and puffed up.

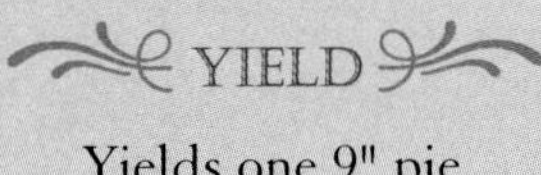

Yields one 9" pie.

CAFÉ ECCELL

College Station

In December of 1947, residents celebrated the opening of College Station's first city hall. The modern, one-story structure, designed by Texas A&M architecture students under Mayor Ernest Langford's guidance, was located in the Northgate area across Wellborn Road and adjacent to the railroad tracks.

It remained city hall until 1972, when the College Station utility company took over the building for their operations. Then, in the early 1980s, the police department acquired it as a recreation area, and it also served as a campus voting precinct and community hall. The building remained virtually unused until the fall of 1988, when it was renovated and opened as Café Eccell in August of 1989. Today, Café Eccell stands as a historic landmark for College Station.

Café Eccell's food is described as a unique ensemble of multi-regional cuisine that blends Mediterranean, Asian, Progressive American and Latin American flavors. Offering an unpretentious atmosphere, guests can enjoy an intimate formal dinner or a casual get-together with friends. From sandals and shorts to tuxedos and evening gowns, all are welcome in their relaxed, "no pressure" dining room. Their wood-burning pizza oven is unique to College Station, and their handmade dough and sauces make for an extraordinary pizza menu. Fresh seafood is shipped in two or three times a week, and they serve only "Certified Angus Beef." Desserts and bread are prepared daily by the pastry chef. Generally, they accept no reservations, but may accommodate large parties if you call ahead.

Café Eccell, 101 Church Avenue, College Station, Texas 77840, (979) 846-7908, or visit www.cafeeccell.com. The Café Eccell is open Sunday through Thursday from 11 a.m. to 10 p.m. and on Friday and Saturday from 11 a.m. to 11 p.m.

Jalapeno Buns

2 1/4 cups unbleached flour
1 ounce milk powder
1 pinch salt
2 tablespoons sugar
1/3 cup cheddar cheese
2 tablespoons jalapenos, diced
2 tablespoons onions, diced
3 tablespoons butter, softened
1 egg
3 tablespoons yeast
1 cup water

Combine the water, yeast, butter (microwave for one minute) and egg in a small mixing bowl. Add the cheese, jalapenos, onions and sugar. Add the flour, milk powder and salt. Mix at low speed for 15 minutes. Place dough onto the work surface and cut into 3 3/4 ounce portions. Roll into balls and place onto a lined sheet pan. Brush a bit of olive oil onto your palm and flatten the balls out slightly to produce a wider bun. Set aside to rise until the desired size is reached (approximately triple in size). Place into the oven at 350 degrees for 12 to 15 minutes. Remove from oven and allow to cool.

Makes 11 to 12 buns.

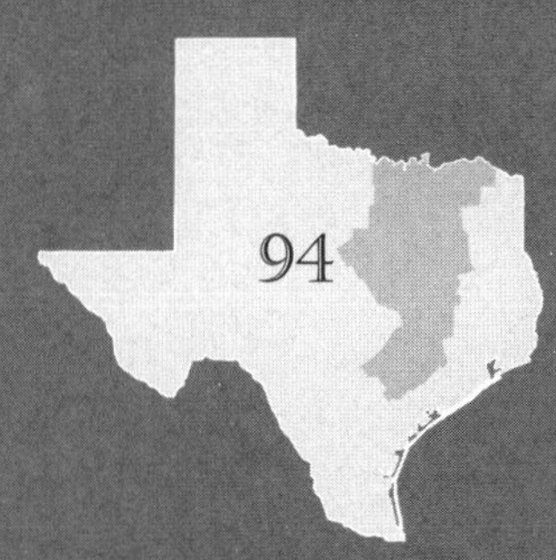

Three Bean Salad

- 1 cup black-eyed peas, canned
- 1 cup northern beans, canned
- 1 cup black beans, cooked
- 1/2 teaspoon chipotle peppers
- 1/8 cup vegetable oil
- 1 teaspoon salt
- 1 teaspoon black pepper
- 1/4 cup white wine
- 1/4 bunch cilantro, chopped
- 1/2 red onion, chopped fine
- 1/2 red bell, chopped fine
- 1/2 green bell, chopped fine
- 1/4 yellow bell, chopped fine

Drain all the water out of the beans. Mix all ingredients well in a bowl. Cover and chill.

Caesar Dressing

- 1/4 cup green onions
- 2 1/2 tablespoons garlic, minced
- 20 anchovies
- 2 1/2 tablespoons Dijon mustard
- 14 egg yolks
- 1 1/2 cups Parmesan cheese
- 1/2 cup red wine
- 1 1/4 tablespoons Worcestershire sauce
- 3/4 tablespoons white pepper
- 3 cups olive oil

Combine and process all ingredients except oil in a food processor for 1 minute. Drizzle in oil slowly while still processing.

1 1/2 quarts.

HOTEL ADOLPHUS

Dallas

The Adolphus, a Dallas landmark for nearly 90 years, is a unique creation of fortune and flamboyance from an extravagant age. The original hotel was built in 1912 by beer baron Adolphus Busch, on the site of the 1880s Dallas City Hall, for an original cost of $1.87 million. Busch spared no expense in erecting his namesake property in what critics have called "the most beautiful building west of Venice." At one time The Adolphus was the tallest building in Texas and it was the first hotel in the world to have central air conditioning.

In 1916, the hotel's Bambooland featured an elegant seven-course lunch for 75 cents. The menu offered a choice of at least six dishes in each category. The Century Room at the Adolphus boasted an Ice Revue starring Olympic skater Dorothy Franey. Most Southwest citizens had never seen skating on ice, and Miss Franey's fourteen-year engagement introduced that unfamiliar art form to Dallas. General John J. "Blackjack" Pershing reviewed parade troops in 1920 from above the porte cochere. Amelia Earhart and Charles Lindbergh were among the famous names that graced the hotel's guest registry in its early years. President Franklin D. Roosevelt reportedly used the hotel's back elevators in order to conceal the great effort it cost him to walk.

The Adolphus was completely restored in 1981 at a cost of approximately $80 million. The rooms were greatly expanded in size as the existing 1,000 rooms were reduced by more than half. The hotel now features 435 guest rooms, including 20 suites. Among the amenities the Adolphus offers are complimentary downtown sedan service, a 24-hour concierge, valet parking, a fitness room and athletic club privileges. Dining options include The Bistro, serving contemporary American cuisine, and the Walt Garrison Rodeo Bar and Grill, serving cocktails and hearty Texas fare.

The award-winning French Room serves classic French cuisine adapted to contemporary American tastes, in a setting that *The New York Times* describes as "a Louis XV fantasy on the prairie… indisputably the most striking and sumptuous restaurant in Dallas." Adolphus Busch created The French Room as the crown jewel of his namesake Dallas hotel. The dining room has been faithfully restored to its original grandeur, reminiscent of Europe's 18th-century palaces and chateaux. Among the architectural features of this opulent setting are murals that span the high, arched ceiling. The muralist, Alexander Rosenfield, also painted the sets for the original production of *Mame* in Philadelphia and the portrait of Laura in the motion picture *Laura*.

Eight faux marble columns border the French Room. Original bas-reliefs, gilt moldings and sconces have been completely restored. The principal backgrounds of ivory, pale green, soft tans, blues and pinks set the tone of the room. The French Room also features hand-blown crystal chandeliers of 17th-century design. They were made in Murano, Italy, by the descendants of craftsmen who made the famous originals more than 300 years ago. The flooring is a verde monte marble, imported from the Orient. Period furnishings, silver, crystal, china and linens have been custom designed for the room.

The French Room is recognized as a product of a culinary revolution that began in France in the 1970s. Its richness, rather than relying extensively on butter and cream, is achieved through reductions of vegetable stocks, purees and emulsions.

The companion French Room Bar is paneled in rich American walnut. The fireplace mantle is made of English Chippendale mahogany, refinished in antique Chinese red. Many of the bar's tables, cabinets, oil paintings and lamp bases are authentic pieces from the 17th, 18th and 19th centuries.

Meeting and banquet facilities include the Grand Ballroom with 5,200 square feet in French Renaissance style and the Century Room with 4,650 square feet. A separate mezzanine contains five conference/classrooms and six boardrooms. The meeting services department is designed to handle every need of the meeting planner, from airport transfers to spouse programs and menu selections.

The Adolphus holds virtually every architectural, interior design and hospitality award in the industry. *Condé Nast Traveler*'s Reader's Choice Award proclaimed it one of the top ten hotels in the United States, an honor consistently supported by the *Zagat Surveys*, *Fodor's*, *Frommer's* and other travel authorities.

The Adolphus, a Noble House Hotel, is located at 1321 Commerce Street, Dallas, Texas, 75202, (214) 742-8200 or (800) 221-9083. The French Room is open for dinner Tuesday through Saturday, from 6:00 to 10:00 p.m. Two courses cost $59.00; three courses are $69.00; four courses cost $77.00; and five courses are $85.00. A tasting menu is available nightly: with wine, it is $125.00; without wine, it is $90.00. A gourmet vegetarian menu is also served each evening for $67.00. All major credit cards are accepted and reservations are recommended.

The French Room Crab Salad

9–12 ounces smoked salmon, thinly sliced

6 fried wonton cups

2 cups shredded crab meat (bite-size chunks)

1 cup shredded smoked trout (1/2-inch pieces)

2 Roma tomatoes, julienne-cut

3 tablespoons chives, finely chopped

24 pieces green beans, blanched and cut into halves

1/3 cup champagne vinegar dressing (recipe on next page)

1 cup mixed greens, julienne-cut

salt and pepper to taste

Gather all ingredients and assemble cooking tools. Make the champagne vinegar dressing (recipe follows).

Place 1 1/2 to 2 ounces thinly sliced smoked salmon in the center of each plate, forming a ring about 3 to 4 inches in diameter. Sprinkle with pepper. Combine crab, trout, green beans, tomatoes, chives and dressing. Mix well, but gently. Add more salt and pepper if needed. Portion out crab salads into wonton cups, filling each cup completely but not packing it. Place the salad onto the salmon ring. Take Salad Sensation or greens and toss with salt, pepper and a small amount of champagne dressing. You just want to give the greens some flavor; do not saturate with dressing. Place a small handful on top of each salad (about 1/8 cup).

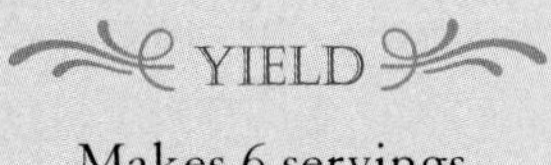

Makes 6 servings.

1 egg yolk

juice of 1/2 lemon

salt and pepper to taste

1/2 ounce champagne vinegar

1 1/2–2 cups grape seed oil

CHAMPAGNE VINEGAR DRESSING:

Combine egg yolk and lemon juice. Mix. Add champagne vinegar and mix. While whisking continuously, add grape seed oil into mixture in a slow, steady stream. Whisk until thick and creamy. Add salt and pepper to taste. If dressing is too thick, add a drop or two of cold water until the proper consistency is reached.

YIELD

Makes 6–8 ounces.

Seared Veal Tenderloin and Schnitzel

with a Mushroom and Asparagus Ragout and a Red Zinfandel and Shallot Sauce

SAUCE:

Sauté shallots, garlic and black peppercorns. Deglaze with zinfandel and reduce au sec (until dry). Add red wine sauce and bay leaf. Reduce by half or until it reaches the desired consistency (enough to coat the back of a spoon). Remove from heat and add thyme (let steep for approximately 10 minutes). Strain and reserve. Cover minced shallots with wine and reduce until dry. Then add to sauce.

RAGOUT:

Sauté bacon until fat is rendered. Add mushrooms and shallots. Cook one minute. Add remaining vegetables. Deglaze with white wine and finish with melted butter.

SAUCE:

8 shallots, sliced

4 cloves garlic, crushed

1 tablespoon black peppercorns

1 bay leaf

3 bottles red zinfandel

1 quart red wine sauce (from 2 gallons veal stock reduced to 1 quart)

1/2 teaspoon thyme

1 cup shallots, minced

1 cup red zinfandel

RAGOUT:

1/2 pound mushrooms, diced

1/2 pound asparagus, blanched (green and white)

1/2 pound tomato concassé

1/2 pound green beans, blanched

1 cup shallots, minced

2 ounces white wine

2 tablespoons bacon, diced

2 tablespoons butter

(continued on next page)

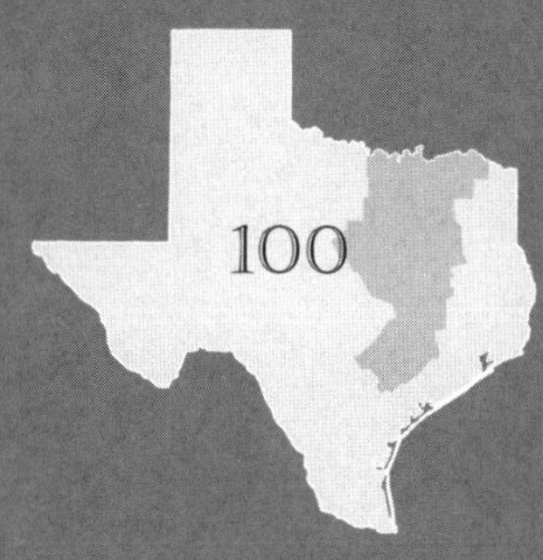

- 2 pounds sweetbreads, blanched
- 4 chicken breasts
- 4 egg whites
- salt to taste
- white pepper to taste
- 3 veal tenderloins (which make 6 medallions)
- 1 cup brioche or regular bread crumbs
- 1 egg
- 1/2 cup flour

SCHNITZEL:

Make a chicken mousse by combining egg whites, chicken breast, salt and pepper. After sweetbreads are blanched, clean all tough tissue and break into smaller pieces. Using chicken mousse, put the sweetbreads together and roll into a log shape with plastic wrap. Then cover with foil. Poach the roulade for approximately 8 minutes. Let cool. Slice schnitzel into rounds and bread with egg, flour and brioche crumbs. Sauté until golden.

ASSEMBLY:

Season veal tenderloin with salt and pepper. Sear tenderloin completely and place in oven at 350 degrees until rare or medium-rare. Top sweetbread rounds with 1 teaspoon of butter after sautéing. Place already cooked sweetbread rounds in a circle on serving plate. Top each sweetbread round with a slice of veal tenderloin. Place vegetable ragout in the middle of the plate and pour mushroom-shallot sauce over each veal tenderloin.

YIELD

Makes 6 servings.

Chocolate Raspberry Tart à la French Room

SHORT DOUGH:

5 ounces powdered sugar

1/4 cup unsalted butter

4 egg yolks, cooked

1 vanilla bean, split and scraped

6 1/2 ounces flour, sifted

1/4 teaspoon baking powder, sifted

FILLING:

12 ounces high quality chocolate, semisweet

10 ounces heavy whipping cream

30 raspberries, depending on size

SHORT DOUGH:

In a small pot, place eggs in cold water. Place on high heat. When the water starts to boil, set timer for 10 minutes. Leave on high boil. When timer rings, remove pot from heat and let cold water run over the eggs to cool. Peel and separate when cool.

In a small mixing bowl, combine the sugar, butter, yolks and vanilla seeds. With a paddle on low speed, cream mixture. Add the flour and baking powder. Mix just until it incorporates. Place dough on a plastic sheet and wrap. Set in refrigerator for one hour. Knead the dough in order to even out the temperature.

Roll out to 1/4-inch thickness and cut out circles using a 3 1/4-inch-diameter round pastry cutter. Bake on a flat cookie sheet at 350 degrees for about 10 minutes or until light golden in color. Let cool at room temperature.

FILLING:

Melt chocolate over a hot water bath, gently (heat not too high). Scald cream. Remove chocolate from the hot water bath and add the cream. Stir gently in a circular motion. On a flat sheet pan lined with wax paper, space six 2 3/4-inch flan rings evenly. Place about 5–6 fresh raspberries in the rings and pour the chocolate filling over them. Fill to the top of the ring. Freeze and remove from molds, using a torch to gently heat the sides of the ring to help loosen

the chocolate disc. Be careful not to overheat the rings—the chocolate will melt!

RASPBERRY SORBET:

2 cups seedless raspberry puree

2 cups water

1 cup granulated sugar

RASPBERRY SAUCE:

1 cup seedless raspberry puree

2 ounces water

Raspberry Sorbet

Combine ingredients and freeze in ice-cream machine according to manufacturer's specifications. Place in freezer until needed.

Raspberry Sauce

Combine ingredients and store in refrigerator until needed.

ASSEMBLING TART:

Center the chocolate disc on top of the short dough. Pour raspberry sauce on a plate, forming a circle with the sauce. Place tart in center of the plate. Scoop raspberry sorbet and place a dollop on top of the tart. Garnish with mint and fresh berries.

INN ON THE RIVER

Glen Rose

Inn On The River has enjoyed a rich history since its turn-of-the-century beginnings. At that time the city of Glen Rose was known as a health resort where thousands of people would come each year for the abundant natural springs and artesian wells.

In 1916, George P. Snyder, a native Californian, built a "drugless sanitarium." People would come for curative mineral baths, fresh-grown food and regimented schedules. Dr. Snyder was so successful that he had to expand his business many times to accommodate the 3,000 patients who annually took their pilgrimage to see him.

In 1919, Dr. Snyder built a two-story structure on his expansive property, which by that time had encompassed a full city block. The building contained 35 bedrooms, 9 bathrooms and a large lobby with twin staircases. That building remains today as Inn On The River. It was one of the seven buildings that created his sanitarium complex. The George P. Snyder Sanitarium, furnished to house a capacity of 250 guests at one time, included a banana grove, a sleeping pavilion, a carbide plant for lighting and a small zoo with an ostrich named Judy. It was declared "the greatest institution in the city of Glen Rose" by the local newspaper in 1924. This landmark sanitarium was so successful that during the depression Dr. Snyder's deposits were credited with saving the Glen Rose bank from bankruptcy.

Dr. Snyder died in 1942 and his family and associates operated the sanitarium until the 1970s. It lay dormant for several years until it was purchased, restored and reopened in 1984 as Inn On The River. At this time, new life was brought to the neglected Inn and the remodeling provided 19 rooms and 3 suites, all with private baths. A conference center was added in 1989. In early 1993, massive internal renovations were made and extensive landscaping additions were completed. An additional meeting room and expanded kitchen facility were added to the conference center.

Because of its outstanding contribution to the heritage of Texas, on March 11, 1985, Inn On The River was recorded as a Texas Historical Landmark. The Inn's structural two-story appearance remains the same today as it did 75 years ago.

The ambling Paluxy River continues to serve as the backdrop to Inn On The River just as it did for the George P. Snyder Sanitarium. Three massive, native, live oak trees, centuries old, stand on the well-manicured grounds of the Inn. These oaks are legendary and enjoy celebrity status. A guest at the sanitarium wrote a song in the 1950s titled, "The Singing Trees." Elvis Presley recorded the song in 1965.

Inn On The River is acknowledged as the largest inn in Texas. It remains a charming, but elegant haven for individual guests and executive retreats.

Inn On The River, 205 SW Barnard Street, Glen Rose, Texas 76043, (254) 897-2929, or visit www.innontheriver.com. They offer dinner Friday and Saturday nights with two seatings, at 6 and 8 p.m. Lunch and other evening meals vary, so please call ahead.

Chilled Peach and Mango Soup

1/4 cup fresh orange juice
1/2 carton mango puree
1 cup peach puree
1/4 teaspoon cardamom
1/8 cup sugar
1/2 cup crème anglais (recipe follows)
1/4 lime, juiced
dash salt

CRÈME ANGLAIS:
1 quart cream
1 vanilla bean
1/2 cup sugar
7 egg yolks

Bring juice and puree to a boil with the sugar. Cool and combine with other ingredients. Mix to taste.

CRÈME ANGLAIS:
Bring all ingredients except yolks to a boil. Temper yolks into mixture and cook gently until anglais thickens. Cool immediately in ice bath.

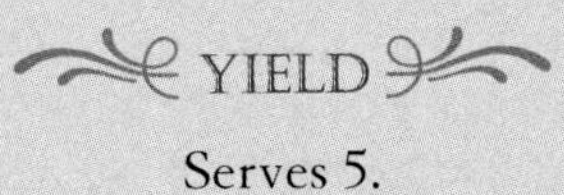

Serves 5.

Citrus Vinaigrette

1/2 cup orange juice, reduced by 2/3
1/4 tablespoon roasted garlic
1/2 shallot
1/4 lime, juiced
1/8 cup champagne wine vinegar
2 teaspoons honey
3/8 cup olive oil
salt and pepper to taste

Reduce orange juice with shallots. Combine reduction and remaining ingredients, except oil, in blender. Emulsify and season with salt and pepper.

Serves 6.

LANDHAUS RAMSEY

Round Top

Perhaps one of the oldest historic properties in Texas now serving as a restaurant facility is the Moore Fort. Colonel John Henry Moore came to Texas in Stephen F. Austin's Colony in 1823. He built this blockhouse and founded the town of LaGrange in 1831 where the La Bahia Trace (road) crossed the Colorado River. It is the oldest structure in Fayette County.

Moore was elected Colonel in the 1835 Battle of Gonzales in the Texas Revolution. He went on to become a famous Indian fighter. In 1839, Moore took command of three companies of volunteers in a campaign against the Comanche. Again in 1840, he fought the Comanche between the Concho and Colorado Rivers. He volunteered for the Texas Rangers in 1861, but was judged too old to fight.

Colonel Moore also founded, in this building, the first Christian church in Fayette County. The Moore Fort was saved, moved to Hackberry Hill near Round Top, and eventually given to the Texas Pioneer Arts Foundation as a Bicentennial gift in 1976 by Mrs. Tanner Smith of La Grange and Harvin and Elizabeth Moore of Houston.

Mrs. Charles L. Bybee and her husband established the Texas Pioneer Arts Foundation to help preserve our great state's history. The foundation's master craftsman, E. J. Lueckemeyer, used not only the 1830 period tools, but also the construction techniques in every detail. He worked with no plans and with only the openings in the walls and floors to serve as guidelines. Fireplaces and chimneys of wrought hewn stone were reconstructed at each end of the double structure. Chinking in the spaces between the walls carefully conforms to the original portholes or notches, which allowed a crossfire against attackers from any approach.

The Moore Fort, an original hand-hewn double log cabin, is nestled amidst a beautiful landscape containing crepe myrtles, lantanas, sages, antique roses and other perennials as part of the Landhaus Ramsey restaurant. Located along Highway 237, this restaurant complex is an excellent example of how a commercial enterprise can be landscaped to fit into the surrounding community. It is a German-American restaurant situated among several of Fayette County's historic landmarks. The newest buildings on the property were built in the 1880s.

Also purchased and restored by Mrs. Bybee and her foundation, numerous other structures were brought on site and strategically placed so that the property was developed around a gorgeous, live oak tree. Specialists from Texas A&M University estimate that the tree is 300 years old and one of the oldest trees of its kind known to exist. The tree provides cool shade for guests on the 1800-square-foot Biergarten and dining deck. The deck was specially designed and constructed so as not to interfere with the tree's root system.

The main building of the restaurant complex came from Frehlsburg, Texas, and was built around 1875. All of the buildings on the grounds relate to German heritage. Additional dining is located inside the completely restored mid-1800s house. The Moore Fort also provides a relaxing atmosphere for small parties or elegant romantic dinners. A variety of gourmet herbs are gardened for both their beauty and their useful, tantalizing purposes in the many dishes that the restaurant proudly serves.

Landhaus Ramsey, Highway 237 to entrance at 109 Bauer Rummel Road, PO Box 269, Round Top, Texas 78954, (979) 249-2080. They are open Thursday from 11 a.m. until 8 p.m., Friday and Saturday from 11 a.m. until 9 p.m. and Sunday from 11 a.m. until 4 p.m.

German Potato Salad

- 1 pound fatback or bacon
- 1 cup onion, chopped
- 4 tablespoons flour
- 4 tablespoons sugar
- 3 teaspoons salt
- ground pepper to taste
- 2 teaspoons celery seed
- 1/2 cup celery, chopped
- 1 cup vinegar
- 1 cup water
- 12 cups cooked potatoes, sliced
- parsley

Cook the bacon until crisp. Drain (reserving 1/2 cup fat) and crumble. Cook onion and celery in fat until just tender. Blend in flour, sugar, salt, celery seed and pepper to taste. Add vinegar and water. Cook and stir until thickened and bubbly. Add bacon and potatoes. Heat thoroughly, tossing lightly so as not to break up the potato slices. Garnish with parsley.

Can be served warm or chilled, but you taste the bacon fat a bit more when it's chilled.

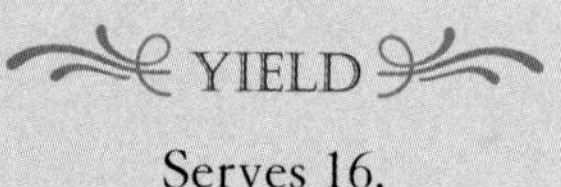
YIELD

Serves 16.

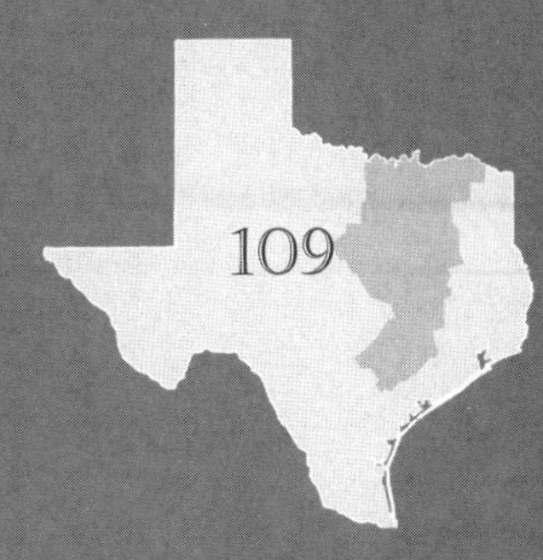

Sauerbraten

2-pound piece good beef (from the upper back hip)

1 cup vinegar from red wine or a 50/50 mixture of red wine and vinegar

2 bay leaves

2 tablespoons whole black pepper

2 onions, large

1 carrot, big

1/2 pound potatoes

1/4 cup bouillon

2 tablespoons crème fraiche (or sour cream)

salt, pepper, oil

Place meat in a high dish. Fill with vinegar (or mixture) until covered. Add bay leaves and pepper grains and place dish in the refrigerator. Leave there for 2–3 days. Turn meat at least once.

Get meat out of marinade and dry. Spice meat with pepper all around. Cut onions, carrot and potatoes in little cubes. Heat oil. Place meat in it and roast until brown from all sides. Add onions until brown, too.

Salt the meat. Add potatoes and carrots, then the bouillon and, optionally, some more red wine (especially if you used only vinegar before). Add also a little of the marinade (without leaves and pepper). Simmer for at least 1 1/2 hours on low heat in a closed pot. Turn once.

Get meat out of the pot and keep warm. Puree the sauce. Let reduce a little. Add crème fraiche or sour cream, and salt and pepper to taste. Cut the meat into slices and serve.

Note: Traditional side dishes are potatoes or Kloesse (dumplings) and some vegetables like Rotkraut (that is, hot, red cabbage). In some areas of Germany, they add raisins and sliced apples to the sauce so that it gets a more sweet-and-sour taste.

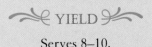

Serves 8–10.

1 pound top round

Dijon mustard

4 or 5 slices bacon

1 onion, sliced

salt and pepper

1/2 cup flour

shortening

Rouladen

Slice top round paper-thin in 8" by 6" strips (you may find it is easier to ask your butcher to do this when you order the meat). Liberally spread mustard over slices of meat. Sauté bacon in skillet until fat is translucent, but bacon is not crisp. (You can also do this in a microwave for one minute.)

Place a slice of bacon on each slice of meat. Distribute onions equally on slices of meat. Roll meat and tie. Season flour with salt and pepper to taste. Sprinkle flour mixture over meat rolls.

Melt shortening in frying pan and brown meat on all sides. Add enough water to half-cover meat rolls. Simmer for 20 minutes, turning occasionally.

YIELD

Serves 4.

LIENDO RESTAURANT

Hempstead

Liendo Plantation was built in 1853 by Leonard Waller Groce, the son of Jared Groce, who was one of the largest, most respected landowners in Texas. Originally a Spanish land grant of 67,000 acres assigned to Justo Liendo, the plantation's namesake, Liendo was one of Texas's earliest cotton plantations. It was considered the social center of Texas, receiving and lavishly entertaining early Texas dignitaries and notorieties. Liendo was considered a typical Southern plantation, having over 300 slaves and being itself built of slave labor. Sufficient in all its needs, it was a self-contained community. Like most Southern plantations, however, Liendo fell on hard times after the Civil War and changed owners several times thereafter.

Liendo has always been recognized for its warm Southern hospitality, but few people know that this same tradition of generosity probably saved it from destruction. Among the more notable statesmen and historical figures that have spent time at Liendo was George A. Custer. At the end of the Civil War, he was stationed at Liendo. It is said that both General Custer and his wife were so impressed with the plantation and the gracious hospitality shown them during their stay, that they made sure Liendo was not harmed in any way in appreciation.

Liendo was also occupied by world-renowned sculptress Elisabet Ney and her husband, Dr. Edmond Montgomery, from 1873 to 1911. She and her husband had emigrated years before from Europe but had never found a new home until they found Liendo. It is reported that, upon arriving at Liendo, she walked out on the balcony, threw out her arms and said, "This is where I will live and die." She lived out her life at Liendo, commuting to her art studio in Austin. She and her husband are buried on the Plantation grounds. She sculpted many notable works, two of the most recognized pieces being the statues of Stephen F. Austin and Sam Houston, which now stand in the state capitol.

The restaurant is located in one of the beautiful homes built on the plantation in 1882. Passing through eleven owners before being purchased by Carl and Phyllis Detering in 1960, this house has served also as a boarding house and antique store. The Deterings have spent 40 years faithfully restoring Liendo to its former glory.

Liendo is recognized as a Texas historic landmark and is listed on the National Register of Historic Places. Open for public viewing the first Saturday of most months, Liendo is also the location of the Civil War Weekend, which is held annually in November. Home tours, folk life demonstrations and local entertainment are some of the weekend's attractions. Other events are held at Liendo Plantation throughout the year. Over time, the restaurant has been surrounded by the town, while the Plantation is on the outskirts of the city. When asking for local directions, be sure to specify which one you are looking for.

Liendo Restaurant, Business 6 in Hempstead, Texas 77445, serves lunch daily from 11 a.m. to 2 p.m. Dinner hours are from 6 p.m. to 9 p.m. every Friday and Saturday. Call (800) 826-4371 or (979) 826-4371 or see www.liendo.com.

Pecan Encrusted Snapper

- 4 fillets of fresh snapper, skinned (6 ounces each)
- 1/2 cup flour
- 2 cups pecan pieces
- 4 egg whites
- salt, pepper and spices to taste
- lemon slice and parsley, for garnish
- tartar sauce to taste

Process pecans in food processor until crumb stage. Mix with white flour to thin somewhat. Mix with salt, pepper and spices (Old Bay if possible). Dust snapper in white flour. Dip snapper fillet in egg whites. Put egg-white-covered snapper in pecan batter and cover with pecans. Press to stick pecans to fish. Shake fish to remove excess batter. Deep-fry in corn oil until fish floats and remove from oil. Garnish with lemon slice and parsley and serve with rice and tartar sauce.

YIELD

Serves 4.

MAIN STREET BISTRO & WINE BAR

La Grange

The building housing the Main Street Bistro & Wine Bar was built in 1914 by the Mohrhousens and the Schmidts. From the beginning it was a 10,000-square-foot general store selling everything from sewing needles to wood-burning cook stoves. The upstairs was a mortuary, operated under the name Koenig Mortuary from 1914 until 1936.

After 42 years of operation the Schmidt family sold the business—but not the building—to a company that continued to operate the Dry Goods/General Mercantile Store. Later, Charlie Tobias operated his furniture store in the building and later John Schaefer also sold furniture there.

In 1997 the Schmidt family restored and updated the building, while maintaining its original architectural integrity. In 1998 Anna Schmidt opened Tim's on the Square, named after her brother Timothy Schmidt. Tim's on the Square served soups, baked potatoes, salads and sandwiches to a large local lunch crowd, along with 16 flavors of Blue Bell ice cream.

In 1999, the current owner, Susan Kuehler, arrived as the General Manager for Tim's. She expanded the menu and the operating hours to include dinner and Sunday Brunch. Tim's Café on the Square, as it became known, started serving choice beef, fresh seafood and authentic pasta dishes, along with homemade desserts, soups and salad dressings.

In February 2001 Susan Kuehler and Mike McCathern purchased Tim's Café on the Square and changed the name to Main Street Bistro & Wine Bar. "Main Street" tells everyone they can find them in the charming, historic, downtown La Grange. "Bistro" is a hint that the fare will be a little out of the ordinary.

Mike and Susan offer the same fabulous food and attentive staff, just with a new name. They expanded the wine and beer list, added a few appetizers and decided to go to a seasonal menu in order to offer their guests the best and freshest in-season products.

The restaurant offers services you would expect in a small-town atmosphere. They will split any entrée for you for a small fee or, if you like, you can split it yourself. The extra plate is no charge. Also, you may bring your own bottle of wine in and the corking charge is only $5 per bottle. They emphasize that this is a non-smoking facility.

The Main Street Bistro & Wine Bar, 155 Main Street, La Grange, Texas 78945. Call (979) 968-9665 or visit www.mainstbistro.com. They are open Monday through Wednesday from 11 a.m. until 4 p.m., Thursday through Saturday from 11 a.m. until 10 p.m. and Sunday brunch is served from 10 a.m. until 2 p.m.

Shrimp and Crawfish Bisque

- 5 or 6 scallions, white and green parts finely chopped crosswise
- 1/2 stick unsalted butter, cut into small pieces
- 1/4 cup flour
- 2 cups milk
- 2 1/2 cups heavy cream
- 2 teaspoons coarse kosher salt
- 1/2 teaspoon freshly grated nutmeg
- 1/2 teaspoon paprika
- Tabasco sauce to taste
- 2 pounds small fresh or frozen shrimp
- 1 pound fresh or frozen crawfish tails
- 3/4 cup pureed roasted red bell peppers
- 1/2 cup sherry

In a large, deep kettle, sauté the scallions in the melted butter until softened, 3 to 4 minutes. Blend in flour and cook, stirring over low heat for 5 minutes. Stir in the milk and cream and cook, stirring until slightly thickened.

Stir the salt, spices and Tabasco to taste and pureed roasted red bell peppers into the soup mixture, blending well. Add the shrimp and crawfish.

Heat gently approximately 3–5 minutes until the shrimp and crawfish are cooked. Important! Do not let it boil—it will break!

After shrimp and crawfish are cooked add the sherry, stir and serve.

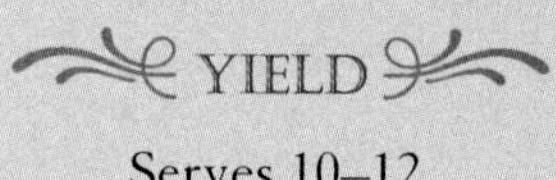
YIELD

Serves 10–12.

Pecan Crusted Catfish

served with a Lemon Thyme Butter

Place half the pecans, flour and Creole seasoning in a food processor and process until pecans and flour are incorporated creating a "pecan flour." Whisk egg in a mixing bowl and add the milk. Place the catfish fillets in the milk and egg mixture, coating both sides, then dredge in pecan flour. Pan-fry the fillets in a large skillet in 4 tablespoons of butter over medium heat.

PECAN LEMON THYME BUTTER:

Melt remaining butter in a medium size pan. Add remaining pecans and toast over medium high heat. After pecans are toasted add the juice from the lemons, the Worcestershire sauce and the fresh thyme leaves. Cook another 3 to 5 minutes over medium heat until you can smell the thyme. Pour over cooked catfish fillets and serve.

Serves 6.

3 cups pecan halves or pieces

1 1/2 cups flour

2 teaspoons Creole seasoning
to taste

1 medium egg

1 cup milk

6 catfish fillets (5 to 7 ounces each)

3/4 cup butter

3 lemons, cut in half

1 tablespoon Worcestershire sauce

2 sprigs fresh thyme

kosher salt and freshly ground
pepper to taste

Mike's Peach Cobbler

2 pounds fresh or frozen peach pieces

1 1/2 cups sugar

8–10 ounces peach nectar

4–6 drops almond extract

2 tablespoons pumpkin pie spice

1 teaspoon real vanilla extract

BATTER:

1 cup flour

1 cup sugar

3/4 cup milk

1 tablespoon baking powder

4 drops almond extract

1 teaspoon real vanilla extract

1 teaspoon pumpkin pie spice

1 stick butter

Place peaches in a large bowl with the ingredients at left and stir well. Cover and place in the refrigerator overnight to allow all the flavors to come together. If you started with frozen peaches, cover and let mixture sit on the counter until thawed before placing in the refrigerator.

BATTER:

Measure flour, sugar, baking powder and pumpkin pie spice in small mixing bowl. Stir dry mixture to evenly distribute spices and baking powder. Add milk and almond and vanilla extracts and stir just until smooth. Mixture should be the consistency of pancake batter.

Preheat oven to 400 degrees. Melt 1 stick of butter in a deep 9 × 12-inch pan or a large stainless steel bowl. Pour batter over the bottom of the hot buttered baking dish. Stir and pour peach mixture over the batter. IMPORTANT: do not stir peaches into the batter.

Place in 400-degree oven for 10 minutes. Then reduce heat to 250 degrees and bake another 45 to 60 minutes. Cooking time depends on size of dish and thickness of batter. Test with a knife in the middle of the pan to make sure the batter is completely done (not gooey). The final cobbler should be a golden brown and the crust will have the consistency of a fluffy biscuit.

Remove from the oven and let stand for 10 to 15 minutes. Serve with your favorite ice cream (vanilla bean, peach or cinnamon are all very good choices) or my favorite—pour clod heavy cream over it. Enjoy.

YIELD

Serves 8.

THE MANSION ON TURTLE CREEK

Dallas

The Mansion on Turtle Creek is the flagship property of Rosewood Hotels & Resorts. Cotton magnate Sheppard King and his wife brought the grandeur of 16th-century Italy to Dallas in 1925 when they built The Mansion, which was their home for 10 years. Sheppard W. King was the son of a Confederate war veteran who migrated to Waxahachie in 1882. A president and partner of the cotton brokerage house of King, Collie and Company, Sheppard King made a fortune in the cotton business and later became involved in oil, setting up offices in New Orleans, Milan and Liverpool.

After marrying Bertha Wilcox in 1891 and moving to Dallas, they built their first home in 1908 and had it demolished in 1923. They traveled throughout Europe with their architect before building their second home, the 16th-century, Italian Renaissance-style structure now known as The Mansion. Today, it is a world-class hotel and restaurant, widely recognized as one of the top hotels in the world.

The King Mansion occupies 10,000 square feet on three levels. Painted rusty pink, the stucco-covered, solid, brick walls vary in thickness from 15 to 36 inches. The marble stairway has attracted attention since its earliest days. Imported marble was lavishly installed both upstairs and down—even on the unique, cantilevered stairway. It was considered such an engineering feat that contractors from St. Louis, Kansas City and Denver came to watch the stairway's construction. Among the great works of art brought from Europe by the Kings are two tall pairs of early-19th-century Spanish cathedral doors featuring hand-carved, helmeted faces and two ornate columns entwined with carved grapes, vines and leaves. The columns can be seen at the entrance to the restaurant.

Rosewood Hotels bought the property in 1979, spending two years and $21 million in restoring the Mansion to its original grandeur. The primary dining room today was the original living room, while other rooms have also been converted to modern usage. The original dining room, which now serves as the Lower Bar, was a creation of the great French architect M. Jacques Carre, then director of the Ecole des Beaux Arts de Fontainebleau. Its inlaid ceiling is composed of 2,400 separate pieces of wood that took six carpenters eight weeks to install. A unique mural depicting points of Italy originally covered the upper third of all four walls. The fireplace in this room is a reproduction of one in England's Bromley Castle. The Honorary Chairman of Rosewood Hotels & Resorts, Caroline Rose Hunt, shares her private collection of hunt trophies, paintings and lithographs on the forest green walls.

At the north end of the dining room is a space referred to as the Library. It retains many of its original elements, including an intricately carved plaster ceiling. Charming cherubs are carved on an imposing stone mantel, which was brought to Dallas from Germany.

The south end of the Dining Room is referred to as the Living Room. Stained glass windows bear the coat of arms of barons who witnessed the signing of the Magna Carta at Runnymede. The silver leaf that originally enhanced the two tall pairs of early-19th-century Spanish cathedral doors was revealed during the renovation, after the removal of six coats of paint.

At the east end of the Dining Room is the Veranda. Now glass-enclosed for all-season dining, the 125-foot veranda still has its original Spanish tile floor with corner insets depicting the life of Don Quixote. In addition to the magnificent main dining facilities, the Mansion also offers five private dining areas. The FDR Suite, Burford Room and Sheppard King Suite are on the second floor of the house and serve as private meeting and dining rooms. In the Hunt Suite, celebrated Chef Dean Fearing envisioned a new concept, true Southwest cuisine. That was a decade ago, and Chef Fearing continues to innovate, boldly stirring pots on the forefront of the American culinary scene. The Hunt Suite was added in 1995.

No self-respecting mansion was built without a silver vault in those days, and this mansion is no exception. The silver vault of yesterday, set on solid, bedrock, Texas limestone, with a nine-foot-deep basement, is now the Wine Cellar. The elegant Wine Cellar is a memorable spot for an intimate private dining experience.

The Mansion on Turtle Creek, 2821 Turtle Creek Boulevard, Dallas, Texas 75219, (800) 527-5432, can also be reached at www.mansiononturtlecreek.com. The restaurant is open for lunch Monday through Saturday from 12 noon to 2:30 p.m., brunch on Sunday from 11 a.m. to 2:30 p.m. and dinner nightly from 6 p.m. to 10:30 p.m. Dress is semi-formal with gentlemen required to wear jackets. Ties are recommended.

Warm Lobster Taco

with Yellow Tomato Salsa

4 lobsters, 1 pound each

6 7-inch, fresh flour tortillas

3 tablespoons corn oil

1 cup grated jalapeno Jack cheese

1 cup shredded spinach leaves

yellow tomato salsa (recipe follows)

Jicama Salad (recipe follows)

I created this dish in early 1986 and it quickly became my signature appetizer on the Mansion on Turtle Creek menu. The name "Lobster Taco" perfectly illustrates the casual elegance that characterizes Southwest cuisine. Its appeal is rooted in the combination of rich lobster and a simple flour tortilla. The salsa and salad garnishes produce an explosion of color that promises exciting dining.

—Dean Fearing, Executive Chef

Preheat oven to 300 degrees. Fill a large stockpot with lightly salted water and bring to a boil over high heat. Add lobsters and cook for about 8 minutes or until just done. Drain and let lobsters cool slightly. Wrap tortillas tightly in foil and place in preheated 300-degree oven for about 15 minutes or until heated through. Keep warm until ready to use.

Remove meat from lobster tails, being careful not to tear it apart. Cut meat into thin medallions (or medium-sized dice, if meat breaks apart).

Heat oil in a medium sauté pan over medium heat and sauté lobster medallions until just heated through.

Spoon equal portions of warm lobster medallions into the center of each warm tortilla. Sprinkle with equal portions of grated cheese and shredded spinach.

Roll tortillas into a cylinder shape and place each one on a warm serving plate with the edge facing the bottom.

Surround the taco with Yellow Tomato Salsa and garnish each side with a small mound of Jicama Salad.

YELLOW TOMATO SALSA:

In a food processor, using the steel blade, process tomatoes until well chopped. Do not puree. Combine tomatoes and their juices with shallot, garlic, cilantro, vinegar, chilies, lime juice and salt, mixing well. Add maple syrup, if needed, to balance flavor and sweeten slightly.

Cover and refrigerate for at least two hours or until very cold.

Note: For a crunchier, more typical salsa, put tomatoes through a fine dice in a food grinder.

YELLOW TOMATO SALSA:

2 pints cherry tomatoes or

1 pound yellow tomatoes

1 large shallot, very finely minced

1 clove garlic, large, very finely minced

2 tablespoons fresh cilantro, finely minced

1 tablespoon champagne or white wine vinegar

2 Serrano chilies, seeded and minced

2 teaspoons lime juice

salt to taste

1 tablespoon maple syrup (use only if tomatoes are not sweet enough)

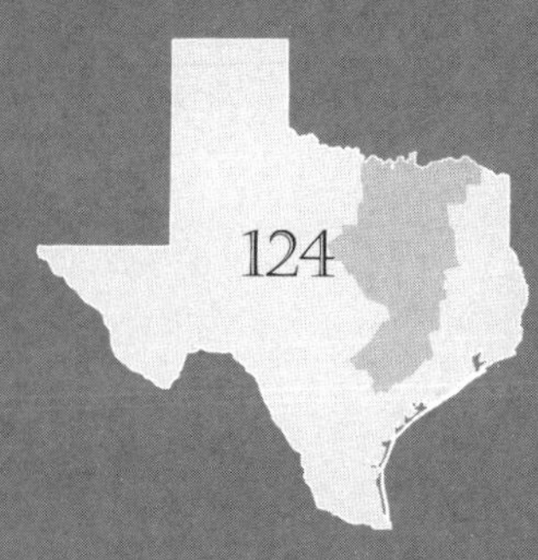

- 1/2 small jicama, peeled and cut into fine julienne strips
- 1/2 small red bell pepper, seeds and membranes removed, cut into fine julienne strips
- 1/2 small yellow bell pepper, seeds and membranes removed, cut into fine julienne strips
- 1/2 small zucchini (only part that has green skin attached) cut into fine julienne strips
- 1/2 small carrot, peeled and cut into fine julienne strips
- 4 tablespoons cold-pressed peanut oil
- 2 tablespoons lime juice
- salt to taste
- cayenne pepper to taste

Jicama Salad

Combine vegetables, oil, lime juice, salt and cayenne to taste and toss to mix well.

ADVANCE PREPARATIONS:

1. Lobsters may be boiled up to a day ahead. Remove tail meat and slice. Store covered and refrigerated.

2. Yellow Tomato Salsa must be prepared at least 2 hours (but no more than 8 hours) ahead and refrigerated, covered, until cold. Adjust seasoning.

3. Jicama Salad may be prepared several hours ahead and refrigerated. In that case, omit salt until almost ready to serve.

4. Cheese and spinach for tacos may be shredded several hours ahead. Wrap tightly and refrigerate.

Serves 6.

Tortilla Soup

Caroline Rose Hunt, creator of Rosewood Hotels and The Mansion on Turtle Creek, enjoyed this soup at the venerable Argyle Club in San Antonio and suggested its adaptation for the menu of The Mansion on Turtle Creek.

This hearty soup, which is suitable on warm spring days as well as cold winter nights, has been on the menu since The Mansion on Turtle Creek opened.

When Tortilla Soup is ordered, it is brought to the table in a tureen for individual service by the waiter, who garnishes each bowl according to the customer's desire.

—Dean Fearing, Executive Chef

3 tablespoons corn oil

Heat oil in a large saucepan over medium heat.

4 corn tortillas, coarsely chopped
6 cloves garlic, finely chopped
1 tablespoon chopped fresh epazote or cilantro
1 cup fresh onion puree
2 cups fresh tomato puree
1 tablespoon cumin powder
2 teaspoons chili powder
2 bay leaves
4 tablespoons canned tomato puree
2 quarts chicken stock
salt to taste
cayenne pepper to taste

Sauté tortillas with garlic and epazote over medium heat until tortillas are soft. Add onion and fresh tomato puree and bring to a boil. Add cumin, chili powder, bay leaves, canned tomato puree and chicken stock. Bring to a boil again, and then reduce heat to simmer. Add salt and cayenne pepper to taste and cook, stirring frequently, for 30 minutes. Skim fat from surface if necessary.

1 breast chicken, cooked, cut into strips
1 avocado, peeled, seeded and cubed
1 cup shredded cheddar cheese
3 corn tortillas, cut into thin strips and fried crisp

(*continued on next page*)

Strain and pour into warm soup bowls. Garnish each bowl with an equal portion of chicken breast, avocado, shredded cheese and crisp tortilla strips. Serve immediately.

Note: Soup may be made one day ahead and reheated before serving.

YIELD

Serves 8 to 10.

THE MELROSE HOTEL

Dallas

The Melrose Hotel provides a central location to the arts and business districts of modern Dallas. Originally the site of the Mellersh family farm, owner Colonel George Mellersh built his home here in 1876. The severe depression of the 1890s forced the family to abandon the house, which fell into ruin and was eventually used as a sheep barn. In 1904 the site was purchased and restored by a prominent banker and real estate promoter, Ballard M. Burgher. The house remained in the possession of the Burgher family until its demolition for construction of The Melrose Hotel in 1924.

The Melrose, built at a cost of $2 million, was designed and constructed as both a transient and apartment hotel, and has operated as such since the day the doors first opened. The building was designed by C. D. Hill, a noted Dallas architect who also designed the Municipal Building, Houston's Warwick Hotel and Fair Park's Coliseum. Hill's work also includes a number of distinguished residences in the Lakewood and Highland Park areas of Dallas, as well as the Oak Lawn Methodist Church, which faces The Melrose on Oak Lawn Avenue.

Upon its completion the hotel was known for its old-world atmosphere of hospitality and comfort. Each of the 385 rooms had an outside exposure, while 100 units included kitchen facilities. The hotel changed ownership in 1933 to The Melrose Company and was remodeled in the 1950s.

On July 10, 1955, the *Dallas Times Herald* ran an article about the newly built luxury swimming pool, which still remains a part of the property but is buried under today's parking lot. In 1964 and 1980 The Melrose again changed hands. In 1981 and 1982 the new owner, Banyan Realty Corporation, closed the hotel for a complete renovation, during which the number of rooms was reduced from 385 to 184. Both the exterior and interior renovations were aimed at preserving the qualities that originally gave The Melrose its character and charm.

Throughout its history the property has seen the entrance on Oak Lawn go from rose garden to driveway to rose garden and back again. It has been both permanent and transient home to thousands of people, including Elizabeth Taylor, Arthur Miller and Luciano Pavarotti. In 1983 The Melrose Hotel was declared a historical landmark by the Dallas Landmark Commission.

In December of 1991 a group of investors purchased The Melrose and began a renovation program for the hotel. In 1999 the hotel was sold to an investment group headed by Berwind Property

Group, which also assumed the property's management and completed the guest room renovations as well as enhancements to the lobby, the Landmark Restaurant and the Library Bar. The company also owns and manages the historic Great Southern Hotel in Columbus, Ohio, and The Melrose Hotel in Washington, DC.

Over the years The Melrose Hotel has been many things to many people: a home where a child was married, the site where an important business deal was finalized or the place where one went for that first special date or social occasion. Every passing day becomes another memory and contributes to the continuing history of the hotel.

At The Melrose, dining becomes an extraordinary experience. Long acclaimed for his culinary creativity, Executive Chef Wiley Bates III delights both hotel guests and loyal followers with his eclectic menu served in the award-winning, elegant and recently renovated Landmark Restaurant. The restaurant has earned the acclaim of "One of the Area's Finest Restaurants" by *Zagat Restaurant Review*. Before or after dinner visit the Library Bar, voted "The Top Place To Sip & Sup" by *The Wall Street Journal*.

The Melrose Hotel, Dallas, located at the corner of Oak Lawn and Cedar Springs Avenues, 3015 Oak Lawn Avenue, Dallas, Texas 75219. Call (214) 521-5151. Breakfast is served Monday through Friday from 6:30 a.m. to 11 a.m. and Saturday and Sunday from 7 a.m. to 11 a.m. Sunday brunch is served from 11 a.m. until 2 p.m. Lunch is served Monday through Friday from 11 a.m. until 2 p.m. Dinner is served Monday through Thursday, 6 p.m. to 10 p.m. and Friday and Saturday from 6 p.m. to 11 p.m.

Goat Cheese Terrine

- 4 goat cheese, 11-ounce logs
- 1/4 cup red onion, minced
- 3 tablespoons chives, minced
- 3 tablespoons dill, minced
- 1 tablespoon black pepper
- 2 teaspoons salt
- 10 asparagus spears
- 1 Idaho potato
- cooking oil spray

Spray a ceramic terrine mold with coating of cooking oil spray. Line the mold with plastic. Slice the potato very thin and place in a steamer pan. Steam for about one minute until the potato slices are barely cooked. Place the potatoes along the bottom of the inside of the mold so that they are the same height on both sides of the mold. Each slice should slightly overlap the other. Place the remaining potatoes on the inside of the mold all the way around overlapping the first bottom layer. Place half of the goat cheese (2 logs) into the mold and press it down evenly. Lay the asparagus into the goat cheese, 5 on each side. Put a layer of goat cheese (1 log) over the asparagus. Put another layer of potatoes on top of the goat cheese lengthwise. Place the 4th log of the cheese into a mixture of the remaining ingredients and fold over the potatoes. Cover with plastic and weigh down with another terrine mold until set.

YIELD

Serves 8.

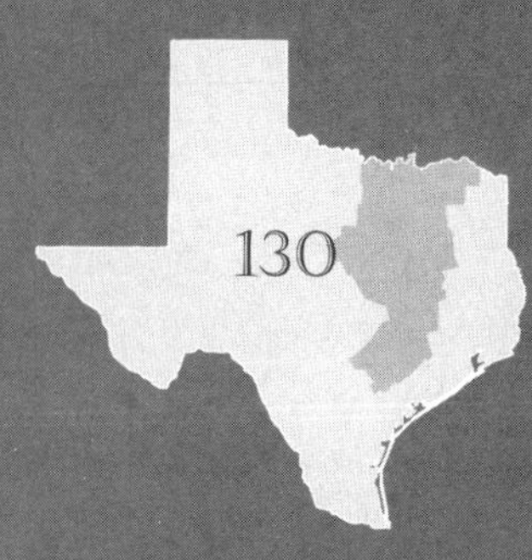

Portobello Mushrooms

1 portobello mushroom
1 ounce balsamic vinaigrette
salt and black pepper

Clean the stems and gills off of the portobello mushroom. Toss with balsamic vinaigrette and let sit for 1 hour. Season the mushroom lightly with salt and pepper. Grill it over low heat until it is tender all the way through. Dump the excess balsamic vinaigrette back over the mushroom.

YIELD

Serves 1.

Chestnut Flour Crepes

1 1/2 cups chestnut flour
1 cup flour
2 eggs
3 1/2 cups whole milk
1/2 teaspoon salt
1 tablespoon thyme, chopped
2 tablespoons sugar

Combine all the ingredients except the eggs and mix until smooth. Add the eggs. Heat a dipper of batter—enough to lightly cover the bottom of an oiled crepe pan. Turn over when lightly brown and place on plate. Fill with desired ingredients.

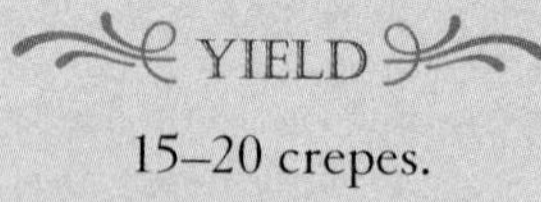

YIELD

15–20 crepes.

Morel Mushroom Flan

1 ounce dry morels

1 quart heavy cream

1/4 cup shallots, sliced

8 eggs

2 tablespoons thyme, chopped

1 tablespoon salt

1 tablespoon white pepper

Combine the morels, shallots and the cream and simmer for 10 minutes. Puree the morel mix in a blender. Temper with eggs and mix. Add the remaining ingredients. Put 3 ounces in a timbale mold covered with foil and bake in a water bath for about 30 minutes at 300 degrees.

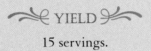

15 servings.

THE MERRY HEART TEAROOM

Granbury

Granbury derives its name from Hiram Brinson Granberry of Mississippi. In 1851, Hiram came to Texas, opening a law office in Sequin. He later turned to building concrete houses. In Waco he practiced law and worked on newspapers.

In 1861 Hiram Granberry organized the Waco Guards and led them into battle in the Civil War. He was taken prisoner in 1862 at Fort Donelson and was sent to Johnson Island. Late that year he was released at Vicksburg in a prisoner exchange, and he went back to Texas to reorganize his unit. The new company served at Fort Hudson in the famous engagement with the Farragut Fleet. They also participated in the Battle of Chickamauga.

After the disaster at Missionary Ridge, Granberry was promoted to Brigadier General, and his unit was assigned to the Army of Tennessee. He was killed at the Battle of Franklin in 1864. His body was kept in a vault in Fort Worth National Bank until preparations were completed in Granbury for his final internment. No one is certain why they changed the spelling of his name, but the two are often incorrectly assumed to be unrelated.

Granbury is unique in the state of Texas for a number of reasons. It is one of the few pioneer towns with so many original stone buildings still intact and in use. Most of its buildings were constructed between 1870 and 1900 from hand-cut limestone laboriously taken from two local quarries. Many of the stones were cut exactly to fit specific portions of the buildings. Most were completely load-bearing. There are no steel supports used in construction.

Prior to 1850, the town center was a wilderness of huge oak, pecan and cottonwood trees. The area abounded with buffalo, deer, antelope and other, smaller game. It was a favorite camping and lookout area for the Indians. Raiding parties would leave their families and excess gear at Comanche Peak and make forays against the settlements to the south and west. The Brazos River was known as the "Dead Line," as it was perilous to cross over to the west side into Indian territory.

Davy Crockett's widow, Elizabeth, and his son, Robert, settled in what is now Hood County in the 1850s. They built two small log cabins near the early frontier settlement of Acton. The foundation of one of the Crockett cabins is now beneath an old rock ranch house, and it features an escape tunnel to a nearby creek bed. The tunnel was used to hide from Indians.

A Texas Centennial Marker, the first historical marker erected in Texas, marks the site of Elizabeth's cabin. Elizabeth died in 1860 and is buried in Acton Cemetery, the smallest state park in Texas. A statue was erected at her gravesite by the state of Texas in 1911 to honor this pioneer mother. Robert Crockett became a Hood County Commissioner and his son, Ashley, was Granbury's first newspaper publisher in the early 1970s. Crockett Street is named in honor of the family.

The Merry Heart Tearoom is located in a building constructed in 1906. It shared a common north wall with City National Bank, which added a deed restriction to ensure that the building could be only one level, because they did not want their windows blocked. The first occupant was a dry goods store. Since the only storage place at the time was the attic, an elevator shaft was included that is still in place in the ceiling. The original tin ceilings are also still there. The south wall looks like sheetrock, but it is the original limestone plaster wall.

Granbury Printing occupied the building until the early 1980s when it was purchased and remodeled. In 1988, Diane Rawls Davis took over the building and opened the first antique co-op on the square. In 1990, she opened a tearoom at the back of the shop, named after her personal motto: "He who is of a Merry Heart hath a continual feast." (Proverbs 15:15) Her success has caused the Merry Heart Tearoom to be voted best in Hood County according to a newspaper poll. The restaurant seats 100. Reservations are suggested but not required. Group rates are available upon request.

The Merry Heart Tearoom, 110 N. Houston Street, Granbury, Texas 76048. Call (817) 573-3800 or (800) 354-1670 or email merryheart2@hotmail.com. Open Monday through Thursday from 11 a.m. until 3 p.m., Friday and Saturday from 11 a.m. until 9 p.m. and Sunday from 11 a.m. until 3 p.m.

Chicken Salad

9 cups water
7 boneless chicken breasts
1/2 medium yellow onion, diced
1/2 carrot stick, diced
1/2 celery stalk, diced

1 cup lemon nonfat yogurt
1/4 cup mayonnaise
1/4 cup green onion, diced
1/8 cup celery, diced
1/2 cup red grapes, cut in half
1/8 cup almonds
1 teaspoon Mrs. Dash
1/2 teaspoon salt

Bring the water to a boil. Add diced yellow onion, diced carrot, diced celery stalk, and boneless chicken breasts. Boil until fully cooked. Remove the chicken from the water and cool with ice.

Mix all the remaining unused ingredients in a large bowl. Chop the chicken into small pieces and mix together. Serve on a bed of lettuce, as sandwich filler or over a sliced tomato.

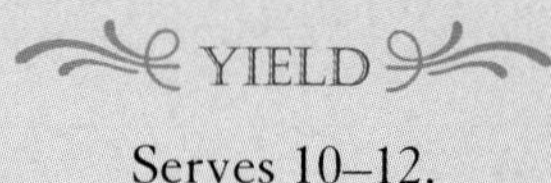
YIELD

Serves 10–12.

Pumpkin Bread

4 eggs
2/3 cup water
1 teaspoon salt
1 1/2 teaspoons baking powder
2 teaspoons cinnamon
2 teaspoons baking soda
1 teaspoon nutmeg
3 1/3 cups flour
3 cups sugar
15 ounces pumpkin
spray for pans

Put ingredients in order in a mixer. Mix continuously. Scrape down the sides of the bowl and mix well. Divide into 4 well-sprayed pans. Bake at 325 degrees for 45 minutes to one hour or until top springs back.

YIELD

4 loaves.

Cherry Crisp
with Rum Sauce

21 ounces cherry pie filling

3 cups yellow cake mix

3/4 cups margarine or butter

2 cups pecans

RUM SAUCE:

1 1/2 cups evaporated milk

1 1/2 cups fresh milk

1 1/4 cups sugar

1/4 cup butter

2 tablespoons cornstarch

3 ounces rum

Grease a 9 × 13-inch pan and add the pie filling. Cover with the cake mix. Dot with margarine or butter. Cover with pecans and bake at 350 degrees for 35 to 40 minutes.

RUM SAUCE:

Heat first 4 ingredients in double boiler. When hot, dissolve 2 heaping tablespoons cornstarch in a little water and add to boiler. Stir until thick. Remove from heat. When cool, add 3 ounces of rum.

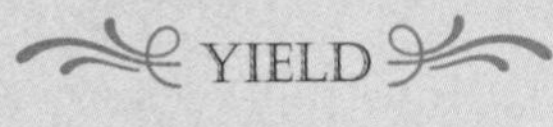

Serves 8.

MESSINA HOF WINERY & RESORT

Bryan

Nestled among forty acres of vineyards on a 100-acre estate lies Messina Hof Winery, the Vintage House Restaurant and the Villa, an elegant antique-appointed ten-room bed and breakfast. Messina Hof is owned by Paul and Merrill Bonarrigo, who chose the name Messina Hof to reflect their family heritages. Winemaker Paul Bonarrigo's heritage lies in Messina, Sicily and Merrill's family hails from Hof, Germany. When it was founded in Bryan, Texas, in 1977, Messina Hof was one of only three Texas wineries. Today Texas, the fastest-growing wine-producing state in America, boasts over 50 wineries.

The winery's lakeside Guest Center is located in the restored Howell House, a local historical landmark. This French manor home was constructed in the early 1900s by the Ursuline Sisters and later purchased, restored and lavishly furnished by the Howell family. The Howells were prominent in the Bryan community and Mr. Howell served as Ambassador to Uruguay.

Paul and Merrill purchased the home, moved it to its present location and carefully reconstructed it to retain its former grace and elegance. The Guest Center still has its original masonry and hardware and the Burgundian trusses that adorn the ceiling. Sections of the original home were also incorporated in the building of the Vintage House Restaurant and Gallery and the Villa.

The Rose Garden, which highlights the front of the Guest Center and is a popular site for weddings, was planted as a tribute to Mrs. Howell. Her rose garden of 3,500 white rosebushes was her pride and joy. The Bonarrigos have planted 350 pink floribunda and antique roses to bring back the beauty of times past.

The Vintage House Restaurant is bordered by the vineyard and serves only the freshest and finest vineyard cuisine. The romantic setting is enhanced by a wall of oak barrels where the award-winning Papa Paulo Port is aged. Family heirlooms, tables and 11-foot, majestic, stained glass windows dating from the 19th century infuse the atmosphere with old-world charm. Other items of interest include etchings of the State Capitol Building, which were gifts to the winery from Texas Speaker of the House, Billy Clayton, and a miniature grape press, a gift from Joseph Duhacsek.

The Villa is the ultimate in charm, old-fashioned service and privacy. As you approach the building along the rose-lined walkway, you immediately notice the unique front doors, which are from

Louis Pasteur's country home. The doors open into the Great Room, which is accented by the Bonarrigo family dining table dating back to the 1400s. As you gaze upward, you see a brilliant chandelier from the turn of the 20th-century and the hand-painted glass panel that is from the Louvre in Paris.

The Villa has 27 stained glass windows, including the colorful, half-circle windows on the front of the Villa that date back to the 1700s and were hand blown in Spain for a Catholic Church in Donna, Texas. Each room of The Villa is individually appointed with furniture thematically chosen according to the room's name.

The bedroom suite in the Lancelot & Guinevere Room dates back to the 1600s and was handcrafted by monks in England, and the torchéres were once in Yorkshire Castle in England. You will find luxury, elegance and history in whichever room you select.

Each year, Messina Hof Wine Cellars holds an annual Texas Artist Wine Label Competition and this year's theme was "Crepe Myrtles." Beautiful and colorful entries were received this year, so the competition was tough. A panel of five judges are selected to determine the first-, second- and third-place winners of the competition. The judges are chosen from the Arts Council of Brazos Valley, the local artistic community and one member of Messina Hof. The first-place winner receives $700.00 and the winning artwork is displayed on Messina Hof's Private Reserve Wine labels.

Winery tours and wine tastings at $5.00 per person are conducted Monday through Friday at 1 p.m., 2:30 p.m. and 5:30 p.m., Saturday at 11 a.m., 12:30 p.m., 2:30 p.m., 4 p.m. and 5:30 p.m. and Sunday at 12:30 p.m. and 2:30 p.m.

The Vintage House Restaurant, 4545 Old Reliance Road, Bryan, Texas 77808. Call (979) 778-9463 or (800) 736-9463, visit www.messinahof.com or email: wine@messinahof.com. The Vintage House Restaurant is open Wednesday through Saturday for lunch from 11 a.m. to 4 p.m. and for dinner at 5 p.m. until 10 p.m. They serve Sunday brunch from noon to 6 p.m. Reservations are recommended.

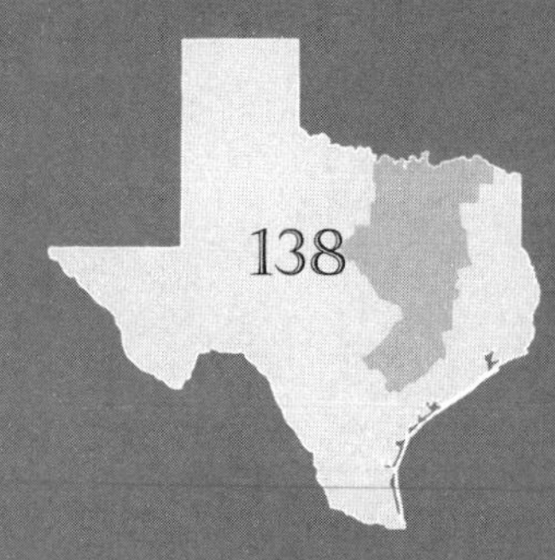

1/2 pound wild rice

6 tomatoes

1/2 teaspoon salt

1 1/2 minced garlic cloves

1/2 cup parsley

1 can mushroom stems and pieces

2 tablespoons basil, chopped

1/2 cup Romano cheese, grated

6 tablespoons olive oil

6 teaspoons bread crumbs

sprigs fresh basil with stem, for garnish

dash of pepper

Paul's Stuffed Tomatoes

From *The Ultimate Wine & Food Pairing Cookbook*, by Merrill Bonarrigo

Wine Recommendation:
Messina Hof's Sauvignon Blanc

Cook rice in salted boiling water following directions on the package. When half cooked, drain and put into a large bowl. Meanwhile, cut a slice from the stem end of each tomato and scoop out tomato pulp with a melon scoop. Add tomato pulp to rice. Also add salt, minced garlic, parsley, can of mushroom stems and pieces, basil, 1/2 of the Romano cheese and a dash of pepper for taste and blend well; then, fill hollow tomatoes. Replace cap of tomato over filling.

Arrange tomatoes in a well-greased baking dish, pouring olive oil evenly over each. Garnish with bread crumbs and the remaining Romano cheese. Cover and bake at 350 degrees Fahrenheit for about 45 minutes.

Garnish with sprigs of fresh basil with stem.

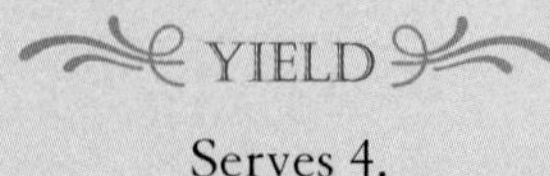

Serves 4.

PRESENTATION:

Insert sprig of basil gently into center of tomato cap, creating the look of green leaves. Remove the cap and rest against the side of the tomato to reveal the filling.

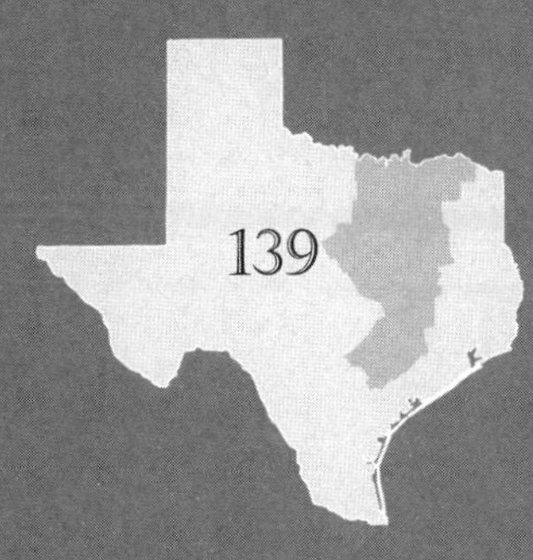

Salmon Napoleon

6 ounces salmon fillet
1 teaspoon chopped garlic
1 teaspoon capers
1 teaspoon red onion, diced
1 teaspoon red bell pepper, diced
1 teaspoon tomato, diced
1 ounce white wine (Chardonnay recommended)
1 tablespoon whole butter
3–4 tablespoons olive oil
1 potato cake
3/4 cup sautéed spinach

Season and pan sear salmon fillet. In a hot sauté pan add olive oil, then the red onion, red bell pepper, garlic and capers. Deglaze with Chardonnay and tomatoes. Cook until the mixture is almost dry, swirl in the whole butter to make the sauce. Cut the salmon in half. Serve on sautéed spinach, then top with a potato cake, then the other half of the salmon. Finish with the sauce.

YIELD

Serves 1.

Garden Chicken

1 breast of chicken, 6 ounces
6 or 7 slices mushrooms
1 teaspoon chopped garlic
1 teaspoon capers
2 tablespoons tomatoes, diced
3 or 4 quarters artichoke hearts
1 ounce olive oil
1 or 2 ounces Messina Hof Chardonnay white wine
1 tablespoon whole butter

Grill the chicken breast. Use a hot sauté pan, add olive oil, then the mushrooms, capers, garlic, artichoke hearts, then the tomatoes and the wine to deglaze the pan. Continue to cook until the mixture is almost dry. At the last minute before serving, swirl in the whole butter to make the sauce.

Serve with wild rice and a vegetable.

YIELD

Serves 1.

NEWPORT'S SEAFOOD

Dallas

During the late 1800s, industry began to spring up in what is known as The West End Historic District. The building that Newport's currently occupies housed the Dallas Brewery and Bottling Works around the turn of the century. This local company brewed and distributed Dallas Spirits, Tipperary and Dallas Black beers.

Pure artesian spring water, drawn from the cavernous well, was used to make these beers. As a result of prohibition, the Brewery was converted into the Grain Juice Company. Unfortunately, it went bankrupt in 1926.

Blackland Properties purchased what was left of the original brewery in 1982 and began the first major restoration of the West End. During this restoration, the now-famous well was uncovered. At 31 feet wide and 55 feet deep, the well contains over 35 feet of water. Divers found smooth brick walls and flooring, with a smaller well in the center that is 12 feet in diameter. Due to downtown development since the turn of the century, the artesian spring that fed the well is primarily inactive today.

Mounted over the well today is the majestic ship model, which was discovered in a European antique shop. It originated from the Seaman's Chapel in Copenhagen, which served as a church for seagoers, where they would pray for a safe journey before setting sail.

Newport's Seafood was the West End Historic District's first upscale restaurant, opening in 1984, and it helped set the stage for the revival of downtown Dallas. Its concept is simple. Newport's purchases fresh fish from brokers on all coasts every single day. It prepares and serves it with sincerity, honesty and pride. The concept seems to work, because Newport's has thrived for almost 20 years in a town that some believe has the most restaurants per capita in the country.

Awards have set this restaurant apart. By the end of their first year of operation, Newport's was honored by *GQ* magazine as one of the 100 best restaurants in the United States. Their wine list is superior, having won the prestigious *Wine Spectator Magazine*'s Award of Excellence for the past five years.

Newport's Seafood, 703 McKinney Avenue, Dallas, Texas 75202. Call (214) 954-0220 or visit www.newportsrestaurant.com. They are open for lunch Monday through Friday from 11:30 a.m. until 2 p.m. Dinner is served seven nights from 5 p.m. until 10 p.m.

Crispy Thai Shrimp Cakes
with Coconut-Lemongrass Aioli

SHRIMP CAKES:

Process shrimp in food processor for 10 seconds. Combine with remaining ingredients in large bowl and blend thoroughly. Wet hands and form into appropriately sized cakes. Sauté on medium heat until golden brown.

COCONUT-LEMONGRASS AIOLI:

In blender, whip egg yolks and lemongrass until doubled in size. Add lime, coconut milk and cilantro. Very slowly, pour a small stream of oil into blender until thickened, very similar to mayonnaise. Season with salt and white pepper to taste.

Serves 4.

SHRIMP CAKES:

1 pound raw shrimp, shelled (small inexpensive shrimp will do)

1 1/2 inch galangal, or ginger, finely chopped

2 tablespoons red curry paste

1 egg

2 tablespoons Nam Pla (Thai fish sauce)

8 Kaffir lime leaves, vein removed and finely chopped

1/4 tablespoon white pepper

oil for frying

COCONUT-LEMONGRASS AIOLI:

3 egg yolks

1 sprig lemongrass, finely chopped

1 tablespoon lime juice

1/2 cup unsweetened coconut milk

2 cups vegetable oil

1/2 bunch cilantro, chopped

salt and white pepper to taste

Newport's Lobster Bisque

LOBSTER STOCK:

- 2 tablespoons tomato paste
- 1 whole fresh lobster, cut in half, or 3–4 empty lobster shells
- 1 yellow onion, coarsely chopped
- 2 or 3 carrots, very coarsely chopped
- 2 or 3 stalks celery, coarsely chopped
- 5 sprigs fresh tarragon
- 2 tablespoons paprika
- 4 tablespoons olive oil
- 1 gallon cold water
- salt to taste

BISQUE:

- 1 cup dry sherry
- 1/2 gallon fresh lobster stock
- 1 quart heavy cream
- 2 whole vanilla beans, split lengthwise
- salt to taste
- white pepper to taste

Note: If you happen to have fresh lobster stock, this recipe is extremely easy. Do not substitute for the lobster stock, as the dish will become another kind of bisque entirely.

FIRST MAKE THE LOBSTER STOCK:

Sauté first 7 ingredients in olive oil on very high heat until vegetables are browned and almost caramelized. Add water and bring to a rolling boil. Turn heat down to low and simmer for 1 1/2 hours or until reduced to 1/2 gallon of liquid. Strain. If using a whole, fresh lobster, remove the lobster after cooking for 50 minutes, reserve the meat for garnish or another use, then return the shells to the pot for the remaining time.

BISQUE:

Bring all ingredients to a boil, then reduce heat and simmer for approximately 45 minutes, or until thickened. Garnish with fresh lobster meat, if desired.

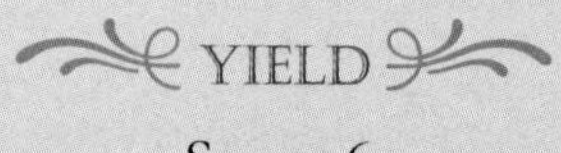
YIELD

Serves 6.

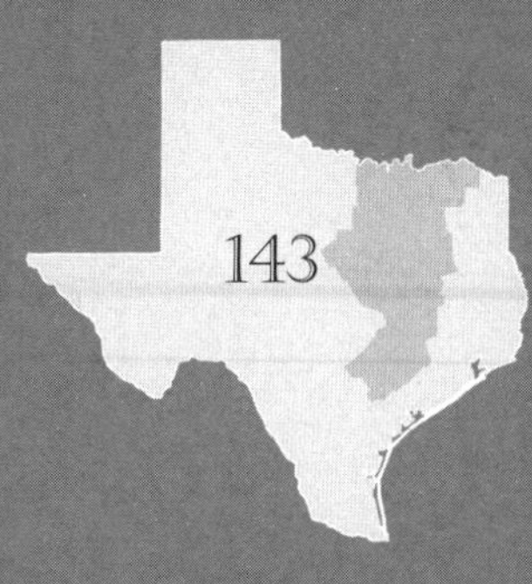

Tarragon-Dijon Salmon Fillets

- 4 8-ounce fillets of fresh salmon
- 2 cups milk
- 1 cup heavy cream
- 2 ounces butter
- 2 ounces flour
- 2 tablespoons fresh tarragon, chopped finely
- 2 tablespoons Dijon mustard
- salt and white pepper to taste

After cleaning and boning salmon, place in refrigerator until ready to use. Bring the milk to a simmer in a 2-quart saucepan, whisking to avoid a skin from forming on the surface. In a second saucepan, make the roux: gently melt the butter and add the flour. Stir the mixture over medium heat for about 2 minutes, until the flour has a toasty smell but is not browned. Remove from heat and cool slightly for 30 seconds to one minute. Whisk the simmering milk into the roux.

Return the sauce to the stove and bring it back to a simmer while whisking. Add the heavy cream, and continue whisking until the sauce has reached a desirable consistency. Extra cream may be added to thin the sauce if necessary. Once the sauce has reached a desirable consistency, add the fresh tarragon and Dijon mustard, salt and pepper to taste and whisk to incorporate.

Keep the sauce warm while you grill the salmon fillets. Once the salmon has been grilled to your desired temperature, place on plate and surround the fillet with the sauce. Rice pilaf, steamed vegetables or grilled vegetables may be served with the entrée, if desired.

YIELD

Serves 4.

THE NORTHWOOD INN

Waco

The Northwood Inn was built in the early 1900s as a carriage house on the Cameron Estate. The Cameron family was one of the prominent families in establishing what is now the thriving city of Waco. After being sold to the Burgess family in the late 1940s, it was remodeled into the lovely home of today. It was sold to the Dossett family who, in turn, sold it to Tom Keubler, who opened it as a restaurant in 1982.

The Northwood Inn is now under the ownership of the Lundys, who are dedicated to preserving the history of the property, as well as offering Central Texas a place for fine food in a unique atmosphere.

The changing seasons only add to the beauty of the surroundings. There are several rooms available for intimate rehearsal dinners or private business meetings. This lovely setting is often chosen for weddings and receptions. Lunch parties of ten or more are welcome.

Holding to the traditions of fine dining, the professional staff is trained in the art of tableside presentations, as in Café Diablo, Bananas Foster, Cherries Jubilee and Chateaubriand.

The Northwood Inn is located at 1609 College Drive, Waco, Texas 76708. Call (254) 755-8666 for more information or visit www.the-northwood-inn.com. It is open Monday through Saturday with seatings from 6 p.m. to 10 p.m. It closes when the last diner leaves.

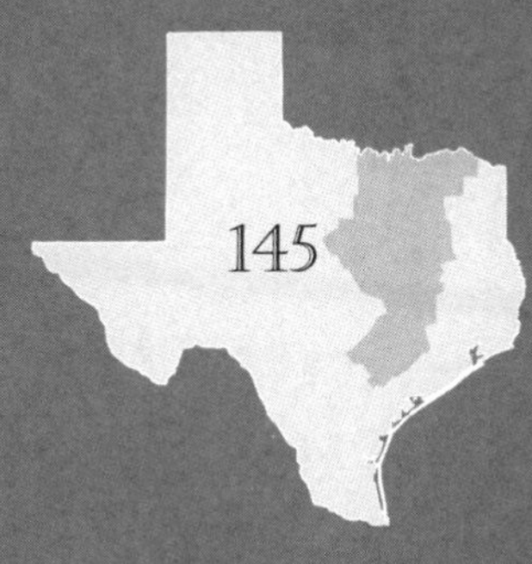

Herbal Brie Shrimp

Blend flour and 1 tablespoon of softened butter. Sauté shrimp in unsalted butter and garlic for 1 1/2 minutes each side. Remove from pan. Add clam juice to pan. Heat to boil. Whip in flour and butter mixture. Cook for 2 minutes.

Add herbs and blend in Brie cheese. (Thin sauce with 1–2 tablespoons white wine, if necessary.) Salt and pepper to taste. Add shrimp. Heat thoroughly and pour sauce onto 4 small plates. Arrange shrimp over sauce. Serve immediately.

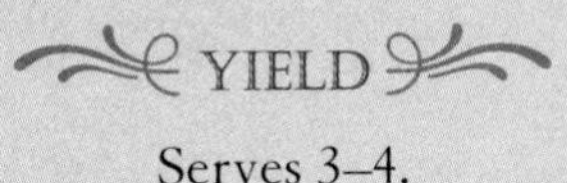

Serves 3–4.

- 12 large shrimp, peeled and deveined
- 2 tablespoons unsalted butter
- 2 teaspoons fresh chopped garlic
- 2 teaspoons fresh chopped basil
- 1 teaspoon fresh chopped lemon thyme
- 2 tablespoons Brie cheese
- 8 ounces clam juice
- salt and pepper
- 1 tablespoon flour
- 1 tablespoon softened butter
- 1–2 tablespoons white wine

Red Leaf and Bibb Salad

2 small heads red leaf lettuce

1 small head Bibb lettuce

8 cherry tomatoes, halved

1/2 cucumber, peeled, seeded and sliced

4 large mushrooms, sliced

TOMATO SHALLOT DRESSING:

3 large, ripe tomatoes, peeled and seeded

1 tablespoon olive oil

3 tablespoons red wine vinegar

1 1/2 cloves fresh shallot, peeled and chopped

salt and pepper to taste

Rinse lettuces in cold water and gently tear. Pat dry. Toss lettuce together. Prepare dressing below.

TOMATO SHALLOT DRESSING:

In blender or processor, puree tomatoes with oil and vinegar until smooth. Add shallots and blend 30 seconds. Add salt and pepper to taste.

To assemble, place lettuce on plate. Arrange tomato, cucumber and mushrooms. Drizzle desired amount of dressing over salad.

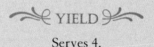

YIELD

Serves 4.

Broiled Lamb Chops
with Crème de Menthe Jelly

LAMB MARINADE:

Combine all ingredients. Marinate chops 2 hours. For whole lamb racks, marinate 24 hours.

CRÈME DE MENTHE JELLY:

Blend in saucepan over low heat.

Broil lamb chops to desired temperature. Serve warm sauce over chops.

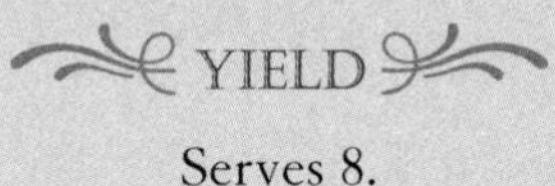

Serves 8.

8 lamb loin chops, about 5 ounces each

LAMB MARINADE:

2 cups olive oil

1 cup sherry

1/2 cup orange juice

2 tablespoons fresh garlic, chopped

2 teaspoons fresh mint, chopped

1/2 small onion, diced

1 teaspoon salt

1 teaspoon pepper

CRÈME DE MENTHE JELLY:

2 parts mint jelly

1 part white Crème de Menthe

Grand Marnier Cream for Fresh Seasonal Berries

- 2 egg yolks
- 1 1/2 ounces Grand Marnier
- 1/2 ounce sherry
- 5 tablespoons sugar
- 3 ounces heavy whipping cream

Place sugar, sherry, Grand Marnier and egg yolks in stainless steel mixing bowl or top of double boiler. Cook over double boiler, whipping constantly until sugar dissolves and mixture has thickened to a soft, whipped cream texture. Blend in heavy cream. Chill.

Pour cream over available berries of your choice.

YIELD

Serves 2.

THE NUTSHELL EATERY & BAKERY

Granbury

The moment you enter The Nutshell you are sure to notice the flavor and history of this historic building. It was constructed in 1885 by A. P. Gordon, who set out to make a living in "wet goods." This, of course, was early American shorthand for the saloon business. Other activities on the premises were suspected under cover of the rooms upstairs, reported to be used as "hotel rooms" by some of the patrons.

After a period of time, Gordon converted the facility to a dry goods store. The building was filled from floor to ceiling with tools, fine fabric and grocery items. He was known for the wide selection of merchandise he carried and his fair prices. People believed that "if ole A. P. didn't have what you wanted, then no one did."

But the saloon is what gives The Nutshell its claim to fame (or perhaps infamy). Historians say that a bartender at the old saloon named John St. Helen was really John Wilkes Booth, the man who assassinated President Lincoln. Booth is reported to have been put up to killing the President by disloyal members of his cabinet. These same individuals helped Booth escape and planted another hapless individual in the barn on the Garrett farm. The stand-in was killed, identified as Booth and buried, without the benefit of modern forensic tools available to verify his guilt.

It was widely reported that Booth broke his left leg as he jumped to the stage of Ford's Theater to make his escape. John St. Helen frequently quoted Shakespeare, walked with a limp on his left side and was reported to drink more heavily than usual on the anniversary of the President's murder. At one point when St. Helen thought he was dying, he called several local men and a priest to his bedside and confessed that he was, in fact, John Wilkes Booth. He also indicated where they might find the pistol he used to shoot Lincoln. One of the men present recovered the gun and it has been in a safety deposit box in Austin ever since.

When St. Helen failed to die as he expected, he disappeared from Granbury and was never heard from again, under that name. A few years later in 1903, a man named David George killed himself in Enid, Oklahoma. His suicide note said he was the secretive John St. Helen from Granbury and the presidential assassin, John Wilkes Booth. Both *Unsolved Mysteries* and the television news magazine

20/20 investigated this legend and presented their analysis. No conclusive evidence was offered, but circumstantial findings give Granbury a minor claim to an unfortunate chapter in American history.

The first floor of the Gordon building has been a restaurant and bakery since 1970. The Nutshell Eatery & Bakery, 137 E. Pearl, Granbury, Texas 76048, (817) 279-8989, is open daily 7 a.m. to 5 p.m. and Friday and Saturday nights from 5 p.m. to 9 p.m.

Sour Dough Bread

STARTER:

Let this mixture sit overnight unrefrigerated. This must be done the night before. The mixture should be bubbling and smell of fermentation when ready.

IN THE MORNING:

Mix until dough is not sticky. Place in bowl and brush lightly with oil. Cover until it doubles in bulk. Punch down and place in loaf pan. Let rise. Bake 350 degrees for 35 minutes.

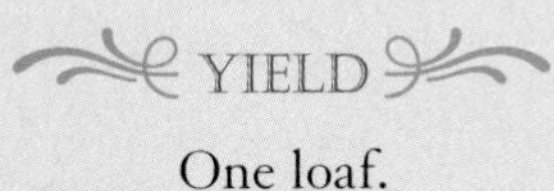

One loaf.

STARTER:

2 cups water

1/2 cup fresh potato, grated

3/4 cup sugar

IN THE MORNING:

2 cups sour dough starter

3/4 cup oil

1 tablespoon salt

4 to 5 cups flour

Chocolate Cream Pie

Mix sugar, cocoa, flour and salt. Add milk and beaten egg yolks. Cook over medium heat stirring constantly until it boils. Remove from the heat. Add vanilla and butter. Pour into a baked pie shell.

MERINGUE:

Beat the egg whites, sugar and cream of tartar until stiff. Cover pie and brown in oven. Enjoy!

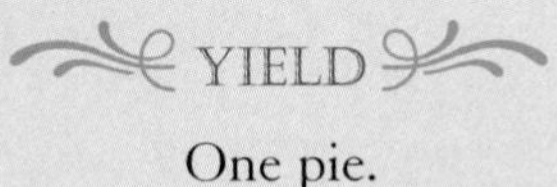

One pie.

1 cup sugar

1/2 cup cocoa

4 tablespoons flour

salt to taste

3 egg yolks

2 cups milk

1 teaspoon vanilla

2 tablespoons butter

baked pie shell

MERINGUE:

3 egg whites

1/2 teaspoon cream of tartar

1/4 cup powder sugar

THE NUTT HOUSE RESTAURANT

Granbury

The first building on this site was a 12-foot-by-16-foot log structure, which served as a store with a wagon yard in the rear. Later, contractor Jim Warren built the current hand-hewn two-story limestone structure for two blind brothers, Jesse F. and Jacob Nutt, to serve as a mercantile store. The Nutt family first settled in the area in the 1850s. Several of their clan followed, and Granbury boasts two century-old homes on East Bridge Street that were originally built for Nutt families.

Jesse and Jacob Nutt were successful with their store and, together with Thomas Lambert, donated the 40-acre site that became Granbury, the county seat of Hood County. In 1919, after the family grocery store was remodeled, the second floor of this building became the Nutt Hotel, which was famous in the area for its dining room. One of the first buildings in historic Granbury to be restored, the Nutt House Restaurant was reopened on this site by Nutt family descendants Mary Lou Watkins and Joe Nutt in 1970.

Granbury is rich with Wild West legends. Many people say that the notorious outlaw Jesse James is buried in Granbury and not in Missouri. Historians say that Jesse James was shot by one of his own gang members in 1882. But others say that a substitute was shot and passed off to law enforcement as the famous outlaw. They were fooled, and Jesse escaped to Granbury. He worked on the railroad during the 1880s, spending some time in Granbury before moving on.

Legend says that James returned to Granbury when he was more than 100 years old to live out his remaining years with his grandson. Before dying he spent a lot of time with a new friend, Oran Baker, who happened to be the Hood County Sheriff. Following Jesse's death in 1951 at the age of 103, Baker conducted a postmortem examination of the body.

Sheriff Baker wrote a story for the newspaper in 1966 where he reported that he had found 32 bullet wounds on the body of the man he believed was in fact Jesse Woodson James. He further stated that he had discovered a rope burn scar on his neck, consistent with other stories of Jesse's life. The Granbury Cemetery contains a headstone erected by James family descendants who also believe that their famous ancestor is buried in Granbury.

The famous Texas chef Grady Spears has recently taken over operation of The Nutt House, creating a unique dining sensation. His following among Texas diners is legendary.

The Nutt House Restaurant, 121 East Bridge Street, Granbury, Texas 76048, (817) 573-5612, is open for dinner Wednesday through Sunday from 5 p.m. to 10 p.m., and lunch Friday, Saturday and Sunday from 11 a.m. to 3 p.m. The Javalina Bar, in the front of the building, is open Tuesday through Saturday 4 p.m. to 11 p.m. and Sunday 11 a.m. to 8 p.m.

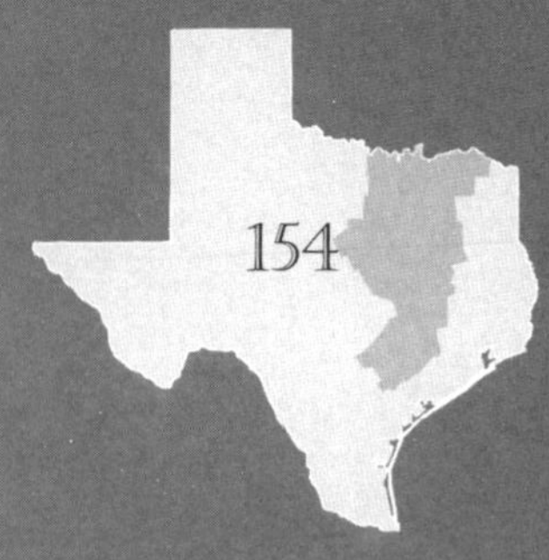

Nutt House Ranch Meatloaf

- 2 pounds Nolan Ryan ground sirloin
- 3 eggs
- 1 cup seasoned breadcrumbs
- 4 cloves garlic, minced
- 1 red onion, chopped
- 2 tomatoes, diced
- 1/2 cup cilantro
- 1/4 cup Worcestershire sauce
- 1 1/2 cups Monterey Jack cheese, grated
- 2 tablespoons Tabasco sauce
- 1/2 cup brown sugar
- kosher salt to taste

Preheat the oven to 350 degrees. In a large bowl, combine all the ingredients, mixing well. Place the mixture in a greased loaf pan. Bake for 45 minutes at 350, then increase the heat to 425 degrees and cook for an additional 15 minutes or until the meatloaf is firm to the touch. Remove and serve warm.

YIELD

Serves 6–8.

Bread Salad
with Oven-Dried Tomatoes and Texas Cheeses

- 12 cups Romaine lettuce, torn into large pieces
- 2 cups oven-dried tomatoes
- 3/4 cup slivered onion
- 1/2 cup olive oil
- 2 cups grated Asiago or Parmesan cheese
- 2 teaspoons fresh minced garlic
- 3 limes, juiced
- 6 cups day old bread
- kosher salt and freshly ground black pepper, to taste
- 1 cup soft goat cheese

In a large bowl, combine the oil, cheese, garlic and lime juice, mixing well. Add the bread and toss to coat. Then add the tomatoes, slivered onion and chopped Romaine, gently tossing to coat the lettuce. Top each salad with dollop of goat cheese and salt and pepper to taste.

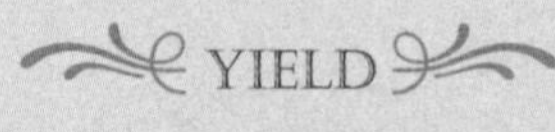

Serves 8.

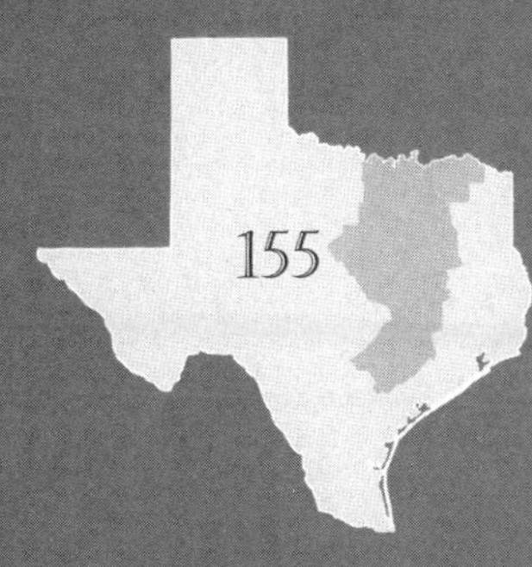

Mary Lou's Buttermilk Pie

Preheat the oven to 350 degrees. In a bowl, combine the sugar and cornmeal. Add the eggs and buttermilk, mixing well. Add the butter, vanilla, lemon rind and lemon juice. Pour into the pie shell and bake for 45 minutes.

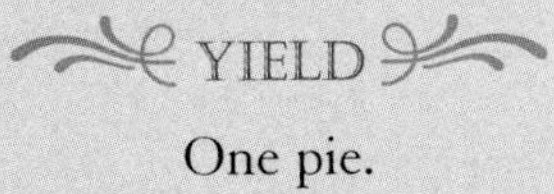

One pie.

1 pie crust

2 cups sugar

2 tablespoons cornmeal

5 eggs, beaten

2/3 cup buttermilk

1/2 cup melted butter, (chilled)

1 tablespoon vanilla

2 tablespoons lemon rind

3 tablespoons lemon juice

RADISSON PLAZA HOTEL

Fort Worth

When The Hotel Texas opened in 1921, it was representative of Fort Worth's change from a rowdy cattle town to a financial and cultural center, a young and growing city to be reckoned with by all of Texas and the Southwest. Dependence on cattle, meatpacking and the railroad had diminished. The catalyst for this change was the 1917 Oil Boom in Ranger, 80 miles to the west. Fort Worth became the center of that booming industry, where fortunes were made—or lost—overnight. The city's leaders, primarily the cattle barons on whose land the oil was discovered, found themselves with new wealth.

In 1919, a group of prominent business leaders met to plan the building of a first-class hotel. They included Amon Carter, William Monnig, W. K. Stripling, W. C. Stone Street, Van Zandt Jarvis and O. K. Shannon. The group formed The Citizens Hotel Company and raised $1.2 million among themselves. Under the company's first president, retail merchant William Monnig, the group launched a campaign in which more than 800 people, virtually all citizens of Fort Worth, pledged an average of $2,250 each to the venture, for a total of $1.8 million.

Originally the hotel was to be called The Winfield Hotel in honor of the leading citizen Winfield Scott; however, Mr. Scott died in 1911 before seeing his dream come true. As the enthusiasm grew, the investors recognized Fort Worth's pride in its heritage and decided the building should be known as "The Hotel Texas." Fort Worth, more than any other city, had lived the Texas legend.

At that time, the city's tallest building was six stories high. The new hotel, built to be a showplace, would rise fourteen stories, with an exterior of deep red brick and terra cotta, with distinctive arched windows on the ground floor and the crest. Opened on September 30, 1921, with elaborate fanfare, The Hotel Texas became an immediate source of pride to all citizens. Known not only as the home of cattle barons and oil tycoons, it became a kind of town square, where social, cultural and business life came together for all people.

The front doors of The Hotel Texas opened onto a room often described as the South's greatest lobby. It was bright and spacious, two stories in height and filled with beautifully upholstered furniture, Turkish carpet, polished woods and rows of ferns in large, glazed spots. The lobby featured an abundance of bright Texas sunlight admitted by the large, arched windows.

Those who designed and built the hotel were determined that "it would be Texas in name and Texas in atmosphere." Thus, almost every gathering place in the new hotel represented some aspect of the state. The Cactus Room, decorated in the soft yellow and pale green of the cactus bloom, located near the Crystal Ballroom on the top floor, paid homage to the rugged Texas plains and the brilliant cactus flower.

After an elevator ride to the top floor, guests stepped through a paneled entrance of etched glass into a marble hallway running the entire south end of the building. Called the Bluebonnet Promenade, it was a pre-function area for the magnificent Crystal Ballroom. The delicate blue color scheme, custom designed and painted furniture, chandeliers and fixtures, all suggested the state flower.

The Crystal Ballroom of The Hotel Texas, located on the hotel's top floor, was the center of Fort Worth's social and entertainment life in the 1920s and 1930s, hosting, over the years, the city's most elegant debutante balls, wedding receptions and important business and civic gatherings. The crystal chandeliers for the original Crystal Ballroom came from the Ritz-Carlton in New York. In 1925, the fundraising drive to establish the Fort Worth Symphony Orchestra was initiated at a luncheon in the hotel's elegant Crystal Ballroom.

In 1936, Dallas was chosen to host the Official Texas Centennial Celebrations, marking 100 years of independence from Mexico. In a move typical of Fort Worth's feisty spirit, the late Amon G. Carter, a newspaper publisher determined not to let Fort Worth slip into Dallas's shadow, devised a scheme. His city could siphon off thousands of people attending the event in Dallas by luring them to the frontier fiesta and its naughty-but-nice Casa Manana. Broadway showman Billy Rose was hired to produce the show and immediately began an advertising campaign, encouraging people "to go to Dallas for education and come to Fort Worth for fun." From his post in The Hotel Texas's Crystal Ballroom, Rose auditioned local beauties for what became the most successful extravaganza in Texas for its time.

In the 1940s, the big dance bands played in the ballroom. During World War II, the hotel became home of the Air Force Officers Club. The Civil War Air Patrol was also headquartered here. In 1948, The Hotel Texas had 600 rooms. The price per night for a single occupancy was $3.50 and $4.00 for a room with air conditioning. For double occupancy, the price was $5.00 and with air conditioning was $5.50.

In 1952, the 14th floor was remodeled and redecorated. The Bluebonnet Promenade was redone in shades of gray and cinnamon and renamed The Silver Lounge. The wood panels covering the walls were bleached white and then brought to a silver-platinum finish, and were so beautiful, people didn't believe they were real.

President John F. Kennedy spent his last night in the hotel before his assassination in Dallas in November of 1963. The suite Jackie and he stayed in was called "Kennedy Suite" and "White House–Fort Worth." President Kennedy spoke at a large gathering outdoors in front of the hotel, then at a breakfast in his honor, inside the hotel, prior to departing for Dallas.

The Hotel Texas remained open until the early 1960s. Purchased and reopened in the early 1960s, Sheraton operated the hotel until the late 1970s and built the east tower during that time, adding approximately 250 rooms to the hotel. Sheraton closed their doors in 1977. Woodbine Development purchased and renovated the hotel, in 1979 and 1980, reopening in January 1981 as The Hyatt Regency Fort Worth. On December 1, 1991, the management of the hotel changed and the hotel is now flying the Radisson Banner.

In 1981, the hotel was named to the National Register of Historic Places, insuring protection to the familiar façade, and dedicated by then-Vice President George Bush and Mrs. Ruth Hunt.

Since the hotel's opening, the registry has recorded names of the world's most famous people. Tex Richard signed Jack Dempsey for the Dempsey–Tunney fight for the world boxing title in a 10th floor bedroom. Rudolph Valentino, who died in 1926 at the age of 31, danced tango here with his wife, Natacha Rambova, in the Crystal Ballroom of the 14th floor, while tables were overturned and women all but swooned. Natalie Wood and Robert Wagner were among the thousands of honeymoon couples who made The Hotel Texas a stop. Lawrence Welk, at the height of the Depression, serenaded diners with his accordion and nine-piece band. Will Rogers, President Franklin D. Roosevelt, Lyndon Baines Johnson, Elvis Presley, Barry Goldwater, John Tower and a then-Vice President Richard Nixon were just a few of the guests to stay here.

More recent celebrity guests include Bob and Gloria Hope, President and Mrs. George Bush, Vice President and Mrs. Dan Quayle, Luciano Pavarotti, Christy Brinkley, Tanya Tucker, Michael Keaton, Red Skelton, Tina Turner, Carol Channing and The Harlem Globetrotters. Tennis greats such as Andre Agassi, Pete Sampras, Jim Courier and John McEnroe were here for the 1992 World Davis Cup finals. The legends of golf are here yearly for the Colonial Golf Tournament, including Fuzzy Zoeller, Ian Baker-Finch, Arnold Palmer and Jack Nicklaus.

Since the change in management on December 1, 1991, they have undertaken a multi-million dollar renovation program and to date have completed the Grand Ballroom, from floor to ceiling, and the Cactus Bar & Grill, as well as other amenity and security items.

The Radisson Plaza Hotel, 815 Main Street, Fort Worth, Texas 76102. Call (817) 870-2100, or visit www.radisson.com/ftworthtx. The Café Texas is open seven days a week for breakfast from 6 a.m. until 11:30 a.m. Café Texas then begins to serve lunch, which runs until 1:30 p.m. The Cactus Bar & Grill is open for dinner seven days a week from 4:30 p.m. until 10 p.m.

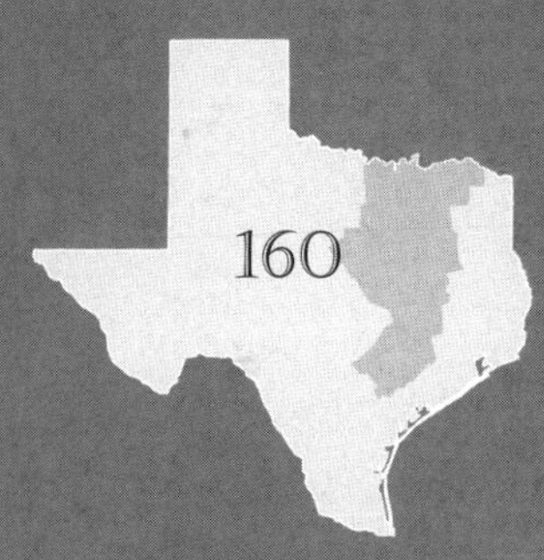

Tortilla Soup

- 1/2 ounce tortilla chips
- 2 slices avocados
- 2 tablespoons Monterey Jack cheese
- 1/2 cup steamed rice
- 1/2 cup chicken taco meat
- 12 ounces chicken broth
- chopped scallions for garnish

Using a 16-ounce soup bowl, place all the ingredients in the bowl then add the broth.

YIELD

Serves 1 or 2.

Bread Pudding with Vanilla Sauce

- 2 cups sliced croissants
- 1 cup diced fruit Danish
- 6 ounces milk
- 8 ounces heavy cream
- 4 eggs
- 1/2 cup sugar
- 1 teaspoon vanilla
- 1/2 teaspoon nutmeg
- 1 teaspoon cinnamon
- 1/2 cup raisins (optional)

VANILLA SAUCE:

- 1 box instant vanilla pudding
- 2 cups milk
- dash vanilla
- dash nutmeg

Preheat oven to 325 degrees. Mix well the milk, cream, eggs, sugar, vanilla, nutmeg and cinnamon. Place sliced croissants, fruit Danish and raisins in a cake pan. Then pour mixture over all and bake for 45 minutes.

VANILLA SAUCE:

Whip until liquefied. Pour on top of bread pudding and serve.

Serves 4–6.

RANCHMAN'S CAFÉ

Ponder

Also known as the Ponder Steak House, Ranchman's Café is one of very few historic eating establishments in Texas that actually started out as a restaurant. The Brock family built the original part of the building in 1903. It was built for the purpose of housing a café in one side, which was rented and operated by the Horton family, and a barber shop in the other. During the 30s depression it was taken over by the Brocks and turned into a dry goods store. It remained such until 1948 when "Pete" Jackson and her husband, who owned a grocery store a couple of doors down, bought the building and opened Ranchman's Café.

Over the years Ranchman's has built a national reputation for serving some of the finest T-bone steaks, largest chicken-fried steak and highest meringue pies to be found anywhere. The restaurant has been written up in *Southern Living*, *Gourmet*, *Cowboys & Indians* and *Texas Highways* magazines, to mention a few, as well as newspapers as far away as Sydney, Australia. They have served more celebrities than the staff can name, including President Jimmy Carter's mother, who purchased the old outhouse from Pete and had it shipped back to Georgia.

The current owner, Dave Ross, explains their success by saying, "This is as Texas as you can get." The true Ranchman's experience is gained by ordering a 24-ounce Porterhouse steak and sharing it with a friend (or two?). Not only is the meat hand-cut in their own kitchen, but everything served in the restaurant is made from scratch. If you liked the pie you had there last year or even in the 1970s, you will still like it today, as Evelyn Stack is still there after 30 years, making fresh pies daily. Guests wanting a baked potato with their meal must phone ahead because they refuse to microwave theirs.

It is not only Dave's preference to serve the best of everything, but also a tribute to Pete, who insisted on the very best for her customers. And your drinks will certainly be to your liking, since this is a dry county and you must BYOB. Dave says it is not at all uncommon to see coolers carried in by guests—even those arriving in limousines.

Dave purchased the café in 1992. He was no stranger to the place, however, having worked here as a cook for Pete in 1973 while attending the University of North Texas nearby. He was even there to help add the 50-seat addition in 1978. Dave used to ride his bicycle out to the café for a taste of their famous pies, which are still made daily, from scratch naturally.

The atmosphere of Ranchman's is simple. One can literally drive up to the door, and the tables are not cluttered with tablecloths. People feel very relaxed before they ever walk inside to sit down. Perhaps that is the reason so many famous people come from all over the world to dine at the Ponder Steak House. Movies filmed in the area such as *Bonnie and Clyde* introduced several notable Hollywood figures to Ranchman's Café. Warren Beatty and Faye Dunaway enjoyed their visits there and apparently also recommend it to their friends. Famous customers have included singer-songwriter Eric Clapton, author Larry McMurtry and actresses Cybill Shepard, Lauren Hutton and Jacqueline Bisset.

Ranchman's Café, 110 West Bailey, Ponder, Texas 76259, (940) 479-2221, or visit www.ranchman.com. The café is open every day at 11:00 a.m. until 10:00 p.m. They are closed only on Christmas Eve, Christmas Day, New Year's Day and July 4th. They offer live country and western and bluegrass music every Friday and Saturday night as well as the first Sunday afternoon of each month.

Ranchman's Chicken and Dumplins

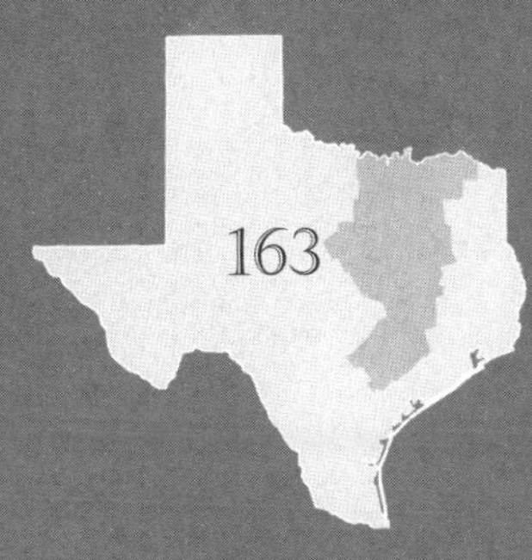

1 chicken

1 quart flour

4 eggs

1/4 cup water

2 teaspoons salt

1 cup milk

1 onion, diced

2 stalks celery, chopped

chicken bouillon

Boil the chicken in 2 gallons of water until tender. Let cool and then remove meat from bones. Chop meat and giblets. Reserve broth. Cool overnight, and then remove fat from the top.

Mix flour, eggs, water and salt in mixer with dough hook for 15 minutes, or until smooth. Divide into 2 balls. Roll each ball out with flour until thin as pie dough. Cut dough into 2-inch-by-1/2-inch pieces. Toss dumplins with flour so they don't stick.

Cook dumplins in chicken base and plenty of water for 1/2 hour. Drain the dumplins and add them to the chicken stock with the chicken meat, diced onion and celery. Add chicken bouillon to taste, and sufficient water to fill pot enough to cover dumplins. Add milk.

Serves 4.

- 2 eggs, beaten
- 1 cup sugar
- 1 cup buttermilk
- 1/2 stick butter
- 2 tablespoons flour
- 1 teaspoon lemon flavor or juice
- 1/2 teaspoon vanilla
- 1 pie crust

Ranchman's Buttermilk Pie

Beat the eggs separately. Melt the butter. Stir in the flour. Add the lemon flavor or juice. Add vanilla, buttermilk, sugar and beaten eggs. Mix well and pour into an unbaked piecrust.

Bake in a 350-degree oven for 30 minutes or until the center rises to a mound and has a golden yellow color.

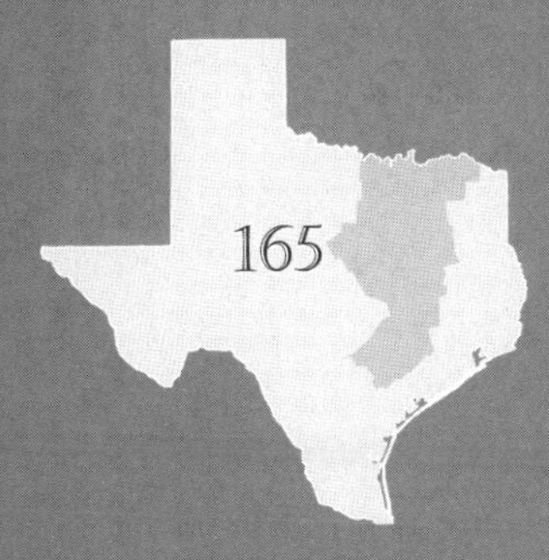

Ranchman's Caramel Pie

3 egg yolks

2 1/2 cups milk

1 1/2 cups sugar

1/2 stick margarine

1/2 cup flour

1 teaspoon vanilla

1 pie crust

Mix egg yolks, milk, 1 cup sugar and 1 teaspoon flour in a saucepan on the stove. Heat slowly to a simmer. While the milk mixture is heating (not boiling), place the 1/2 cup of flour and margarine in a small pan and cook it, stirring to make a roux. It does not need to brown—just thicken—and it will look a little curdled. About 5 minutes. Remove from heat, saving for later.

Heat 1/2 cup of sugar in a small skillet and stir very little, if at all, until all the sugar is liquid and has an even, dark-brown color. Watch this 100% of the time, as it can burn or catch fire. Be fully clothed, as molten sugar is hard to get off and it hurts.

As soon as the sugar is ready, pour and scrape it into the milk mixture. Watch out for the sizzle, splatter, spray and steam. If your vent hood isn't on now, it's too late. Stir in the caramel with a whisk until it is dissolved and evenly colored.

Add the roux and keep the heat on low while whisking it until it's thick. It will be really thick. Turn off the heat and add the vanilla, mixing until blended. Immediately pour it into a precooked pie crust and top with meringue. Bake as instructed to toast the meringue.

ROGERS HOTEL

Waxahachie

This very spot in Ellis County was not only the site of the very first structure in the area, but has repeatedly been the site of the best hotel facilities. Emory and Nancy Rogers first settled in the area in 1847, living in a tent on the very site of the current hotel. Construction of a log cabin not only gave them a more permanent place to live, but also provided lodging for numerous visitors to the area.

The Rogers were so well known for their generosity toward settlers and even Indians traveling through the area, that their home also became a place for social gathering, religious services and town meetings. The first elections were held in their home, and the name Waxahachie was given to the new county seat.

The attraction of many people to the area caused Emory Rogers to build a two-story hotel on the site and he opened it to the paying public as the Rogers Hotel around 1855. The hotel passed to new ownership 15 years later, and then in 1882 a fire destroyed the structure completely.

Recognizing the continuing need for a hotel and the value of that particular site, a new and much larger hotel was built the following year. This building survived until another fire destroyed it in 1911. The replacement hotel, which still stands today, was built at a cost of $120 thousand. It opened for business in 1913. Four stories high, it offered hot and cold water for every room, and some of the rooms had private baths. Later, a steam heating system was added, along with electric lights and fans. Each room was connected by telephone to the outside world and all outside windows had bug screens installed.

The lobby of the hotel offered sample rooms and parlors, along with a restaurant serviced by a large kitchen in the rear. Elevators took some guests to upper floors, and the roof was turned into a terrace garden. In addition to serving food and offering lodging, the hotel also housed a billiards parlor and a barbershop.

Due to the decline of business after the end of World War II, the hotel was closed for a number of years, but has recently been renovated and reopened with modern amenities set in an old-world style and atmosphere. Emory's Bistro serves new American cuisine set in a turn-of-the-century dining room.

The Rogers Hotel, 100 North College, Waxahachie, Texas 75165, (972) 938-3688 or (800) 556-4192, or visit www.rogershotel.com or email info@rogershotel.com. Emory's Bistro serves lunch Monday through Friday 11 a.m. to 2 p.m. and Saturday 11 a.m. to 3 p.m. Dinner is served on Thursday, Friday and Saturday evenings from 6 p.m. to 10 p.m. They are closed Sundays.

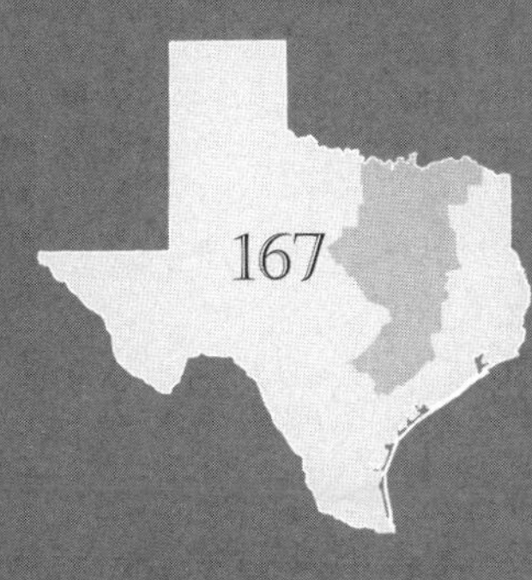

Brazilian Chicken

- 4 chicken breasts
- 15 ounces coconut cream (Coco Lopez)
- 1/2 cup peanuts
- 1/2 cup green peppers, diced
- 1/2 cup onions, dried
- 1 tablespoon jalapenos, chopped
- 2 tablespoons cilantro, chopped
- 1/2 cup tomatoes, diced
- 2 cups heavy cream
- 1 tablespoon ginger, chopped
- Salt and pepper to taste

Sauté chicken in butter until done. Add peppers, onion, jalapenos, tomatoes, heavy cream and sauté. Add coconut cream, peanuts, cilantro and ginger. Salt and pepper to taste. Heat and mix well. Serve over white rice.

Serves 4.

Pumpkin Lobster Bisque

- 30 ounces pumpkin, canned
- 1 quart chicken stock
- 2 quarts heavy cream
- 2 tablespoons nutmeg
- 1 tablespoon cinnamon
- 1/2 cup brown sugar
- 2 tablespoons cumin
- 1 lobster, cooked and diced
- sour cream, for garnish

Mix all ingredients together. Simmer 45 minutes. Top with sour cream.

Serves 8.

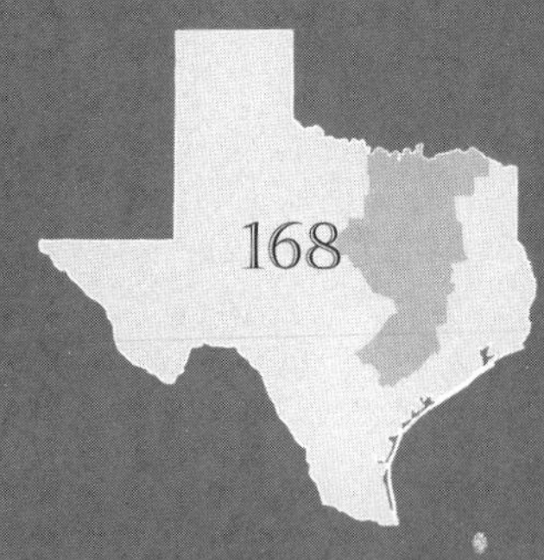

1 loaf dry, white bread, cubed

4 eggs

1/2 cup sugar

3 cups half and half

1 tablespoon vanilla

1/4 cup butter, melted

2 tablespoons cinnamon

CARAMEL BOURBON TOPPING:

2 cups sugar

1 cup bourbon

1 pint heavy cream

Emory's Classic Bread Pudding
with Caramel Bourbon Topping

Make caramel sauce first and let set.

Mix all ingredients. Pour over bread cubes placed on bottom of 9 × 13 pan. Bake at 350 degrees for 45 minutes.

CARAMEL BOURBON TOPPING:
Heat sugar in saute pan until brown. Stir constantly. Add bourbon slowly. Add cream slowly, while still warm. Let set. Pour over bread pudding and serve while warm.

Serves 8.

TWO GRANNIES

Glen Rose

Need a hug? Visit Two Grannies. Everyone who comes though the door, whether it is your first time there or you have known them for years, gets a hug from the grannies. Built in 1892, their building has served as a hardware store, a drugstore and at one time housed the Glen Rose Post Office.

Its charming edifice was also a Chinese restaurant before June and Gloria decided to serve some of the best down-home cooking in Texas. The cook yodels, June dances, Gloria sings and one of the cooks does the cancan to entertain their guests. On Friday and Saturday nights a pianist who played for the Granbury opera for 21 years delights patrons with highbrow music in a lowbrow setting. Beautiful country quilts of all shapes and styles adorn the walls.

A different menu is served at every meal, which might explain why loyal local patrons frequent the establishment. Some might come for the hug, but the food is truly delicious. What else would you expect when one of the grannies actually serves you your meal, and the other one comes to check and make sure you are satisfied with it?

Lunch buffets are very popular with all patrons. The grannies' motto is, "If you don't get enough to eat, it ain't our fault!" Anything your grandmother would have made for you, they will offer, and it will be at very reasonable prices. The chicken fried steak is so good it should be the official Texas State Meal.

"Two Grannies" is really a misnomer. It should be called "Two Great Grannies," not just because they are great and serve great food, but because they are both really great grandmothers. Gloria Whitley has seven grandchildren and eight great grandchildren with one more on the way. June Thomas proudly boasts seven grandchildren and one great grandchild.

Glen Rose is on the map not only because of the Historic Glen Rose Square, which offers a number of quaint shops, but also because of the Dinosaur Valley State Park nearby. Over the course of thousands of years, the meandering Paluxy River has worn down its streambed to expose numerous dinosaur tracks. At Carl Baugh's Creation Science Museum visitors can view fossilized footprints of dinosaurs and man together.

Two Grannies, 109 West Barnard Street, Glen Rose, Texas 76043, (254) 897-9773. They are open for lunch on Thursday, Friday and Saturday from 11 a.m. until 2 p.m. and dinner 5 p.m. until 8:30 p.m.

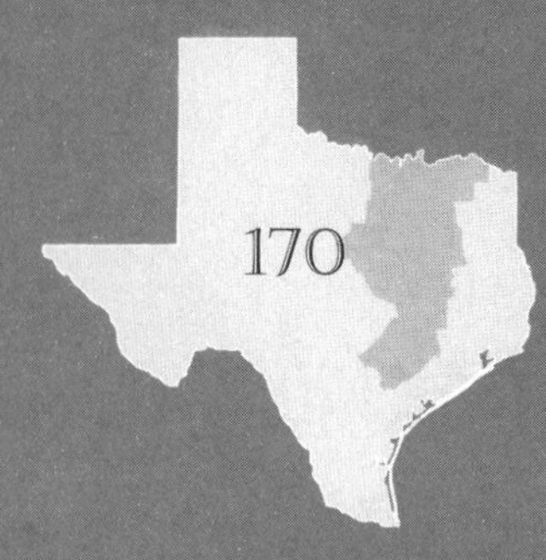

Brown Sugar Pastry

1/2 cup margarine
1 cup plain flour
1/4 cup brown sugar, packed
1/2 cup chopped pecans

Place all ingredients in a pie pan. Do not mix. Bake in 400-degree oven for 15 minutes.

Remove from oven and stir well with fork at once. Put out into 9-inch pie plates.

This is good for any cream filling or chiffon pie.

YIELD

One pie crust.

South of the Border Cake

2 cups flour
2 cups sugar
2 eggs
1 teaspoon salt
1 teaspoon soda
1 can crushed pineapple, 20 ounces

ICING:
6 ounces cream cheese
1/4 cup butter
2 cups powdered sugar
nuts
coconut

Mix ingredients at left. Bake in 13 × 9 × 2-inch pan at 425 degrees for 45 minutes.

ICING:
Mix the cream cheese and butter together over low heat until creamed together. Add powdered sugar. Put over cake while still hot. Add nuts and coconut as desired.

Serves 8.

4

South Texas Plains

Ranch Country. From San Antonio to the Rio Grande much of the scenery looks like the Southwest. Native American, Mexican and Spanish heritages are the focus. The struggles and fight for freedom are aptly depicted in the many museums, and the numerous missions are fine examples of that heritage. The Alamo is the most memorable attraction from its era. Cattle ranching is a major part of the region. Other cities include Laredo, Eagle Pass, Port Isabel and McAllen.

LA MANSIÓN DEL RIO HOTEL

San Antonio

Sixteen years after the fall of the Alamo in 1852, four brothers of the Society of Mary arrived in San Antonio to establish a school. They occupied the second floor of a livery stable on the west side of Military Plaza and immediately began construction of a limestone building on College Street. The bells of the new school, originally known as St. Mary's Institute, tolled for the first time on March 1, 1853, summoning students.

Winters were hard and sometimes provisions were scarce, but corn bread was always served three times a day washed down by river water. During the next 54 years, construction was finished on the original structure. By 1875, it was a well-proportioned structure of rough limestone, typically European in style and the largest building complex in San Antonio. Livestock was kept at Mission Concepcion, then run by the brothers. This gave the school fresh milk, cheese and butter. In the summer the boarding students spent their time at the mission in somewhat of a camp atmosphere.

As the need for education grew, St. Mary's became a junior college and finally grew into a senior college. In 1894, a new campus was acquired for boarding students and the original property was able to increase its enrollment of day students. The College Street campus grew and prospered as St. Mary's Academy until 1924 and after that as St. Mary's University Downtown College. In 1934, the law school was set up downtown and remained on College Street until December of 1966, when it moved to the Woodlawn campus.

Seeing the value of the property and its location, a former St. Mary's law student purchased the property, and work began on a new hotel. The exterior was made Spanish in style and a six-story addition was added at the rear, overlooking the river. The designs and furnishings were well planned, reflecting the city's cultural ties to Spain and Mexico with graceful Spanish arches and columns, cloistered courtyards and romantic interiors accentuated with the antiques of Colonial Mexico and Spain.

In April 1968, La Mansión del Rio opened its doors as a luxury hotel, just in time for Hemisfair, San Antonio's 1968 World Fair. Additional guest rooms, the formal restaurant and the ballroom were added eleven years later. La Mansión del Rio is designated as a historical treasure by the Texas Historical Commission and the San Antonio Conservation Society.

San Antonio's crown jewel of hospitality, La Mansión del Rio Hotel overlooks the historic Paseo del Rio, or River Walk, in the heart of downtown. In 2001, the hotel completed a $15 million renovation. Three hundred thirty-seven guest rooms and meeting spaces were meticulously refurbished with inlaid, carved wood furniture accented with granite and iron. Spanish starburst tapestries and chenilles, custom Axminster carpets from England, crystal chandeliers, sconces and ambient lighting in the guest rooms—all accentuate the hotel's romantic Spanish Colonial style.

Often called the River Walk's most elegant restaurant, Las Canarias reflects the old-world charm of Colonial Spain. Built on three levels that descend to the River Walk, it offers diners a choice of tables on a riverside veranda, in an interior courtyard or on one of three indoor levels that capture the ambience of historic San Antonio. The legendary Sunday Champagne Brunch is truly a feast, as well as a local tradition.

La Mansión del Rio Hotel and Las Canarias Restaurant, 112 College Street, San Antonio, Texas, 78205, located on the River Walk. Hours for the restaurant are Monday through Saturday 6:30 a.m. to 11:30 a.m. Lunch is served 11:30 a.m. to 2:30 p.m. Dinner is served seven days at 5:30 p.m. until 10:30 p.m. Sunday brunch is available from 10:30 a.m. to 2:30 p.m. Call (800) 292-7300 or (210) 518-1000 or check the web at www.lamansion.com

Crab Cakes

- 1 pound jumbo lump crab meat
- 2 tablespoons red onion, diced small
- 2 tablespoons celery, diced small
- 2 tablespoons red pepper, diced small
- 2 slices white bread (no crust)
- 1/2 cup skim milk
- salt and pepper, lemon juice, Tabasco, Old Bay seasoning, Worcestershire sauce—to taste
- fresh breadcrumbs as needed
- butter or olive oil, for searing

Mix all ingredients together, except for milk and butter, white bread and breadcrumbs. Take the fresh bread and mix with skim milk and let the bread absorb all the milk. Mix bread/milk with crab and seasoning mixture. Weigh out crab cake to 3 ounces. Shape like a pancake. Roll the cake into the breadcrumbs.

Pan sear in either butter or olive oil until cooked through.

YIELD

6 crab cakes.

Creamy Balsamic Vinaigrette

- 1 cup balsamic vinegar
- 1 teaspoon shallots
- 1/2 teaspoon garlic
- 1 tablespoon Dijon mustard
- 1 tablespoon tarragon, chopped
- 2 cups cottonseed oil
- 1 cup olive oil
- salt and pepper to taste

Mix garlic, shallots, vinegar and mustard. Slowly emulsify with oils. Add tarragon and season with salt and pepper.

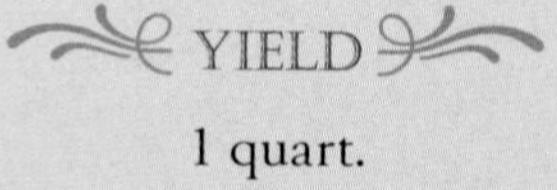
YIELD

1 quart.

LA POSADA HOTEL/SUITES

Laredo

The history of La Posada begins with Alexander Graham Bell and the telephone. In April of 1884, only eight years after he received his patent for his new talking device, Laredo needed a telephone exchange to serve not only the local phone customers, but also long distance in the states and the international business. Laredo was considered the gateway to Mexico and was a geographically logical site for a switching center.

The Erie Telegraph and Telephone Company opened the first exchange in April 1884 at 1101 Zaragoza Street. The building itself had been constructed some time earlier as a residence. The precise year is unknown, but records show that the de la Garza family lived there for a number of years prior to the house's being used by the phone company.

By 1912, the phone exchange had outgrown its location and moved to a much larger facility. The building was again sold as a residence in 1912, for the Bruni family. Antonio Henry Bruni was the great-great grandson of the American patriot Patrick Henry, famous for saying, "Give me liberty, or give me death!" The site served as business offices until 1994, when it was purchased by the owners of La Posada Hotel next door and reopened as The Tack Room, a popular restaurant and bar.

In 1916, Laredo had grown to the point that it needed a new high school. It was built next door to the old telephone exchange, where it served to educate generations of students for decades. By 1960, a newer school had been built, and the old high school building was sold to one of its former students who dreamed of opening a luxury hotel. La Posada opened its doors in July 1961 and it has welcomed politicians, celebrities, industrial leaders and numerous blushing brides.

La Posada is a site rich in Texas history and Spanish tradition. It was along the banks of the Rio Grande River, the current site of the hotel, that Don Tomas Sanchez first settled the area. By 1836, the Republic of Texas had grown to include the community of Laredo. After the Texans defeated Santa Anna at San Jacinto, Laredo became the capital of the short-lived Republic of the Rio Grande. The capitol was the present Republic of the Rio Grande Museum located on the grounds of La Posada Hotel.

The popularity of Laredo, its sister city Nuevo Laredo and La Posada Hotel resulted in the expansion of the hotel, first in 1966, and again in 1983. In 1994, the Fasken family purchased La Posada

Hotel/Suites and continues to operate it today. The facility reflects its Spanish heritage, while maintaining strong ties to the history and traditions of Texas.

The Tack Room Bar and Grill at La Posada Hotel/Suites, 1000 Zaragoza Street, Laredo, Texas 78040, (956) 722-1701, or visit www.laposadahotel-laredo.com. The Tack Room restaurant hours are Monday through Thursday from 5:30 p.m. to 10 p.m., and Friday and Saturday it is open from 5:30 p.m. to 11 p.m. The bar is open Monday through Thursday from 5 p.m. to 12 a.m. and on Friday and Saturday from 4 p.m. to 12 a.m.

Angels on Horseback

36 large shrimp

salt and pepper

1/4 pound bacon

BARBEQUE SAUCE:

5 ounces Worcestershire sauce

5 ounces soy sauce

1/2 lemon, juiced

5 ounces tomato puree

1 1/2 tablespoons dark brown sugar

1 cup heavy whipping cream

Season the shrimp with salt and pepper. Wrap in bacon. Broil the shrimp until done, about 10 minutes. Brush them with barbeque sauce (recipe follows).

Serves 8.

BARBEQUE SAUCE:

In a small saucepan combine the Worcestershire sauce, soy sauce, lemon juice, tomato puree and dark brown sugar. Stir on medium heat until sugar is dissolved. Bring to a boil and simmer for 5 minutes. Remove from heat. In a large saucepan add cream and bring to a boil. Then simmer until the cream sticks to the back of a spoon. Stir in barbeque sauce base to taste.

Bring the mixture back to boil and simmer again until it coats the back of a spoon.

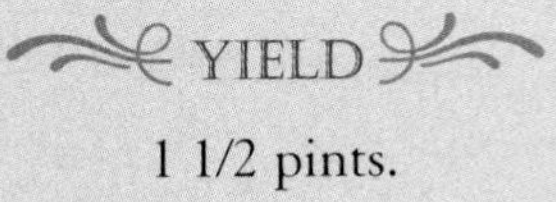

1 1/2 pints.

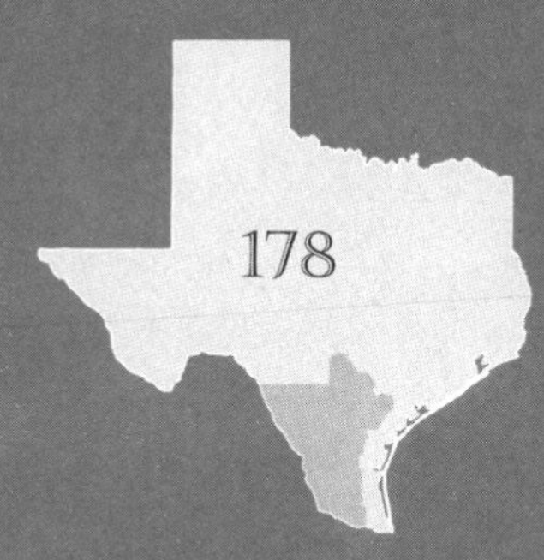

Canadian Beer Cheese Soup

2 tablespoons unsalted butter

12 ounces Canadian beer

6 ounces heavy cream

16 ounces extra milk cheese

salt and pepper to taste

chopped jalapenos and croutons, for garnish

In the soup pot, add butter and cook for three minutes. Add heavy cream and beer. Bring to a boil. Reduce heat and simmer for 10 minutes. Add cheese and season with salt and pepper. Ladle into bowls and serve with chopped jalapenos and croutons.

YIELD

Serves 4.

Churrasco

4 8-ounce pieces of filet mignon

salt

fresh ground pepper

CHIMICHURRI SAUCE:

1/2 cup extra virgin olive oil

1 cup parsley, chopped

1 tablespoon crushed red pepper

1/2 cup garlic, chopped

2 tablespoons white vinegar

salt and black pepper to taste

2 tablespoons red vinegar

cumin and oregano to taste

Pound filet mignon with a mallet to 1/8 inch thickness. Season with salt and pepper and partially grill on both sides—enough to sear the outside. Marinate with Chimichurri Sauce (recipe follows).

CHIMICHURRI SAUCE:

Add all ingredients to food processor and pulse. Let stand for 2 minutes. Marinate tenderloin for about 3 hours and finish cooking them on the grill for about 10 minutes.

Serves 4.

LITTLE RHEIN STEAK HOUSE

San Antonio

The Little Rhein Steak House is located on a site historically rich and diverse. The Coahuiltecan Indians founded a settlement here before 1500. In the early 18th century, Spanish soldiers and Canary Islanders established a village on the site. The Mexican General Santa Anna encamped here during the Battle of the Alamo.

During the late 19th century, German immigrants settled the area, designating their neighborhood as the Little Rhein District. The Steak House derives its name from that district. This building was constructed around 1847 and is believed to be the first two-story structure in San Antonio. The lower level was hidden under silt until it was rediscovered in 1950. The structure was utilized as an early Texan home, a boarding house, a German saloon, a hangout for desperados and a historical museum. Because of its historical significance, the building is protected by the San Antonio Conservation Society.

Frank W. Phelps established the Little Rhein Steak House in 1967. Collectibles chosen by the founder line the walls of the Little Rhein. The unique brass lights once illuminated the old Federal Courthouse in Chicago. The wooden booths are from the old Katy Depot.

The Little Rhein Steak House is located near the River Walk in downtown San Antonio at 231 South Alamo, 78205, (210) 225-2111. They are open every day from 5 p.m. to 10 p.m.

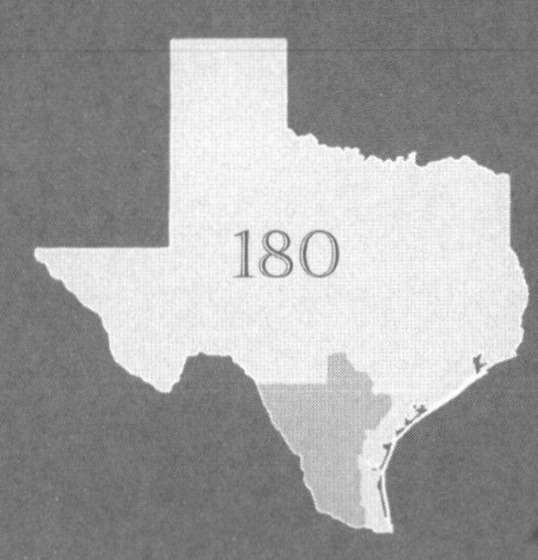

5 pounds dried black-eyed peas

2 1/2 tablespoons seasoning salt

1 tablespoon salt

1/2 tablespoon paprika

1/4 teaspoon garlic, ground

1/4 teaspoon cumin

1/2 teaspoon black pepper

1 1/2 cups celery, chopped

1/4 pound butter

1/2 onion, chopped

1 1/2 cups green bell pepper

3/4 cup diced red pepper

pinch cayenne pepper

Texas Caviar

Put peas and all ingredients in a pot. Use enough water to cover peas. Cover and simmer for 1 1/2 hours. Remove from heat if done. Chill. Serve with crackers.

YIELD

Serves 15–20.

THE MENGER HOTEL

San Antonio

When William Menger emigrated from Germany to San Antonio, his first business venture was operating a brewery and a boardinghouse. With hotel experience under his belt, he enlarged the boardinghouse, and the Menger Hotel was created in 1859. At the time it was not only the height of frontier sophistication but was also considered to be "the finest hotel west of the Mississippi River."

Next door to the world famous Alamo, The Menger attracted such notable patrons as Generals Robert E. Lee and Ulysses S. Grant; Sam Houston; Presidents Taft, McKinley and Eisenhower; Roy Rogers; Mae West and Oscar Wilde. Teddy Roosevelt did more than just stay at the Menger while hunting javelinas. He was so impressed with the patrons he came back years later and recruited Rough Riders in the hotel bar for the Spanish-American War.

Built originally of limestone with just 50 rooms, the hotel was immediately inadequate for the business it drew, and 50 more rooms were added the following year. A complete renovation in 1949 doubled the number of rooms while adding a new main lobby. The original three-story lobby was retained with its gorgeous leaded-glass skylight. Another renovation in 1989 increased the room capacity to 318.

The Menger Bar, patterned after the House of Lords Pub in London, cost $60,000 to build—more than three times the cost of the original hotel. This was due in great part to the architect having to actually travel to London to make his construction plans precise, and the cost of importing cherry wood booths and ceiling panels from France. Today it is a priceless gathering spot for tourists by day and locals at night.

While renovations have added amenities such as a heated pool and massage facilities, the Menger Hotel retains its old-world charm with original wrought-iron balconies and much of the original furniture, art and accessories from the hotel's early days, purchased personally by William Menger in New York and Europe.

Many of the patrons from the early days are also said to still inhabit the hotel. Guests periodically report seeing ghosts idly passing time in the hotel. But don't ask the manager, Ernesto Malacara, to discount the stories. He reports having seen an elderly woman knitting in the lobby. Malacara thinks that the location of the hotel, on top of the Alamo battlefield, has some bearing on these ghostly encounters. Sightings are so rare, however, serious ghost hunters are regularly disappointed.

The Menger Hotel, 204 Alamo Plaza, San Antonio, Texas 78205, (210) 223-4361, is located in the heart of San Antonio, next door to the Alamo and one block from the River Walk. Or access www.historicmenger.com. Restaurant is open Sunday through Thursday 6:30 p.m. to 10 p.m. and Friday and Saturday from 6:30 p.m. to 11 p.m.

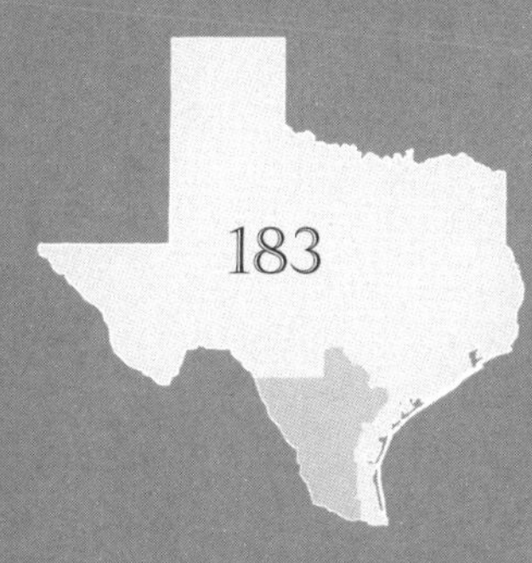

Original Menger Chicken Salad

- 2 pounds chicken breasts, grilled and diced
- 2 teaspoons cilantro
- 4 teaspoons green onion, diced
- 2 teaspoons fresh garlic, minced
- 4 teaspoons Thai pepper, minced
- 6 teaspoons sugar
- 8 teaspoons fish sauce
- 2 cups cucumber, diced
- 2 teaspoons lime juice
- salt to taste
- 24 thin slices lime, for garnish

Mix all ingredients together and marinate for at least two hours. Serve in a pineapple boat on a bed of lettuce. Garnish with thin lime slices.

YIELD

Serves 6–8.

Menger Tortilla Soup

- 1 1/4 pound ground beef
- 1/2 pound yellow onion, diced
- 3/8 pound Anaheim peppers, diced
- 1/4 pound poblano peppers, diced
- 16 ounces tomatoes, canned
- 1/4 cup tomato paste
- 1/2 gallon chicken stock
- 1/4 ounce ground cumin
- 1/4 bunch fresh cilantro, chopped
- 1/4 ounce fresh garlic, chopped
- dash ground black pepper, or to taste
- 16-ounce package red corn tortillas
- 1 cup mixed cheeses, Monterey Jack and cheddar

Brown meat and drain well. Add onion and peppers and sauté. Add diced tomatoes, tomato paste and sauté. Add chicken stock and seasonings. Bring to a boil and reduce to simmer. Simmer for one hour.

When ready to eat, top with tortilla strips (red corn tortillas) and Monterey Jack and cheddar cheese mix.

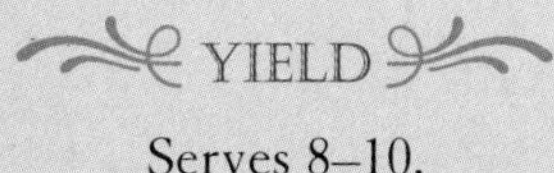

YIELD

Serves 8–10.

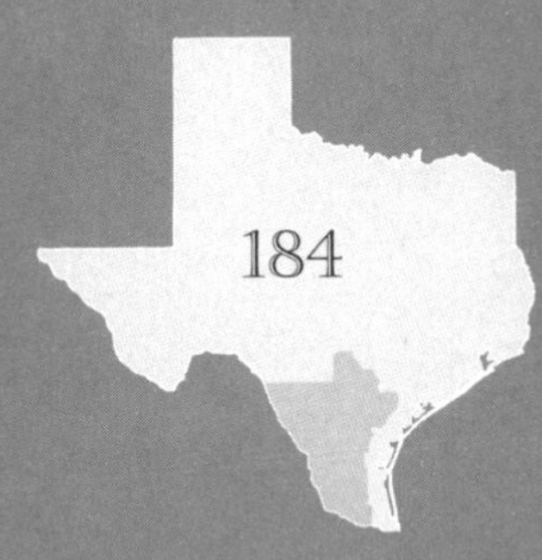

6 6–8 ounce top butt steaks

Dijon mustard

8 bay leaves

juniper berries

1–2 teaspoons mix of garlic, salt and pepper (equal parts of each)

2 cups burgundy wine

1 cup water

flour, for thickening

STUFFING:

6 slices raw lean bacon

2 whole onions, chopped

1/2 pound mushrooms, sliced

Rinder Rouladen

(Stuffed Beef Rolls)

Mix the three stuffing ingredients together. Pound the top butt steaks flat. Season with the garlic, salt and pepper mix. Paint with Dijon mustard. Stuff and roll into logs. Roll the Rouladen in flour and then sauté in oil until golden brown. Add burgundy wine and water, bay leaves and juniper berries, and bring to a boil. Cover with aluminum foil and let simmer in 335-degree oven for about one hour. Take the Rouladen out of the pan and thicken gravy with flour. Add salt and pepper to taste.

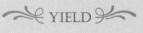

YIELD

Serves 6.

THE YACHT CLUB HOTEL AND RESTAURANT

Port Isabel

During the boom of the 1920s, Port Isabel and South Padre Island were recognized as potential resort communities. Plans for the sleepy, coastal, shrimping town included interconnected waterways, which would serve as the transportation system of the area. It was to be the Venice, Italy, of the Gulf Coast.

In 1926, the Yacht Club Hotel was built by four investors to be a private club. The original membership consisted of the most prominent Rio Grande Valley families, with members from Laredo, Rio Grand City and San Antonio. It was the perfect place for the wealthy to escape to a sporting paradise. When the crash of 1929 came, although the local agriculture and military based economy was not affected as harshly as other parts of Texas, it became clear that the Yacht Club could not operate privately.

Mr. John Shary of Sharyland in the lower Rio Grande Valley bought out the original members and opened the doors to the public in 1929. The John Shary Yacht Club was well received and earned the reputation as being "the place to eat" while vacationing, and was visited by such important people as Charles Lindbergh, President Warren G. Harding and Governor Shrivers.

The beaches of South Padre Island were accessible by a one-car, wooden Model T Bridge with two runners. This bridge was operational from the mid-1920s until the great hurricane of 1933. The Yacht Club survived but the bridge did not. From that point until the 1955 bridge was built, island visitors were shuttled from the Yacht Club by ferry. An "Island Sand Taxi" then took the visitors to the Gulf-side Casino, which was located on the Gulf, less than a mile north of the current (1975) bridge.

The hotel and restaurant fell on hard times following World War II and Shary's death in 1947. The hotel then went through various stages of renovation and disrepair. The 1960s were the toughest years for the Yacht Club, or the "Laguna Madre Hotel" as it was renamed. It eventually went out of business and was boarded up. Hurricane Beulah dealt a destructive blow to the vacant building in 1967. Bud and Tille Franke of South Padre Island brought it back to life in 1969. Refurbished, the Yacht Club reopened its doors in 1971, minus the right viewing tower.

Later owners Ron and Lynn Speiers reestablished the fine reputation the restaurant used to enjoy. The current owners, John, Barbara and their son Sean Allen have maintained the exceptional standards the hotel and restaurant has enjoyed in the past. Port Isabel would continue to be recognized as the "Shrimp Capital of the World" as well as a very popular sport fishing area. When they offer fresh seafood, no one doubts that they mean fresh. In fact, patrons can bring their own fish in to be prepared for their dinner, or they can let the staff get them.

The Yacht Club Hotel, Restaurant and Bar, 700 Yturria Street, Port Isabel, Texas 78578, (956) 943-1301. The restaurant is open daily at 6 p.m. and the bar opens at 5:30 p.m. Closing time is seasonal.

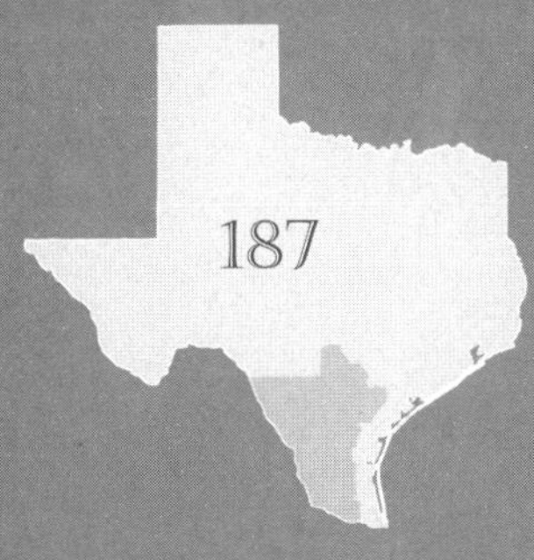

Snapper Pontchartrain

1 red snapper fillet (6 ounces)

SAUCE:

2 shrimp, peeled and deveined

2 sea scallops

1 teaspoon shallots

1 teaspoon garlic

1/2 cup mushrooms

1/2 ounce fresh squeezed lemon juice

1/2 ounce white wine

1/2 teaspoon shrimp base

1 medium green onion, sliced

2 ounces heavy cream

butter or olive oil, for sautéing

Lightly sauté snapper in a pan with butter or olive oil, 2 minutes on each side. Finish cooking for an additional 2 minutes in a preheated oven at 375 degrees.

SAUCE:

Sauté shrimp and scallops in butter or olive oil for about 2 minutes. Add the shallots, garlic and mushrooms and sauté for an additional 3 minutes. Add the lemon juice, white wine, shrimp base, green onion and heavy cream. Cook and stir for 2 minutes. Pour over snapper and serve.

Serves 1.

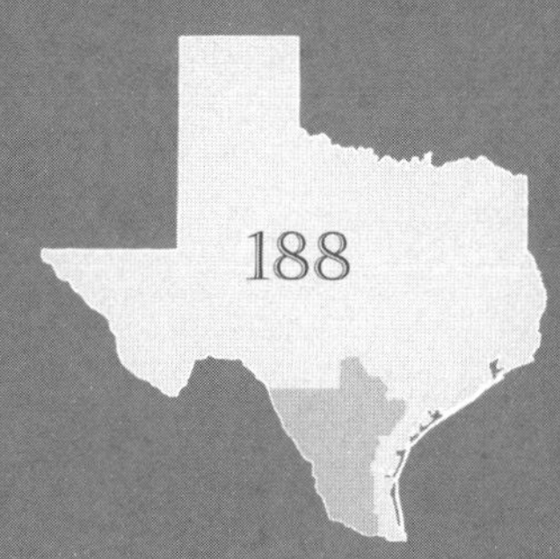

Red Snapper Fillets in Bouillabaisse Sauce

- 2 tablespoons olive oil
- 2 teaspoons garlic, finely chopped
- 3/4 cup onions, finely chopped
- 3/4 cup leeks, well washed, finely chopped
- 1/2 cup fennel leaves, finely chopped
- 1/2 cup celery, finely chopped
- 1/2 teaspoon saffron threads
- 1 cup ripe tomatoes, peeled and chopped
- 1/2 cup dry white wine
- 1/2 cup fish broth or bottled clam juice
- 1 bay leaf
- 1/8 teaspoon cayenne pepper
- 1 1/2 pounds skinless red snapper fillets, cut into 4 portions
- salt and freshly ground black pepper
- 2 tablespoons fresh parsley leaves, chopped

Heat the oil in a saucepan and add the garlic, onion, leeks, fennel, celery and saffron. Cook, stirring over medium-high heat until wilted, about 3 minutes. Add the tomatoes, wine, fish broth, bay leaf and cayenne pepper and cook for 10 minutes more.

Put the fillets in a skillet large enough to hold the pieces in one layer. Season with salt and pepper. Pour the sauce evenly over the fish. Cover and simmer for about five minutes, or until cooked. Sprinkle with the parsley before serving.

Serves 4.

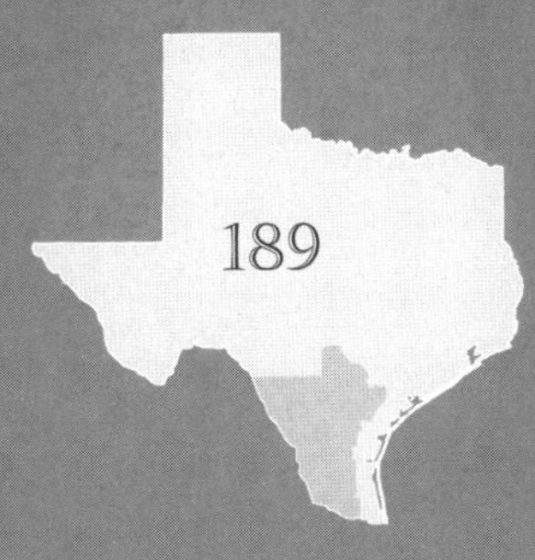

Key Lime Pie

FILLING:

16 ounces cream cheese

15 ounces condensed milk

8 ounces whipping cream

6 ounces lime juice

3 egg yolks

2 teaspoons green food coloring

CRUST:

1/2 cup margarine, melted

2 cups graham crackers, crushed

CRUST:

Mix margarine and crumbs and press into 3-inch springform pan.

FILLING:

In a mixer add cream cheese, condensed milk and whipping cream. Mix until smooth. Add egg yolks, lime juice and food coloring. Mix until blended. Pour mixture into crust and freeze overnight.

One pie.

5

Hill Country

Central Texas Paradise. Rolling hills, spring-fed rivers and dude ranches are all part of this magnificent area that draws visitors from throughout the world. German immigrants inhabited Boerne, New Braunfels, Comfort and Fredericksburg and left their colorful imprint. Dining is a great attraction, especially in Austin, New Braunfels and Kerrville. Bandera, Georgetown and San Marcos are other historic towns in the Hill Country.

ANTLERS HOTEL

Kingsland

Travel back in time as you enter the Antlers Hotel, a turn-of-the-century railroad resort, situated on 15 acres on the banks of Lake LBJ. The original two-story structure has six suites with wide front and back porches. There is also a bunkhouse once used by the train crews and several other cabins on the property.

The hotel first opened its doors on May 1, 1901, as a resort built by the Austin & Northwestern Railroad for vacationers coming to the hill country. In 1923 the railroad sold the hotel, and for seventy years it was closed to the public. After extensive renovation, The Antlers reopened in 1996 and is once again welcoming travelers.

Historic Antlers Hotel is a luxurious, antique-filled establishment. The original pot-bellied stove in the dining room, 12-foot-high ceilings and the grand staircase add a hint of history, but all the modern conveniences have been added.

Tucked in the woods and around the orchard are small houses, which are great for families, friends or a romantic stay. Each cabin features a living room, one or two bedrooms, an equipped kitchen, bath, central air and heat, outdoor grill, TV/VCR and telephone.

The House served as the movie set for *Texas Chainsaw Massacre* in 1973. Unfortunately, movie stardom brought vandals, and the house only had one window and five unbroken spindles when it was moved. The month of rebuilding produced the Old Town Grill, offering diners a new sense of renewed elegance. The Old Town Grill is an 1890 Victorian house on the grounds of the Antlers Hotel. The entire property is listed on the National Register of Historic Places.

Imagine spending the night in a real train caboose. Each caboose offers a living and dining area, bath with a shower, a queen-size bed, two child-size bunks, an efficiency kitchen, telephone and TV/VCR. Climb up the ladder to the cupola—a perfect place to sip morning coffee or watch the sun set.

Stay in the authentic, wooden, 1880s McKinley Coach Railcar. Beautifully restored with two-tier roof, wood paneling and clerestory windows, it has a king-size bed, two twin beds and one-and-one-half baths. The coach will sleep four guests.

The Antlers grounds include 15 acres of woodlands with nature trails, a fruit orchard, a courtyard with working cistern and rolling lawns. A restored 1800s log cabin sits on the waterfront with four docks for boating, fishing, or congregating. Three boat slips are available for guests by reservation.

The Kingsland Old Town Grill, 1001 King, Kingsland, Texas 78639, is open for lunch 11 a.m. to 2 p.m. and dinner from 5 p.m. to 10 p.m. Wednesday to Sunday. Breakfast is available for guests by reservation. Contact (800) 383-0007 or (915) 388-4411 or visit www.theantlers.com.

The chef does not use written recipes, so she shared her advice on ordering one of their famous steaks!

Steak

How do you like your steak? The longer a steak is cooked, the smaller and tougher it becomes!

Rare
Cool red center

Medium Rare
Warm red center

Medium
Hot pink center

Medium Well
A little pink

Well Done
Tough as leather. The Antlers Hotel does NOT recommend well-done steaks.

CARMELO'S

Austin

Established in 1985, Carmelo's is located in the historic "Old Depot Hotel" at Fifth and Red River near the Austin Convention Center. The original building is believed to have been built in 1872 by designer and architect Abner Cook, while the property was owned by Carl Schafer. The Houston and Texas Central Railroad came to Austin in 1871 with its main tracks on Pine (Fifth) Street. The Old Depot Hotel, known as the Railroad House until 1878, was built one block east of the depot and accommodated passengers traveling to other railroads and four stagecoach lines.

Among the various proprietors of the Railroad House was Paul Pressler, who is known to have operated a brewery called Pressler's Beer Garden on the south side of Pecan. He and his descendants owned or occupied the building for more than fifty years. An association and friendship with O. Henry was likely, since O. Henry's home is located across the street in Brush Square.

The bar of Carmelo's, as well as all the private rooms above, occupies the area of the original building known as the Old Depot Hotel, entered on the National Register as a recorded Texas Landmark. In 1964, it was totally restored by Mr. and Mrs. Glenn M. Tooke, Jr. and the 4,200-square-foot masonry addition that currently occupies the restaurant dining room and kitchen was created. The historical marker can be found near the entrance to the restaurant.

Without touching the structure itself, Carmelo Mauro continues remodeling his historic Texas landmark location. An interior designer has brought in new wall coverings, upholstery, draperies and floral arrangements. The floor has evolved from red tile to an elaborate mosaic pattern of cut Italian marble that covers 1,300 square feet.

Carmelo's will accommodate banquets, holiday events, business meetings, wedding receptions or any large party in a private room if desired. Open for lunch weekdays from 11 a.m. to 2:30 p.m., Carmelo's is open for dinner Sunday through Thursday from 5 p.m. to 10:30 p.m. and Friday and Saturday until 11 p.m. Carmelo's, 504 East 5th Street, Austin, Texas 78701, (512) 477-7497 can also be reached at www.Austin360.com/eats/carmelos.

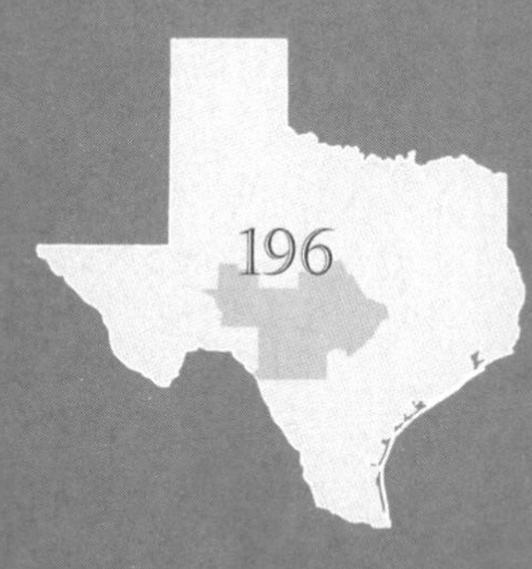

8 large sea scallops

3 ounces shrimp

1 ounce Gorgonzola cheese

1/2 teaspoon salt

4 tablespoons light cream sauce

3 ounces rigatoni pasta

red and yellow peppers, to garnish

Tomato Vodka Sauce (recipe follows)

TOMATO VODKA SAUCE:

12 ounces whole Italian tomatoes, peeled

1 teaspoon shallots

1 teaspoon fresh garlic, diced

3 ounces heavy cream

2 ounces vodka

1 teaspoon lobster base

1/2 teaspoon black pepper

1 pinch basil

Grilled Sea Scallops over Stuffed Rigatoni
with Shrimp and Tomato Vodka Sauce

Cook the pasta first. When it is ready, boil the shrimp and let cool. Melt the Gorgonzola cheese with a light cream sauce until it is paste-like. Dice the shrimp very fine, add to cheese mixture and stuff the rigatoni, then arrange on a plate like a flower. Garnish in the middle with red and yellow peppers and top with scallops. Heat thoroughly and top with Tomato Vodka Sauce.

TOMATO VODKA SAUCE:

Heat skillet and sauté garlic and shallots. Flambé vodka and add tomatoes, cream, lobster base, pepper and basil. Once it reaches a boil, remove from flame and put in a blender. Puree to a smooth, thick consistency. Keep warm.

YIELD

Serves 1.

Carmelo's Mozzarella in Carrozza

RED PEPPER SAUCE:

- 1/2 cup chicken broth
- 1/2 medium yellow onion, sliced
- 1/2 medium red bell pepper, seeded and quartered
- 1/2 cup white wine
- 1/2 cup whipping cream
- 1/2 tablespoon salt
- 1/2 tablespoon ground black pepper
- 1/2 tablespoon chopped parsley

- 2 ounces fresh mozzarella cheese
- 4 slices Italian bread, 1/2-inch thick
- 1/4 cup fresh whole basil leaves
- 4 strips green bell pepper, thin
- dash salt, ground black pepper
- 3 tablespoons Parmesan cheese, grated
- 2 teaspoons parsley, chopped
- 1/2 cup flour
- 3 eggs, beaten
- 4 tablespoons olive oil for frying
- 1/2 cup broccoli florets

RED PEPPER SAUCE:

In a large saucepan, combine all ingredients. Over high heat, bring to a boil, reduce heat and simmer 10 minutes. Remove from heat. Allow to cool 5 minutes. Place mixture in blender and puree to a smooth, thick consistency.

Keep warm.

Heat oven broiler. Cut mozzarella into 6 even slices. Place 3 each on 2 slices of bread. Place basil leaves and bell pepper on top. Sprinkle with salt, black pepper, Parmesan and parsley, leaving some for garnish. Top with remaining bread slices. Dredge all sides of sandwiches in flour and dip in beaten eggs. Pour oil into large nonstick frying pan, heat to medium high. Fry sandwich till lightly browned, or about one minute on each side. Remove from frying pan and place in ovenproof pan. Broil 5 minutes. Slice each sandwich in half. Pour Red Pepper Sauce on platter and arrange sandwich halves on top. Garnish with parsley and broccoli.

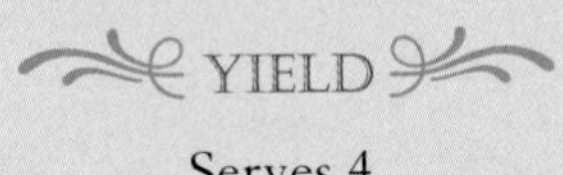

Serves 4.

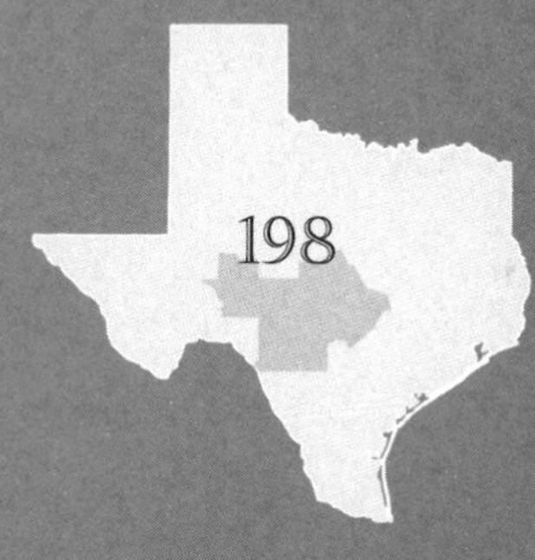

Zuppa di Tartaruga

1/2 pound ground turtle meat (Louisiana farm grown)

1/4 pound ground veal

1 1/2 cups olive oil

1/4 teaspoon thyme

1/4 teaspoon oregano

The following vegetables should be ground, chopped, or finely diced:

- 3 bell peppers, red, yellow and green
- 3 sticks celery
- 1 medium onion

1 1/2 tablespoons lobster base

1 1/2 tablespoons beef base

3 quarts fish stock

1/2 teaspoon black pepper

2 tablespoons tomato paste

1 cup sherry

1/2 lemon

2 chopped eggs

1/4 pound chopped spinach

Sauté meat in olive oil and remove from pot. Add ground, chopped or very finely diced vegetables to the oil with thyme and oregano and sauté. Add more oil if necessary. Return meat into pot and add lobster and beef base, fish stock, pepper and tomato paste. Quarter a half lemon, leaving the skin on, and put it in the blender with the sherry. Add this to soup as it is coming to a boil. Bring to boil and add eggs and spinach at the last moment. Remove from heat immediately after bringing to second boil. Garnish with a cooked rigatoni stuffed with turtle meat.

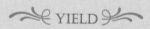

YIELD

Serves 5 to 6.

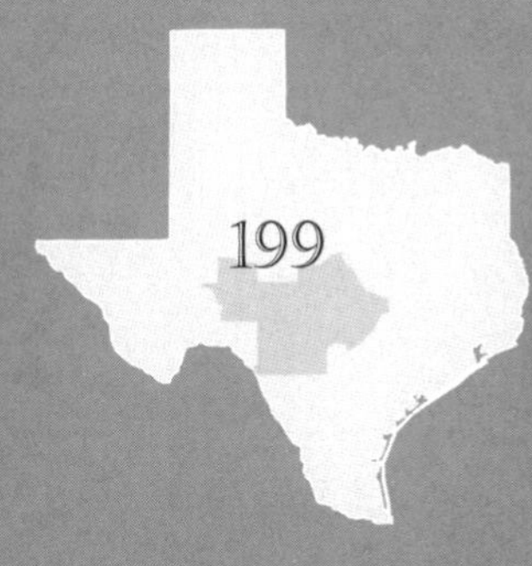

Fettuccine Carbonara

4 ounces cooked fettuccine
1/2 ounce white onions, chopped
1/2 ounce green onions, chopped
1 ounce mushrooms, sliced
1 ounce pancetta, diced
1 tablespoon butter
1 raw egg
4 ounces heavy cream
pepper, to taste

Place butter in a hot skillet, add pancetta, white onions and mushrooms. Cook 3–4 minutes or until nicely sautéed. Add the pasta and toss well. Add the cream and green onions. Pepper to taste. Beat the egg quickly with a fork in a separate bowl and combine with the hot fettuccine mixture. Toss well to coat just before serving.

Serves 1.

THE DRISKILL HOTEL

Austin

Cattle baron Colonel Jesse Lincoln Driskill built his hotel in 1886 to serve as the South's Frontier Palace. His attention to detail and desire to create an architectural masterpiece made Texans very proud. He spent $400,000, an enormous sum of money for the time. A special edition of the Austin *Daily Statesman* described the hotel as "one of the finest in the country" and went on to say that it was "a blessing to the city and state that cannot be overestimated."

Less than two weeks after the grand opening, it hosted the first inaugural ball for Texas Governor Sul Ross. With a tradition established, later governors such as William Hobby, Dan Moody and John Connally also used the Driskill for their inauguration celebrations.

In 1887 Colonel Driskill's livelihood was threatened by a nationwide drought. The following year an exceptionally cold winter wiped out 3,000 of his cattle and he was forced to sell his beloved hotel. A series of owners followed, as well as renovations and improvements that included the first long-distance telephone service in the city.

Desperados, politicians, cattle barons and other notables have all made the Driskill their home. The stained glass dome, fine antiques and inlaid marble floors seem more like a stately grand estate. The leather sofas, plush carpets and Texas accoutrements also remind one of belonging to a private club.

Renowned for its traditional fare, regional sensations and ever-changing, novel creations, the Driskill Grill is a majestic setting for any celebration. Lyndon and Lady Bird Johnson had their first date at the dining room for breakfast there in 1934. The hotel became a lifelong love affair for the couple. He awaited his results of the election for Vice President in 1960 at the hotel. The Governor's Suite on the fifth floor was permanently reserved for LBJ.

Every guest room is unique in its décor. The massive red drapes are beautiful, and wide halls are laden with pastels and oil paintings forming a great gallery. The arched windows and 19-foot ceilings are all part of the grandeur.

For years the Driskill has been host to many famous guests, such as Amelia Earhart, Louis Armstrong, Michael Jordan, Paul Simon, President and Mrs. Clinton, President and Mrs. Bush and Sandra Bullock.

SINCE 1886

The Driskill Hotel Grill, 604 Brazos Street, Austin, Texas 78701. Call (512) 474-5911, or visit www.driskillhotel.com. Open daily for breakfast, lunch and dinner with an a la carte brunch available on Sunday.

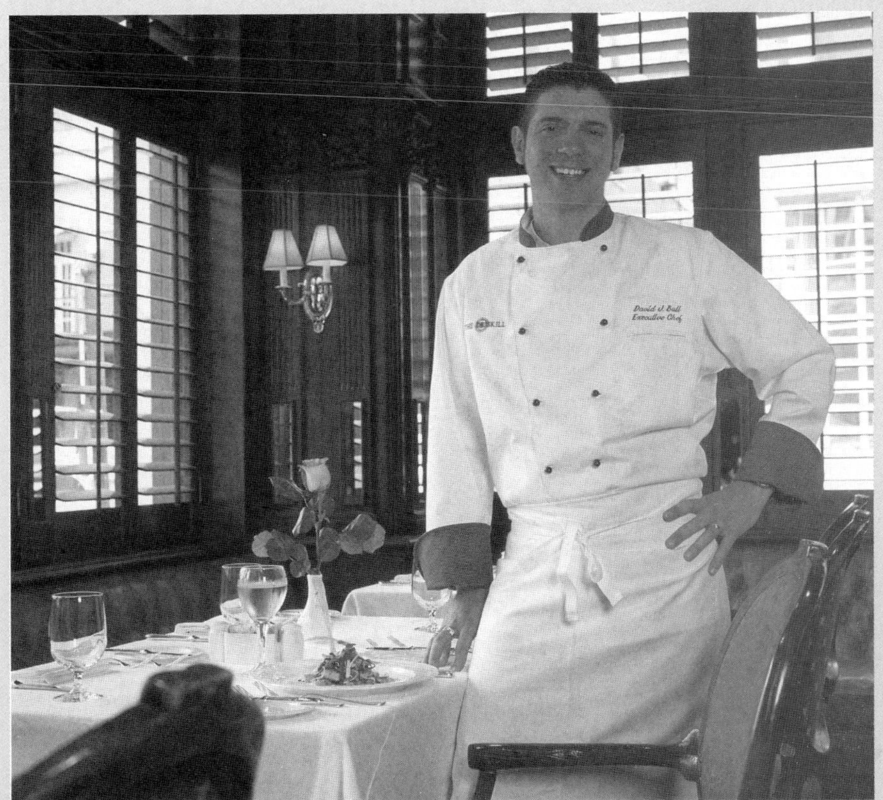

Executive chef David Bull, named Best New Chef of 2003 by Food and Wine *magazine.*

12 sea scallops, cleaned, mussel removed (method to follow)

12 prosciutto, sliced paper thin (method to follow)

8 ounces Cucumber Tomato Salad (recipe to follow)

3 ounces Creamy Vinaigrette (recipe to follow)

CUCUMBER TOMATO SALAD:

1/2 English cucumber cut lengthwise, seeds removed and sliced into half-moon shapes

2 large red heirloom tomatoes, concasséd and thin julienne

2 large yellow heirloom tomato, concasséd and thin julienne

1/2 small red onion, fine julienne

1 teaspoon fresh dill, finely chopped

3/4 cup creamy vinaigrette (recipe to follow)

CREAMY VINAIGRETTE:

1/2 cup sour cream

1/4 cup mayonnaise

1/4 cup white wine

1 teaspoon white truffle oil

1 teaspoon capers

salt to taste

lemon juice to taste

Prosciutto Wrapped Sea Scallops

with Cucumber Tomato Salad

FOR THE SCALLOPS:

Preheat oven to 350 degrees. Wrap prosciutto around the outside of each scallop. Season the scallops with salt and sauté over high heat for 1–2 minutes on each side or until golden brown in color. Place the scallops into a preheated oven and finish cooking for 3–5 minutes.

CUCUMBER TOMATO SALAD:

In a salad bowl, mix all the ingredients together and toss with 3/4 of the creamy vinaigrette. Season with salt to taste.

CREAMY VINAIGRETTE:

Place all ingredients into a blender and puree until smooth. Season with salt and lemon juice to taste. Reserve 1/4 of the vinaigrette for the plate assembly.

ASSEMBLY:

On four large dinner plates place 2 ounces of the cucumber tomato salad in the center of the plate. Place 3 scallops around the salad. Drizzle 1/2 ounce of the vinaigrette around the outside of the scallops.

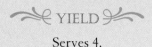

Serves 4.

Jalapeno Mashed Potatoes

3 Idaho potatoes, peeled and cut into even pieces

water as needed

salt to taste

1/4 cup heavy whipping cream

3 ounces whole salted butter

3 jalapenos, roasted, skin and seeds removed, small diced

salt to taste

In a large saucepot cover the potatoes with water, season with salt and bring to a boil. Cook over medium heat until the potatoes are fork tender. Combine the heavy cream and the butter and bring mixture to a boil in a small saucepot over medium heat. Strain the potatoes and push through a food mill or whip until incorporated.

Add the remaining cream butter mixture as needed to obtain proper consistency of mashed potatoes. Add the roasted and diced jalapenos and season with salt to taste. Garnish with sweet corn sauce (recipe to follow).

Reserve hot until ready to serve.

Serves 4.

- 1 ounce canola oil
- 1 shallot, chopped
- 1/4 teaspoon cumin, ground
- 3 ears of corn, shucked—kernels removed
- 2 cups chicken stock
- lime juice to taste
- salt to taste
- maple syrup to taste

Sweet Corn Sauce

In a small saucepot over medium heat add the canola oil. Add the shallot and sauté for 1 minute. Add the ground cumin and toast for 1 minute. Add the shucked kernels of corn and cook for 1 minute. Add the chicken stock, bring to a boil and cook for 5 minutes.

Place mixture into a blender and puree until smooth. Strain through a fine mesh sieve and season with lime juice, salt and maple syrup to taste.

Reserve hot until ready to serve.

YIELD

1 quart.

GREEN PASTURES RESTAURANT

Austin

The mansion was built in 1894 by Dr. E. W. Herndon, a minister from Tennessee. His unique antebellum taste is reflected in the mansion's highly detailed architecture and quality workmanship. The doors of first-growth Louisiana pine and cypress and the mantels of oak and bird's-eye maple are virtually irreplaceable.

The home became the residence of lawyer Henry Faulk in 1916. Faulk's daughter, Mary Faulk Koock, became renowned for her cooking and her flair for entertaining. Her bestseller, *The Texas Cookbook*, continues to be a favorite.

In 1945, Mary and her husband, Chester, converted Green Pastures from a family homestead to a restaurant. Since that time, Green Pastures has been a popular choice for elegant dining in Austin. In addition to lunch and dinner, they offer to host private parties, weddings, receptions, banquets, business meetings and off-premise catering. With an abundance of free parking, Green Pastures' beautifully appointed Victorian mansion and live oak shaded grounds offer the ideal site for a truly memorable celebration.

Green Pastures Restaurant, 811 W. Live Oak, Austin, Texas 78704, (512) 444-4747, or visit www.citysearch.com/aus/greenpastures. The restaurant is open for lunch seven days a week from 11 a.m. until 1:45 p.m. and for dinner Monday through Saturday from 6 p.m. until 9:30 p.m. for the last reservations. Sunday they are closed for dinner.

3 1/2 cups whole wheat flour
3–3 1/2 cups white flour
2 packages active dry yeast
2 cups milk
1/2 cup sugar
3 tablespoons shortening
1 tablespoon salt
2 eggs

Cotillion Rolls

Combine 2 1/2 cups white flour and yeast in large bowl. In medium saucepan, mix milk, sugar, shortening and salt and cook over low heat. Stir until shortening is completely melted and liquid reaches a temperature of 115 to 120 degrees. Add to flour mixture. Add eggs, one at a time, beating well after each addition with electric beater. Beat at high speed for 3 minutes.

Add whole wheat flour and remaining white flour. Mix with a wooden spoon. Knead, adding more white flour if necessary to make a firm dough. When dough is smooth and elastic (5–10 minutes), it is done.

Place dough in a large greased bowl. Turn over once. Cover the bowl and let dough rise for approximately 1 1/2 hours or until double in size. Punch the dough down and allow it to rest for 10 minutes. Shape into desired rolls (cloverleaf or crescents). Cover the rolls and allow to rise until almost doubled for approximately 45 minutes. Bake in 400-degree oven for 15 to 20 minutes.

20 rolls.

Green Pastures' Bread Pudding

4 eggs
1/4 cup sugar
1/4 teaspoon salt
1/2 tablespoon vanilla
2 1/2 cups heavy cream
1 1/2 teaspoons cinnamon to taste
1/4 teaspoon nutmeg to taste
2/3 butter, melted
3 cups bread, crumbled (preferably the Cotillian rolls above)
4 ounces white chocolate pieces
1/4 cup pecans

Crumble bread into a 9-inch pan. Drizzle melted butter over bread and toss. Sprinkle nuts and chocolate over bread. Mix eggs, sugar, salt, spices and vanilla in separate bowl. In saucepan bring cream to a boil. Remove cream from stove and pour into egg-sugar mixture. Mix thoroughly. Pour mixture over the bread, mixing with fingers until thoroughly saturated.

Bake at 350 degrees and check for doneness (35 to 40 minutes).

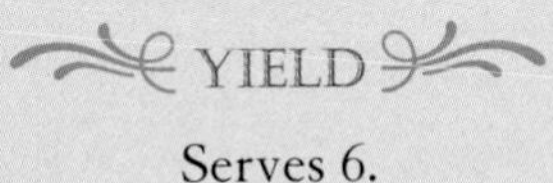

Serves 6.

Green Pastures' Milk Punch

3 gallons vanilla ice cream
1 gallon whole milk
3 cups bourbon
2 cups rum
1 cup brandy

Blend liquors with ice cream until smooth. Pour milk into mixture and stir.

Serves 20.

1/2 pound butter, unsalted

2 1/2 cups sugar, granulated

4 eggs

1 1/2 cups flour

3 ounces cocoa

2 teaspoons baking soda

1/2 teaspoon vanilla extract

2 1/4 cups milk

Green Pastures' Fat Chocolate Cake

Preheat oven to 350 degrees. Lightly coat the inside of two 10-inch cake pans with melted butter and dust with flour.

Cream butter and sugar together. Add eggs one at a time. Sift dry ingredients. Add dry and liquid ingredients to creamed mixture—alternate beginning and ending with dry.

Pour the cake batter into the prepared pans and bake in the preheated oven until a toothpick inserted in the center comes out clean (35 to 45 minutes). Remove from the oven and cool in the pans for 15 minutes at room temperature. Invert onto cake circles and refrigerate uncovered until needed.

YIELD

Serves 8–10.

GRISTMILL RIVER RESTAURANT

New Braunfels

In 1878, Henry D. Gruene built a cotton gin along the Guadalupe River in what would be named New Braunfels. The construction site was selected because there had been an earlier gristmill at that location to grind corn from surrounding fields. Known as the Gruene Cotton Gin, it was powered by steam. Water from the river was channeled into the boiler room, where it was heated with a wood-burning furnace. This rather simple process was successful back then because hand-picked cotton was much cleaner than machine-picked cotton, since the pickers were careful to eliminate seeds and other debris.

The entire Gruene community was dependent on the cotton crop. Henry Gruene had two dozen sharecropper families farming 100 acres each of his land, and they not only made him a profit when the cotton came in, but they also purchased all of their farm supplies from his Mercantile Store. Unfortunately, the cotton gin burned in 1922, and everything was destroyed but the boiler room. Built to house a fire inside, the two-and-a-half story brick boiler room survived with minor damage. Although nothing was done with the remaining structure for several decades, the property was renovated and in 1976, the Gristmill River Restaurant opened in the surviving boiler room.

Located in what is now known as the Gruene Historic District, and below the water tower, the Gristmill River Restaurant boasts a Texas Historical Marker. The current owners, Pat Molak and Mary Jane Nalley, offer typical Southwest meals in a very unusual, historical Texas setting at 1601 Hunter Road, New Braunfels, Texas 78130. Call (830) 625-0684 or visit www.gristmillrestaurant.com. Open daily at 11 a.m., it closes Monday through Thursday at 9 p.m. in the winter and 10 p.m. in the summer. On Friday and Saturday it closes at 10 p.m. in the winter and 11 p.m. in the summer.

2 yellow onions

3/4 cup flour

1 teaspoon Lawry's Seasoned Salt

dash black pepper

1/2 cup buttermilk

12 crackers, finely ground

Onion Rings

Slice onions 3/4 inch thick. Wet rings in water, dust with mixture of seasoned salt, flour and black pepper. Dip rings into buttermilk and roll in finely ground crackers. Deep-fry until golden brown. Season with Lawry's Seasoned Salt and serve.

YIELD

Serves 2.

Beef Tenderloin Salad

TENDERLOIN MARINADE (1 QUART):

Melt margarine over low flame. Add Worcestershire sauce, soy sauce, lime juice, diced cilantro, salt and black pepper. Place garlic in blender with just enough water to cover blades. Blend until smooth and add to marinade. Cook over low flame for another 10 minutes.

Dip beef tips in marinade. Cook to your temperature preference. Add the beef tips to a 3-leaf mixture of leaf lettuce, Romaine lettuce and spinach. Add two ounces of Vinaigrette Dressing along with avocado and mix. Serve in a salad bowl with tomato wedges.

VINAIGRETTE DRESSING:

In a mixing bowl, combine the mayonnaise, Dijon mustard, buttermilk, white pepper, sugar and salt. Mix together with a wire whisk until smooth. Slowly add the salad oil while whisking vigorously. In a food processor, blend together the garlic and onion, then add the red wine vinegar until the onions are in tiny pieces. Slowly add the onion, garlic and vinegar mixture and basil to the dressing while whisking. Keep refrigerated.

Serves 1.

TENDERLOIN MARINADE (1 QUART):

1 pound margarine

1/2 cup Worcestershire sauce

1/2 cup soy sauce

1 cup fresh-squeezed lime juice

1/2 tablespoon garlic

1/4 cup cilantro, diced fine

1 tablespoon black pepper

7 ounces beef tips

leaf lettuce

Romaine lettuce

fresh spinach

4 slices avocado

2 wedges tomato

2 ounces Vinaigrette Dressing (recipe follows)

VINAIGRETTE DRESSING:

6 tablespoons mayonnaise

1 1/2 teaspoons Dijon mustard

dash white pepper

1/8 tablespoon sugar

1/16 tablespoon salt

5 tablespoons salad oil

2 tablespoons red wine vinegar

2 tablespoons buttermilk

2 teaspoons green onions, diced

1/2 teaspoon garlic, diced

1/16 tablespoon basil

GÜERO'S

Austin

As early as 1887, the City Directory of Austin listed a man named Arthur Poteet as operating a grocery store at the northwest corner of South Congress Avenue and Elisabeth Street. In 1895, one of his relatives is listed as proprietor of the South Austin Grist Mill at the same location. In the late 19th century, Charles B. Poteet is listed as operating a corn and feed mill at 1412 South Congress Avenue.

From 1903 through 1941, the Crawford family was listed in City Directories as operating grocers and millers for this location. They also operated as wholesale and retail dealers in hay, grain and what the directory described as "mill stuff." J. M. Crawford was born in North Carolina and moved to Austin in the 1880s. Ruth R. Crawford, his daughter, spent most of her life in a house next door. (That property has been removed and the lot now serves as the parking lot for the current restaurant.) She taught for over 50 years at the North Dallas High School, and she was an employee with the Austin History Center. Her knowledge of the city (especially South Austin) made her a tremendous source of historical information.

In the early 1940s, this location housed the Central Feed Store, and this operation continued into the 1960s. It was a popular stopping place for anyone who needed to purchase baby chickens, baby rabbits, feed, pesticides, seedlings, seeds, fertilizer, potting soils and other assorted farm and garden supplies.

The purchase of this property by the current owners provides an excellent example of the advantages of rehabilitating historic structures for current uses. President Bill Clinton was a guest at this restaurant on one of his trips to Austin in 1995.

Güero's, 1412 South Congress Avenue, Austin, Texas 78704, (512) 447-7688. Open Monday through Friday 11 a.m. to 11 p.m., Saturday and Sunday 8 a.m. to 11 p.m.

Güero's Tacos al Pastor

In Mexico City, these tacos are made from spiced pork cooked on a rotisserie. We have imported this tradition to our restaurant in Austin, Texas—rotisseries and all.

- 1/4 cup granulated garlic
- 1 tablespoon cider vinegar
- 1 teaspoon dried oregano
- 1 teaspoon Anaheim chili powder
- 1 teaspoon freshly ground black pepper
- pinch ground cumin
- salt to taste
- 2 cups fresh orange juice
- 1 1/2 tablespoons achiote paste
- 2 pounds boneless pork loin, thinly sliced
- 1/2 pineapple, peeled, cored and cut into long, thick strips
- 12 corn tortillas, warmed
- 1 onion, finely chopped
- 1 bunch cilantro, finely chopped
- salsa

In a medium-sized bowl, combine the garlic, vinegar, oregano, Anaheim chili powder, black pepper, cumin, salt to taste, orange juice and achiote paste. Add the pork slices and turn to coat both sides. Marinate for at least 1 hour, and not more than 3 hours.

Heat the grill. Place meat over a hot fire and cook, turning once and basting with any leftover marinade during cooking, until crisp. At the same time, grill the pineapple strips, turning as needed, until lightly browned. Both the pork and pineapple should take no longer than about 5 minutes.

To assemble, chop the grilled pork into 1/4-inch pieces. Cut the pineapple into 1/2-inch pieces. Place the pork on the warmed tortillas and top with the onion, cilantro and pineapple pieces. Serve the salsa on the side.

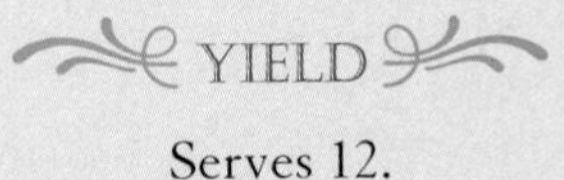

YIELD

Serves 12.

Güero's Black Beans

(Goes great with Tacos al Pastor!)

- 2 1/2 pounds black beans (soaked overnight in water)
- 1/2 pound carrots, diced
- 1/2 pound onions, diced
- 1/2 bunch cilantro, minced
- 1 1/2 ounce cumin
- 1 ounce white pepper
- 1/2 ounce garlic powder
- dash salt

Put beans in a large cooking pot. Fill pot with cold water. (The water should rise 2–3 inches above the beans). Cook for 30 minutes, or until beans are tender. Add diced vegetables. Simmer for an additional 15–20 minutes. Add spices in last 5 minutes of cooking.

YIELD

Serves 12.

GUMBO'S

Austin

Gumbo's is located in the Brown Building in downtown Austin. Originally constructed by Brown & Root as its world headquarters and multi-tenant office building, the Brown Building was built to last. It began as an eight-story structure, which was completed in 1938. The ninth and tenth floors were added in 1949 to accommodate growing demand for class "A" office space in the post-World-War-II economic boom.

Designed by Charles H. Page, the leading Texas architect of the early 20th century, the Brown Building is an Austin treasure. Combining Art Moderne and Art Deco styles, Page created a bold statement. Completed as the Great Depression was ending, the building was a symbol of the promise of Texas power and prosperity for decades to come.

Important architectural features include the Texas granite façade and original aluminum canopy and window along Colorado Street. The original terrazzo floors, art-deco light fixtures and Mississippi red gum wood trim complement the Tennessee marble on the ground floor. On the upper floors a variety of finishes include terrazzo, brass handles, concrete, operable steel windows with marble wainscot and marble trim painstakingly restored.

The construction of the Brown Building is phenomenal. Built upon solid limestone, the steel and concrete structure was considered so strong it was the designated bomb shelter for public officials during the cold war. The marble-clad lobby with original aluminum light fixtures has been remarkably preserved. The art-deco, etched glass pieces above the elevators were originally commissioned by Herman Brown to depict the original businesses of Brown & Root, including the construction of hydroelectric dams, highways and oil and gas refineries. Today, Brown & Root is one of the world's largest construction companies and it came to age in the Brown Building.

Famous tenants have included President and Lady Bird Johnson. Mrs. Johnson ran KTBC Radio from the ground floor while Congressman Lyndon Johnson welcomed his constituents to visit without an appointment in Suite 725. Cactus Pryor, Governor John Connally and Congressman Jake Pickle all worked for KTBC in the Brown Building after World War II. Senator Ralph Yarborough, Congressman Lloyd Doggett and the University of Texas Regent and legend Frank Erwin were all tenants of the building.

The photos that are on display on the residential floors were acquired from the Austin History Center, the Harry Ransom Center, the LBJ Library and the Stephen Clark Gallery. Each floor has a collection of photos, which are either historic or contemporary depictions of Texas by Texas photographers.

In the early 1990s the LBJ Holding Company purchased the Brown Building. They renovated it in a manner that preserved the historic integrity of the building while creating modern living spaces full of light for today's urban dweller. The building was awarded several environmental awards for recycling, energy efficiency and clean air components of the project.

Gumbo's, 710 Colorado Street, #100, Austin, Texas 78701. Call (512) 480-8053. They are open Sunday through Friday for lunch from 11 a.m. until 2 p.m. and dinner from 5:30 until 10 p.m., except on Friday they stay open until 11 p.m. Saturday they are open for dinner only from 5 until 11 p.m.

Pecan-Crusted Shrimp Caesar

7 shrimp, peeled and deveined (size 21/25)

1 cup pecan halves

1 cup egg wash

4 or 5 Romaine lettuce leaves

2 ounces Caesar dressing

3 slices tomato

1 tablespoon Parmesan, freshly grated

1 cup garlic-seasoned breadcrumbs

salt

cayenne pepper

freshly ground black pepper

Blend pecans in food processor with breadcrumbs until coarsely ground. Add salt, pepper and cayenne to taste. Coat shrimp with egg wash, then pecan crust. Fry until golden brown and let drain. Toss Romaine leaves in your favorite Caesar dressing until completely coated. Stack leaves in center of plate and place tomato slices on top. Place three shrimp on tomatoes and the rest around the plate. Garnish with fresh Parmesan.

YIELD

Serves 1.

Crawfish Eddy

6 ounces crawfish tails

1 ounce butter

2 teaspoons green onions, sliced

2 teaspoons parsley, chopped

1 tablespoon blackening spice

1 teaspoon lemon pepper

2 teaspoons flour

1 1/2 ounces white wine

5 ounces alfredo sauce

2 teaspoons tarragon

water as needed

toast points

Sauté crawfish in butter in a medium pan. Add all of the ingredients and bring to a boil. Adjust the consistency of the sauce with flour or water. The sauce should coat the back of a spoon. Spoon crawfish and sauce into a bowl, making sure to pile crawfish in the middle. Serve with toast points.

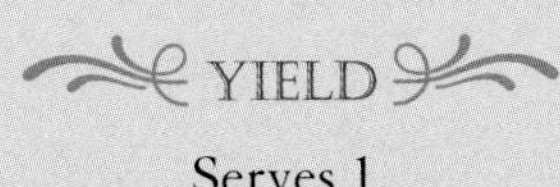

YIELD

Serves 1.

- 4 shrimp (size 21/25)
- 3 ounces crawfish tails
- 2 ounces jalapeno sausage, diced
- 5 ounces alfredo sauce
- blackening spice, as needed
- 1 teaspoon parsley, chopped
- 1 tablespoon green onions, chopped
- 2 ounces white wine
- 1 teaspoon lemon pepper
- 7 ounces pasta
- fresh Parmesan and sun-dried tomatoes, for garnish

Jalapeno Sausage Pasta

In a hot pan, sauté shrimp, crawfish and sausage. Add wine and all other ingredients. Let simmer until shrimp are cooked. Toss with your favorite pasta, and serve. Garnish with fresh Parmesan and sun-dried tomatoes.

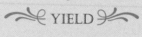

YIELD

Serves 1.

HILL TOP CAFÉ

Fredericksburg

In the late 1800s, the McDonald family operated a stage stop and watering hole about 200 yards north of the current location of Hill Top Café. This was also a stop on the Pony Express circuit. After the demise of both the stage line and the Pony Express, and the advent of the automobile, the old building was dismantled and relocated to its current location.

In about 1918, the Fiedler family (descendants of the McDonalds) used lumber from the old building to construct the building that now houses Hill Top Café. Fiedler's Station, as it would be known for years, was the center of the Hill Top community and served weary travelers on the Mason Highway with grocery items, Magnolia gasoline, beverages, tire service and cold beer. A Fairbanks-Morse "make and break" engine powered the air compressor and block ice kept the drinks cold.

After a fire partially destroyed this building in 1924, renovations included enlarging the front awning to accommodate larger vehicles and acquisition of part of the old bar from the defunct White Elephant Saloon in Fredericksburg. Around this time Willie Fiedler switched to Texaco gasoline and also installed newer gravity flow "visible" gasoline pumps.

With the advent of prohibition, Fiedler became adept at distilling corn liquor and making home brew that he bottled in the old storm cellar. Business flourished as the Fiedlers produced some of the best corn liquor in the county. It didn't hurt that his in-laws were related to the sheriff who always tipped them off when the Revenuers were in the area.

After prohibition, Fiedler's prospered until its sale to Norman Simmons in 1951. The Simmons family ran Hill Top, as it became known, as a successful roadhouse gas station, community beer joint, grocery store and watering hole until the late 1960s, when he sold it to Bill Talbert of Dallas. A big attraction during Simmons's tenure was when his son would land his airplane on the highway out front and take customers for rides over the hill country.

Bill Talbert kept the business the same while adding a motorcycle shop in the old garage. He sold it to Curtis Wilson in 1975, who in turn sold it to the current owners, Johnny and Brenda Nicholas, in 1980.

When the Nicholas couple took over, the place was badly in need of repairs, but the old bar and most of the ambiance (stuffed animals, beer signs, posters and assorted goofy wall hangings) was still in place. Many items which had disappeared have been returned and restored, such as the old pumps, the Fairbanks-Morse engine, the old pre-electric Coke box and many original signs and decorations.

Over the years the café has changed greatly. At one point chili and gumbo were cooked on a two-burner hot plate and burgers, steaks and gulf flounder were cooked on a flat-top/boiler combo purchased secondhand with proceeds from a 1982 recording session Johnny did playing piano on a Fabulous Thunderbirds early recording. The old roadhouse has evolved from providing beer, groceries, a pool table and pumping gas to the current eclectic restaurant known as the Hill Top Café. Johnny still plays the guitar, harp, mandolin and keyboards and has even recorded an album. If you're lucky, you can hear him play live at the café. Every Friday and Saturday night they offer live blues, jazz and boogie-woogie at the piano.

Hill Top prides itself on serving great food in a relaxed, unpretentious atmosphere. The cuisine includes Cajun and Greek influence, reflecting Brenda's Port Arthur upbringing and Johnny's Greek background. The focus has always been on melding these backgrounds with regional products such as local produce, fresh gulf seafood and prime beef and Southwestern flare. Add to this their love of European style and technique. Their demi-glace takes three days to prepare and they do not subscribe to the idea that image rules over substance.

Their philosophy is dictated by one simple rule—it either tastes great or it is sub-par, and they refuse to settle for sub-par. They believe that cooking is an art that requires a God-given talent and dedication to technique and excellence. They constantly strive to be the best. Johnny and Brenda Nicholas believe that travel time is immaterial if the restaurant is excellent. "Our customers don't keep coming back because of the location."

Hill Top Café, 10661 North U.S. Highway 87, Fredericksburg, Texas 78618. Call (830) 997-8922, visit www.hilltopcafe.com, or email hilltopinfo@hilltopcafe.com.

From Fredericksburg, head west on Main. When you hit the "Y" where 290W and 87N split, take 87N 10 miles to the Café. The Hill Top is open Wednesday and Thursday from 11 a.m. until 2 p.m. and 5 p.m. until 9 p.m. They are open Friday and Saturday from 11 a.m. until 2 p.m. and 5 p.m. until 10 p.m. On Sunday they serve brunch from 11 a.m. until 2 p.m., but they also stay open until 9 p.m. for regular dining.

Hill Top Café Greek Quesadillas

1 10-ounce package pocket pita bread

2 cucumbers, peeled and very thinly sliced

1 purple onion, very thinly sliced

16 ounces cream cheese at room temperature

1/3 cup Kalamata olives, pitted

1/3 cup green salad olives, pitted

12 cloves garlic, roasted and chopped

1 teaspoon leaf oregano

1 teaspoon white pepper

3 1/2 tablespoons red wine vinegar or balsamic vinegar

1 teaspoon salt

4 slices Monterey Jack cheese

4 slices longhorn cheddar, mild

6 tablespoons extra virgin olive oil

1 tablespoon butter

1 teaspoon sesame seeds, roasted

Combine softened (room temperature) cream cheese with chopped olives and roasted garlic in a bowl. Mix well to make a spread. In a separate bowl, combine thinly sliced cucumbers and onions. Add white pepper, salt, one heaping teaspoon leaf oregano and red wine or balsamic vinegar. Adjust any of these seasonings to taste. Add olive oil last and mix thoroughly. Allow marinade to work for at least 30 minutes.

Open pocket pita breads by cutting halfway around. Spread cream cheese and olive mixture (about 1/4 inch thick) on inside of one side of pita bread. Place a layer of marinated cucumbers and onions on top of spread. Put one slice each of Monterey Jack and longhorn cheese on top of cucumbers and onions. Close pita bread. Lightly butter both sides of pita bread and cook in a medium-hot skillet until cheese is melted and pita bread is browned on both sides. Remove and cut into quarters or eighths. Garnish with sesame seeds and serve hot.

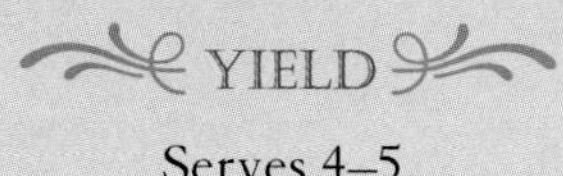

Serves 4–5.

Cheddar & Jalapeno Grits

2 cups instant white corn grits
4 cups boiling salted water
3 large jalapenos (halved and sliced)
1/2 pound unsalted butter
1/2 cup heavy whipping cream
1 cup sharp cheddar cheese, grated
dash salt and black pepper

Slowly stir in grits to boiling water. Reduce heat to simmer. Add jalapenos. Cook for 15 minutes, constantly stirring. Turn off flame. Add butter and cheese. Whip in cream. Add salt and pepper to taste. Serve steaming.

YIELD

Serves 4.

Stuffed Pork Chops

4 large French pork rib chops, with pocket cut below bone
2 links spicy green onion sausage
2 Granny Smith apples, diced small
2 tablespoons brown sugar
2 tablespoons capers
1 tablespoon whole grain mustard
1 1/2 cups green onions, chopped
1 tablespoon extra virgin olive oil
dash salt and pepper

Halve and slice sausage. Render fat in skillet. Strain fat. Add apples, brown sugar and capers. Sauté until apples are slightly soft. Transfer to large mixing bowl. Add remaining ingredients. Let cool. Slice a pocket in pork chop directly below rib bone. Stuff with filling. Grill on a hot grill until desired doneness, turning once.

YIELD

Serves 4.

HUISACHE GRILL

New Braunfels

Sitting next to the rumbling railroad tracks in a hard-to-find location, the Huisache (pronounced wee-sach) Grill first opened in 1994 and quickly became a popular downtown spot in New Braunfels. With a tiny kitchen, and a menu without a hamburger, their goal has been to offer fresh, simply prepared New American cuisine in a comfortable, casual setting, coupled with a dash of small-town charm and some really nice people.

Success brought growth, and in 1999 they expanded into their new space that includes the restored, circa-1870 Tietze Cabinet Shop and the new Wine Bar Room, constructed from recycled and salvaged building materials. Architect Richard Mycue blended the styles of the early Texas Tietze Homestead, the old railroad station and the original fire station into the new construction and design.

In addition to providing much-needed dining and food preparation areas, the new space better facilitates the owners' love of music and the arts. They not only showcase local and regional artists, but also many of the pieces displayed on the wall are available for purchase. Weekends feature a variety of live soft jazz.

The property now includes two historic Tietze homes that have been renovated. The oldest is now the Exquisite Stained Glass Studio, while the larger home is La Maison, shop of French country gifts and furnishings. In addition, they relocated a wonderful old building to the property and restored it as the Princess Be shop. Most recently they reassembled a small vintage cabinet shop obtained from the Heritage Society of New Braunfels. They are also completing a replica of the original palisade the settlers built to provide shelter and storage while building their first home. The German Tietzes camped out in this structure almost a year.

In 1994 the owners planted a small huisache tree at the entrance of the restaurant to commemorate its namesake. A native tree, its beautiful yellow spring blossoms signal what many consider to be the end of winter. Like the restaurant and Grassmarket, the huisache tree has flourished and grown.

Huisache Grill, 303 West San Antonio Street, New Braunfels, Texas 78130, (830) 620-9001 or visit www.huisache.com. The restaurant is open daily from 11 a.m. to 10 p.m. The grill is closed most major holidays.

Cilantro Sauce

- 3 cloves fresh garlic
- 1 teaspoon salt
- 1 teaspoon Dijon mustard
- 1 seeded fresh jalapeno
- 4 bunches cilantro, no stems
- 2 bunches washed parsley, no stems
- 1/2 cup sour cream
- 1/4 cup water
- 3/4 cup salad oil

Blend first 7 ingredients in a food processor and very gradually add the salad oil and water. Continue to blend until smooth. May be made a day ahead of serving.

Serve with tostadas, grilled or fresh vegetables, or as a sauce with spicy chicken or fish.

YIELD

1 1/2 cups.

Shrimp and Crawfish Bisque

- 5 ounces butter
- 3/4 cup flour
- 8 cups whole milk
- 8-ounce bottle roasted red pepper pureed
- 1 tablespoon chicken base or 4 chicken bouillon cubes
- 1/2 pound cooked cocktail shrimp
- 1/2 pound rinsed crawfish tails (may use frozen)
- 1/2 teaspoon white pepper
- 1/2 cup sherry (Do not use cooking sherry.)
- 1 teaspoon parsley, finely chopped

Melt butter in saucepan. Add flour and cook until it reaches a "popcorn" aroma. In a large, heavy-bottom stockpot, add milk, chicken base/bouillon, white pepper and roasted red pepper puree. Heat slowly over medium heat. Do not allow to boil. Add cooked roux to warm milk mixture. Allow to thicken. (This may take up to 30 minutes.) Add sherry, shrimp and crawfish tails. Bring bisque to serving temperature but do not boil.

Garnish with finely chopped parsley.

YIELD

Serves 4.

THE INTER-CONTINENTAL STEPHEN F. AUSTIN HOTEL

Austin

The rapid growth experienced by the Austin community early in the 20th century created a deficit in lodging. Extended hotel accommodations were essential to provide facilities for visitors to the legislature, state institutions, conventions and constantly increasing numbers of tourists. Realizing this, the citizens of Austin subscribed and paid for a bond issue for the construction of a new hotel.

Mr. T. B. Baker of Fort Worth began work on the "Texas" at the corner of Congress Avenue and Bois d'Arc Street (now Seventh Street), one of the more prominent sites in the downtown area. Previous structures housing such businesses as a grocery store, a livery stable, the G. A. Bahn Optical & Diamond Company, the two-story Keystone Hotel and the Bradford Paint building had to be removed to make way for the city's new flagship hotel. Before construction was complete the members of the Business and Professional Women's Club of Austin began a campaign to change the name. Feeling the need for a memorial to Stephen F. Austin, many local civic groups joined the cause.

Stephen Fuller Austin, often referred to as "The Father of Texas," was born in November, 1793, in Austinville, Virginia. Austin came to Texas at the age of 28 to carry out settlement plans for his father, Moses Austin. During the Christmas holidays of 1821, Austin led the first settlers into the rich lands lying between the Brazos and Colorado Rivers (present-day Brazoria County).

Between 1821 and 1828, Austin brought more than 1,200 settlers to the region. In 1835, following three years of imprisonment in Mexico City, Austin urged Texas to join the federalist troops in Mexico in their revolt against dictator Antonio Lopez de Santa Anna. Austin briefly commanded Texas volunteers during the Texas Revolution. He later served as the secretary of state for the Republic of Texas. Austin died in December, 1836, at the age of 43. He never married.

The Stephen F. Austin Hotel opened its doors in May of 1924 with 250 rooms. Complete with individual baths, steel bathroom cabinets, English-style service, running ice water, oriental rugs and a grand marble staircase, the Stephen F. Austin Hotel was built in the same grand style that personified superior hotel construction Baker had used on his other properties. Baker also owned The Menger in San Antonio, The Texas in Fort Worth and The Oriental in Dallas. Only 13 years after its opening, the hotel added five more floors, for a total of 15, and expanded to 350 rooms.

Known as the "Stephen F." among Austin natives, the hotel was the city's first high-rise building. Lyndon B. Johnson once made the hotel his campaign headquarters. In 1971, The Stephen F. Austin Hotel was purchased and became managed by the Hilton Corporation, directed by the Moody family in Galveston. The hotel was placed on the National Register of Historic Places in 1978. The City of Austin has also designated the building as a historical landmark.

In February 1982, the Stephen F. Austin Hotel reopened as the Bradford Hotel after renovations of more than $15 million. The hotel featured "an open, forested atrium; fountains; marble floors; and rare, exotic birds" and the Hippopotamus Lounge and Piano Bar. The Bradford Hotel's board of directors included Robert Mueller, Jr. and then-Mayor Roy Butler. Cecil Warren, who started at the Stephen F. Austin in 1934, was the general manager. Prices ranged from $60 per night for a single room to $500 a night for the Presidential suite.

Substantial remodeling and retrofitting began again in the early 1980s when the hotel was reduced from 400 rooms to 200. In 1987, the combination of an economic downturn in Austin and a decline in the average daily room rates prompted the owners to close the hotel.

Nine years later, a multi-million-dollar renovation project was begun, restoring much of the hotel's grandeur. Early in 2000, Bass Hotel & Resorts took over the hotel and completed the restoration effort. The Inter-Continental Stephen F. Austin opened in May, 2000, for individual guests and conferences.

The most recent renovation in the hotel is the addition of the Roaring Fork Restaurant. Chef Robert McGrath has designed and developed not only a great menu but also a stunning place to eat in downtown Austin.

Six Continents Hotels (formerly Bass Hotels & Resorts) is the world's global hotel company, operating or franchising more than 3,200 hotels and 520,000 guest rooms in some 100 countries and territories. Its hotel brands include Inter-Continental, Crowne Plaza, Holiday Inn, Holiday Inn Express and Staybridge Suites by Holiday Inn. Six Continents Hotels, the hospitality division of Bass PLC of the United Kingdom, hosts more than 150 million guests each year.

Located in the heart of Austin's central business district at Congress Avenue and Seventh Street, the Inter-Continental Stephen F. Austin is in close proximity to a number of business and leisure attractions, including the State Capitol, the Austin Convention Center, the Governor's Mansion, Sixth and Fourth Street entertainment districts, Zilker Park, Paramount Theatre and the Town Lake Hike & Bike Trail (10 miles).

Austin, the city "formerly known as Waterloo," is lush and green with numerous lakes and rivers. Other downtown attractions include Austin Children's Museum, Austin Museum of Art, Bob Bullock Texas State History Museum, Mexican-Art Museum, the LBJ Presidential Library and UT Tower.

Located on the floor above the Roaring Fork is Stephen F.'s, a bar that specializes in more than 75 drinks from around the world and extends out onto the second-floor balcony overlooking Congress Avenue.

The Inter-Continental Stephen F. Austin Hotel, 701 Congress Avenue, Austin, Texas, 78701. Call (512) 583-0000, or visit www.austin.interconti.com. The Roaring Fork, www.roaringfork.com, is open daily from 4:00 p.m. to 10:00 p.m. Sunday through Wednesday and 4:00 p.m. to 11:00 p.m. Thursday through Saturday. Their dress code is "No hairy people in undershirts! Other than that, we want you to be comfortable and we will try not to make fun of you if you don't know how to dress right."

2 pounds cooked king crab legs (jumbo lump crab can be substituted)

1 teaspoon chipotle chilies in adobo sauce, minced, or pureed

1 teaspoon fresh lemon juice

3/4 cup mayonnaise

2 avocados, cut in 1/2"-chunks

1/2 cup diced red onion

1/2 cup Rotel diced tomatoes with chilies

1/2 cup cilantro leaves

2 handfuls arugula

Chef Robert McGrath

Alaskan King Crab and Avocado Salad
with Chipotle Mayonnaise

Using a pair of heavy kitchen shears, split the crab legs and carefully clean out the crabmeat. Move slowly because the crab shells are sharp! Check the crabmeat for any tendons and cartilage. Coarsely chop the crabmeat and set aside in the refrigerator. Fold the minced (or pureed) chipotle chilies in adobo sauce and lemon juice into the mayonnaise then refrigerate until needed.

Cut the top and bottom of the Rotel tomato can out. Gently toss the crabmeat, avocado, red onion, Rotel tomatoes and cilantro together with the chipotle mayonnaise. Using the hollowed tomato can as a mold, fill the empty can with the crab salad and place in the center of the plate. Lift the can off the plate leaving the salad in a tower in the center of the plate. Distribute the arugula around the salad and serve.

Serves 4.

"One-Armed" Rib Eye Steak
with Black Bean and Smoked Onion Sofrito

4 16-to-18-ounce bone-in rib eye steak

kosher salt and fresh cracked black pepper to taste

GARNISH:

2 cups 1/4"-thick julienne of yellow onion

1 cup diced raw bacon

1 cup peeled, seeded coarse-cut tomato

1 cup bias-cut green onion

1 cup cooked, washed and drained black beans

1/2 cup roasted, peeled, seeded, julienne of poblano pepper

1/2 cup coarse-cut roasted garlic cloves

1 cup crumbled queso fresco

1/2 cup chopped cilantro

4 tablespoons whole butter

kosher salt and fresh cracked black pepper to taste

Smoke-roast the onions (on a screen or glazing rack) over hickory in a small smoker, or Weber grill, until they become translucent. Sauté the bacon with the green onion, tomato, black beans, garlic and poblano peppers, then season to taste. Set aside in a warm place.

Heat a cast-iron skillet until very, very hot. Season the steaks thoroughly, but not excessively, and blast-sear them in the cast iron to the desired temperature.

Finish the black bean–smoked onion sofrito with the butter and cilantro then spoon onto the plate. Lay the bone end of the steak against the sofrito. Drizzle a small amount of truffle oil over the steak, then sprinkle the crumbled queso over the plate and serve.

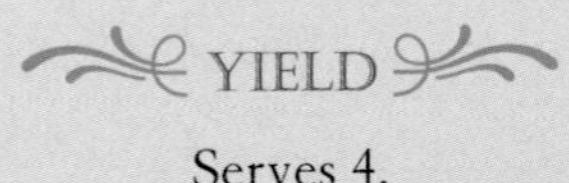

Serves 4.

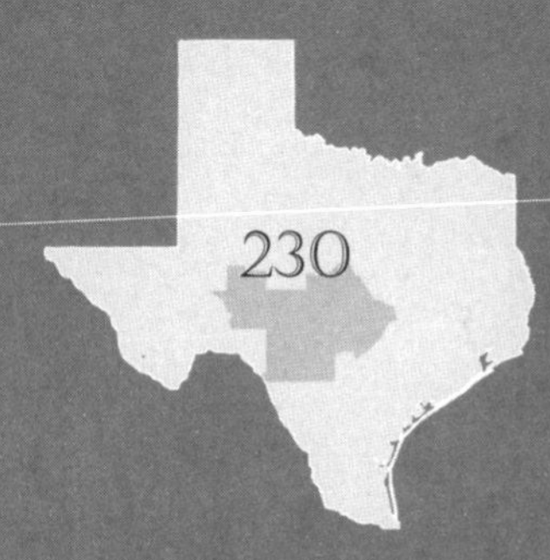

4 boneless rainbow trout

2 tablespoons vegetable shortening

20 whole chives (or baby wild onions)

4 lime wedges

kosher salt and cracked black pepper to taste

SALAD:

2 cups diced watermelon

2 cups cantaloupe balls

2 cups diced honeydew

1 cup bias-cut green onions

1/2 cup 1" chive sections

1/4 cup chopped garlic chives

1 cup raspberry vinegar

corn oil spray

Pan-Fried Canyon Trout

with Salad of Spring Melons and Green Onions

Mix all of the ingredients of the salad together and let sit for 1 hour. Season the trout and spray a hot cast-iron grill lightly with the corn oil. Place the trout cut-side down on the grill for 2 1/2 minutes then turn 90 degrees (to get squared grill marks) for 1 1/2 minutes. Turn over carefully and allow it to cook for 2 1/2 minutes.

Set the salad into the center of the plate and place the grill-marked side up, on top of the salad. Spoon some of the liquid from the salad around the perimeter of the plate. Squeeze the lime wedge over the trout and garnish with the whole chives (or baby wild onions).

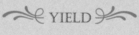

YIELD

Serves 4

JOE'S JEFFERSON STREET CAFÉ

Kerrville

The only Texas Historic Landmark Restaurant in Kerrville is Joe's Jefferson Street Café. Built originally as a home for S. W. and Laura Smith in 1890, it served as the residence for several families for almost a century. The two-story structure has three bedrooms, huge bay windows and porches, ornate fish scale siding and unusually attractive gables overseeing the yard. Other features that make this building unique are the three fireplaces, including the main one in the dining room constructed of Italian marble, the library on the main floor and high ceilings.

The Smiths sold the house and surrounding property in 1895 to Miss Kitty Meridith for $3,000. For unknown reasons, Miss Meridith was unable or unwilling to pay her taxes, so the property was sold at auction by the sheriff to Major Hart from San Antonio. Miss Meridith protested the sale and hired an attorney, who recovered the house and property for her. Months later it was discovered that the foreclosure was performed when Miss Meridith was a minor. The fact that Miss Meridith was also a minor when she bought the house was not considered a significant issue.

Dr. R. H. Preston Wright bought the home from Miss Meridith and spent several years there raising seven children. He was not only regarded as an outstanding civic leader, but also an exceptional host who held elaborate parties. His eldest daughter eventually married Coke R. Stevenson, who served as governor of Texas from 1941 to 1947.

In 1905 a Kerrville businessman, D. H. Comparette, purchased the home, and several generations of his family lived there for the next 72 years. During this time the family had the open porches on both floors enclosed to create more living space. Comparette was responsible for setting up the Kerrville Telephone Company, which he managed until his death in 1952. Bonnie Summers then bought the property and made extensive renovations before opening the house again as the Yellow Ribbon Restaurant.

The current owners, Raymond and Becky Cumpian, bought the restaurant after the name had been changed to Joe's Jefferson Street Café. The house has changed very little over the past 112 years, and a visit is truly stepping back into Texas history.

Joe's Jefferson Street Café, 1001 Jefferson Street, Kerrville, Texas 78028, (830) 257-2929, is open Monday to Friday for lunch from 11 a.m. to 2 p.m., while dinner is served Monday through Saturday from 5 p.m. to 9 p.m.

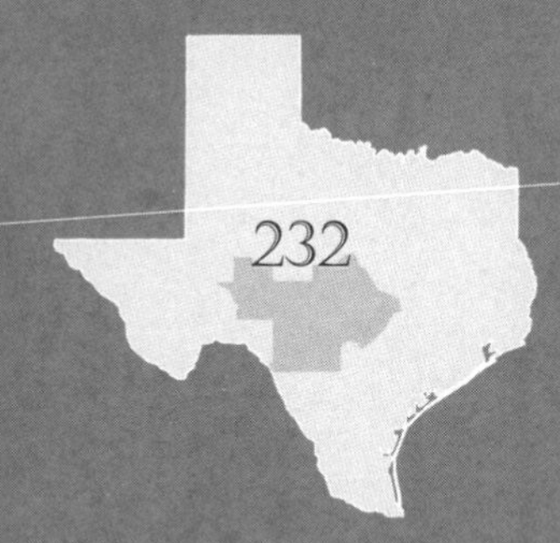

Salmon Oscar

1 fillet of salmon, 8 ounce
1/4 cup fresh crabmeat
4 asparagus spears
hollandaise sauce (recipe follows)

HOLLANDAISE SAUCE:

1 ounce cider vinegar
2 ounces water
1/4 teaspoon Tabasco sauce
4 to 6 egg yolks
1 pint warm clarified butter
1 tablespoon lemon juice
salt and pepper, to taste

Grill the salmon. Boil the asparagus spears and arrange on a plate with the salmon. Cover the salmon with crabmeat. Top with hollandaise sauce.

HOLLANDAISE SAUCE:

Combine vinegar and water, reduce by half. Add egg yolks. Whip over steaming water until yolks ribbon. Gradually add clarified butter, whipping consistently. Add the lemon juice and Tabasco, and adjust with salt and pepper.

YIELD

Serves 1.

Broccoli-Rice Casserole

1–2 bunches fresh broccoli flowerets
2 cups onion, chopped small
4 cups fresh mushrooms, sliced
1 cup water
1 can cream of mushroom soup
2 cups cheddar cheese, grated
1/2 box golden Velveeta cheese, cubed
salt and white pepper to taste
dash Louisiana Hot Sauce
6 cups rice, cooked
8 ounces water chestnuts
oil for sauté

Sauté broccoli with onion. When the broccoli turns bright green, add fresh mushrooms and water and steam for 5 minutes. Add cream of mushroom soup, cheddar cheese, golden Velveeta cheese, salt, pepper and hot sauce. Add cooked rice and water chestnuts. Mix well and serve.

Serves 6.

3-Cities of Spain Cheesecake

GRAHAM CRACKER CRUST:

Mix and line pie pan. For chocolate decadence, add 2 tablespoons of cocoa to mix.

FILLING:

Cream together sugar and cheese. Add eggs and vanilla, and then mix well. Pour into pie shell and bake at 325 degrees for one hour. Let cool for 15 minutes and add topping (recipe follows). After topping is added, cook an additional 15 minutes.

TOPPING:

Mix all ingredients well.

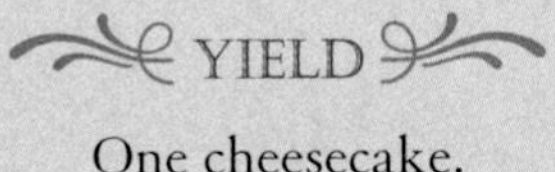

One cheesecake.

GRAHAM CRACKER CRUST:

2 cups graham crackers

1 cup sugar

1/2 cup butter

FILLING:

24 ounces cream cheese

1 cup sugar

5 eggs

2 tablespoons vanilla

TOPPING:

2 cups sour cream

2 tablespoons sugar

2 tablespoons vanilla

THE OLD PECAN STREET CAFÉ

Austin

The Old Pecan Street Café first opened its doors at 314 East 6th (Pecan) Street. This small structure was built around the turn of the century by Oliver Brush, son of S. B. Brush, who built and operated the St. Charles Hotel next door.

Over the years the various tenants have been saloon keepers, Chinese laundries, barbers, shoemakers, saw filers and a drugstore, until 1972, when the Café became the latest occupant.

In 1978 they moved the main dining room and kitchen to 310 East 6th (Pecan) Street. This building was erected by J. W. Simpson in 1905 for his new hardware store. The limestone rubble walls of this structure were originally part of the Radcliffe Platt Livery dating back to 1872.

In the old days Pecan Street was second only to Congress Avenue in cultural and economic importance. It was the center for cigar manufacturers, entertainment establishments, civic halls, fine hotels and restaurants.

The tenants have varied greatly over the years, yet along with the charming architecture of a bygone era, the spirit, quality and color of this street remain a lively and unique part of Austin.

The Old Pecan Street Café is located at 310 East 6th (Pecan) Street, Austin, Texas 78701. It is open from 11 a.m. until 10 p.m. daily and Friday and Saturday until midnight. Sundays from 9 a.m. to 3 p.m. Call (512) 478-2491 for more information. Catering menus and party facilities are also available.

Chicken Poppicotti

Pound rough side of chicken flat with a meat tenderizer. Set aside. Thoroughly blend all other ingredients except spinach. Add spinach and mix slightly.

Stuff breast with mixture and fold over. Sauté each side for 2 minutes, then finish in the oven for 8 minutes at 350 degrees.

Serves 4.

4 double chicken breasts

12 ounces cream cheese

3 ounces cottage cheese

1 ounce Parmesan cheese

1 ounce ricotta cheese

1/2 teaspoon granulated garlic

2 pinches white pepper

4 ounces fresh spinach

THE SALT LICK

Driftwood

Take a deep breath and inhale the aroma of some of the best BBQ the Hill Country has to offer. You've found "The Salt Lick," so named by Hisako Roberts and her husband, the late Thurman Roberts, because "a salt lick is something where all the animals congregate. There is something good, something essential about it."

Family reunions provided them the opportunity to gather and share family BBQ recipes that had been handed down from generation to generation since the Civil War. Their meals were such a success, friends encouraged them to start their own restaurant.

The stones of the building were quarried from their ranch. Everything was done by them with their own hands—building and cooking with care and love, a pride in quality and a job done right.

This is by far one of the most interesting dining adventures that Texas has to offer.

The Salt Lick is about 40 minutes from Austin, Texas on FM 1826. The mailing address is P.O. Box 311, Driftwood, Texas 78619. It is open daily from 11 a.m. to 10 p.m. and the web site is www.saltlickbbq.com The restaurant is reached at (512) 858-4959. They offer a mail-order catalog by calling (888) 725-8542 or shop online at www.saltlickbbq.com. It is a way to enjoy their dinners or smoked meats and sauces all year long.

Following is a recipe used at The Salt Lick, originally from Miz Roxie, Scott Roberts' grandmother and mother of Thurman Roberts.

Blackberry Cobbler

Prepare filling and top crust as directed at right. Preheat oven to 425 degrees. For filling, toss together sugar, flour, cinnamon, nutmeg, lemon peel, lemon juice, salt and blackberries. Place filling in a 9 1/2-inch by 1/2-inch deep pie plate: dot with butter or margarine. Top with crust. Bake 50 minutes or until golden brown.

TOP CRUST:

In medium bowl with fork, lightly stir together flour and salt. With pastry blender or two knives used scissor fashion, cut in shortening until mixture resembles coarse crumbs. Sprinkle in cold water, a tablespoon at a time, mixing lightly with a fork after each addition until pastry just holds together.

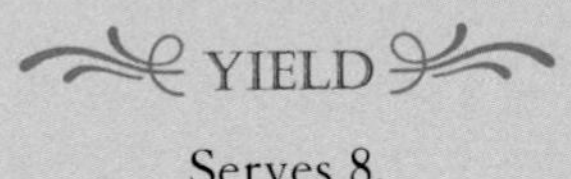

Serves 8.

2/3 cup sugar

1/4 cup flour

1/2 teaspoon ground cinnamon

1/4 teaspoon ground nutmeg

1/2 teaspoon grated lemon peel

2 teaspoons lemon juice

1/8 teaspoon salt

6 cups blackberries

1 tablespoon butter or margarine

Top Crust (recipe follows)

TOP CRUST:

1 cup flour

1/2 teaspoon salt

1/4 cup plus 2 tablespoons shortening

2 to 3 tablespoons water

SCHOLZ GARTEN

Austin

August Scholz (1825–1891), a German immigrant and confederate veteran, built his public bar and café in 1866 over an old boarding house, the year following the end of the Civil War. Mr. Scholz purchased the building and surrounding property in 1862 from Sam Norville for $2,400. Scholz Garten soon became a favorite meeting place for the German population in and around Austin for many of their social activities and German food.

The Biergarten and other rooms were added as the need arose. Mr. Scholz operated his unique tavern and café until his death in 1891. His stepson operated the little bar and restaurant for two more years, then sold Scholz Garten to the Lemp Brewery Company (Falstaff Beer) in 1893, the same year that the University of Texas football team had its undefeated season. Since the university was only two blocks away, the team celebrated its victories at The Garten. Celebrating is just one of the traditions that is still alive here at Scholz Garten.

In 1908 a German singing club, The Austin Saengerrunde (translated: singer-round) purchased the restaurant and bar from the Lemp Brewery and built a six-lane bowling alley near the Biergarten boundaries. It is still in operation today. The Saengerrunde still owns Scholz Garten but leases the bar and restaurant operation.

Undaunted by prohibition Scholz Garten came up with a non-alcoholic brew in 1921 and called it Bone Dry Beer. Food sales became, for obvious reasons, more important and the menu items began to include more regional and traditional Texas favorites. Food sales increased significantly and have continued to be a staple of the business. Good food also became a Scholz Garten tradition. Be sure to take a look at the very large photo on display at the bar taken during prohibition.

Scholz Garten is one of the few establishments that fortunately don't change too much, but when it has, the public seems to make quite a big deal about it. In 1962 Bob Bales, Scholz's operator, decided to do some remodeling and even add, heaven forbid, air conditioning. Bob reported he was almost "run out of town," but the Bales family continued to operate The Garten for 30 more years.

The 1966 Texas Legislature honored Scholz Garten in House Resolution #68 as a gathering place for Texans of discernment, taste, culture and erudition, epitomizing the finest tradition of magnificent German heritage in our state.

The current proprietors, Tom and Liz Davis, emphasize the good food, cold beer, good conversation and good music while you visit Scholz's. As they say, "You probably deserve it."

Scholz Garten, 1607 San Jacinto Boulevard, Austin, Texas 78723, (512) 474-1958 is on the web at www.scholtz@texas.net. The hours are Monday through Saturday from 11 a.m. to 10 p.m. On Thursday, Friday and Saturday they often stay open later if everyone is having fun and someone doesn't want to go home yet.

Guinness Float

In a frosty pint glass add two scoops of vanilla ice cream, then fill with draft Guinness Stout. Serve with two straws (so you can share with a friend).

Snake Bite

In a frosty pint glass pour equal amounts of Harp (an Irish Lager) and Woodchuck Cider (American draft cider) . . . yummy!

YIELD

Serves 1.

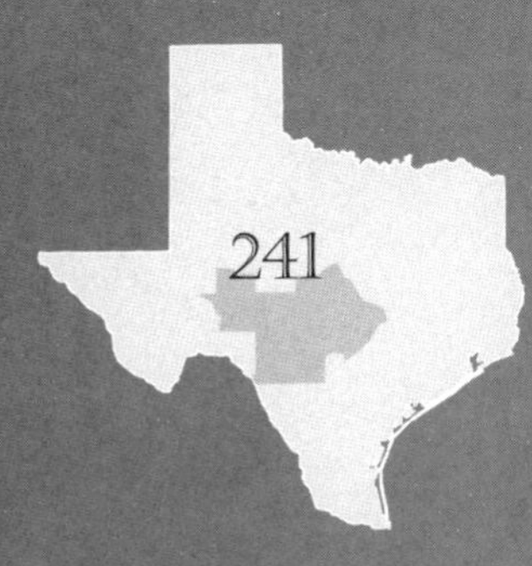

King Ranch Chicken
(a favorite with our lunch crowd)

2 onions, diced
2 bell peppers, diced
1 cup jalapenos, diced
3/4 pound margarine
1 cup flour
2 tablespoons chicken base
5 pounds smoked chicken meat
1 gallon water, boiling
6–8 corn tortillas

Sauté onions, bell pepper, jalapeno and margarine. Add flour and mix well. In a separate pot bring 1 gallon of water to a boil. Add chicken base and return to a boil. Pour boiling water (carefully) into the flour mixture, lower heat and stir until thick and bubbly. Add smoked chicken meat.

Layer a 9 × 13-inch baking pan alternately with the sauce and corn tortillas. Bake in 375-degree oven for 15–20 minutes.

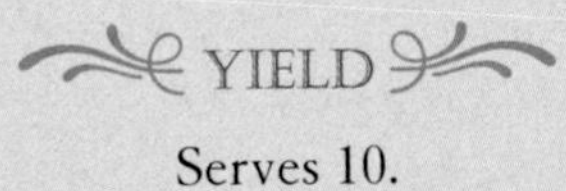

Serves 10.

STAGECOACH INN

Salado

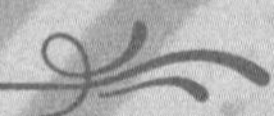

For centuries, this delightful spot had been a campground for tribes hunting the herds of buffalo and other wild game attracted to the mineral water springs. The Spanish traveled through and gave this area the name Salado and in the 1860s W. B. Armstrong, one of the area's first settlers, completed the Old Inn where patrons dine today on the site of an old Tonkawa Indian Village.

The Inn was known as the "Shady Villa," a welcome sight for travelers then and now. It stood at the crossroads of the famous Chisholm Trail and Old Military Road that linked a chain of forts. Its sweeping porch balconies shaded by ancient trees provided comfort for stagecoach travelers, cattle barons, soldiers and countless others. Many famous persons found food and rest inside these walls. Sam Houston slept here and made a major, anti-secession speech from the balcony. General George Custer was a guest shortly after the Civil War. Captain Robert E. Lee, son of the general, passed through Salado as the U.S. Army chased after Pancho Villa.

Salado was a major stop along the Chisholm Trail for cattle barons such as Shanghai Pierce and Charles Goodnight. Many infamous people found shelter here as well, like the James Brothers and Sam Bass. In the wilder days, the cave next to the Inn was reputed to have been used as a hideout for guests not wishing their presence known. Names of these famous people and many more were on the hotel guest register that was stolen in 1944.

The Inn was purchased and restored in the early 1940s by Ruth and Dion Van Bibber. Mrs. Van Bibber created and prepared the famous Stagecoach recipes served today while Mr. Van Bibber hosted with an old-world charm. The waitresses still recite the menu just as was done in the old days when the local housewives would greet the stagecoach or cattle drive with the daily bill of fare. In 1959 Mrs. Van Bibber's nephew, William E. Bratton, purchased the Inn and added room accommodations, meeting facilities, a private club and coffee shop as well as developing the grounds with walking trails, a fishing pond, swimming pools, a heated mineral water spa and tennis courts.

Ownership of the Inn has recently passed to Morris Foster, a native of Salado, who continues the traditions of hospitality and good food that the Inn has been famous for. Vacationers from all over agree that the Indians and the early settlers knew what they were doing when they stopped to rest at Salado.

The Stagecoach Inn, Main Street in the heart of Historic Salado, Texas 76571. The Inn is open daily from 11 a.m. to 4 p.m. and again from 5 p.m. to 9 p.m. Call (800) 732-8994 or (254) 947-9400.

Hush Puppies

- 4 1/2 cups water
- 8 tablespoons margarine
- 3 1/2 cups corn meal
- 3/4 teaspoon baking powder
- 2 teaspoons salt
- 2 tablespoons sugar

Put water and margarine in a pot. Bring to a boil. Place other ingredients together in a mixing bowl and mix well. While water is boiling, pour the dry ingredients into pot, stirring constantly.

Turn off heat as soon as dry ingredients are added. Stir and mix well. Let cool and roll into small log or cylinder shapes.

15–20 hush puppies.

2 cups hot water

8 tablespoons margarine

2 ounces semi-sweet chocolate

10 ounces evaporated milk

2 1/2 cups sugar

3/4 cup flour

1/4 teaspoon salt

1 tablespoon vanilla

2 cups pecans

1 pie shell, uncooked

Fudge Pecan Pie

Combine milk, water, margarine and chocolate and heat. Then add sugar, flour, salt, pecans and vanilla, stirring as necessary.

Pour into uncooked pie shell. Bake at 350 degrees for 35 minutes.

YIELD

One pie.

WALBURG RESTAURANT

Walburg

The Walburg Mercantile building was built in 1882 by Mr. Hy Doering. The original use of the building was as a mercantile market supplying the surrounding farming community with dry goods. Mr. Doering was born in Walburg, Germany, migrating to America as a young man. Upon his arrival in America he purchased many acres in the Walburg area. He built the Walburg Bank, Walburg Mercantile, his home and several barns, naming the town after his birthplace in Germany. He encouraged fellow German immigrants to settle in the area by selling land to them.

To carry on this old-world tradition, two German immigrants have united to bring you a truly authentic German experience in dining and entertainment for over 15 years. European-trained Master Chef Herbert Schwab of Weiden, Germany, awaits your whims of appetite in the kitchen. There he will be applying his masterful culinary skills, which have been featured on *The Eyes of Texas*, *Deep in the Heart of Texas*, *Southern Living*, *Texas Monthly* and *Texas Highways*. His fare has also been sampled by Texas Governor Bill Clements, as well as movie stars Robert Urich, Jane Seymour, Robert Duvall and John Travolta.

Meanwhile you will be entertained by well-known yodeler and accordionist Ron Tippelt from Munich. With his personality and skills as a musician, Ron has become a favorite live entertainer and recording artist, yodeling his way into the hearts of Texans for the last 17 years. Ron and his band, The Walburg Boys, have performed in such places as The Taj Mahal in New Jersey; New Ulm, Minnesota; Wurstfest in New Braunfels and the Munich Oktoberfest, as well as other places all across the United States.

So, welcome to the Walburg Restaurant. Be adventurous and try something new. Enjoy their wide selection of imported beers and wines. Take a stroll to the converted cotton gin that serves as the biergarten. Sit under the canopy of oaks and let the live entertainment surround you. They hope you enjoy your visit to Walburg, and feel that you will take a little bit of Bavaria home with you.

The Walburg Restaurant, four miles off I-35 at exit 268 on CR 972 or mailing address at Box 508, Walburg, Texas 78623. It is closed Mondays and Tuesdays. Open on Wednesdays, Thursdays and Sundays noon to 9 p.m. Fridays it is open from noon until midnight. Saturday hours are 5 p.m. until midnight. Call (512) 863-8440 for more information.

Pork Roast

- 2 pounds boneless pork shoulder
- spices (salt, pepper, marjoram, garlic, caraway seeds)
- 1 cup onions, chopped
- 1 cup soft tomatoes, chopped
- 1 cup celery, chopped
- 1 cup carrots, chopped

Bind roast with string. Rub on spices. Add onions, tomatoes, carrots and celery. Place in oven and bake at 350 degrees for 30 minutes. Baste regularly. Thicken the broth with flour and serve.

YIELD

Serves 6.

Sauerkraut

- 1 slice bacon, diced
- 1 small onion, diced
- 14 ounces sauerkraut
- 2 cups beef stock
- 1 teaspoon caraway seeds
- 2 bay leaves
- 5 juniper berries
- sugar, salt and pepper to taste

Dice some bacon and onions and sauté. Add all remaining ingredients and simmer for 1/2 hour.

Serves 2.

Potato Dumplings

- 1 pound cooked potatoes
- 3 1/2 ounces potato starch
- 1 large egg
- 1/2 teaspoon salt
- 1/2 teaspoon nutmeg
- 1 cup mushrooms, minced
- 12 croutons

Mix potatoes, potato starch, mushrooms and spices with the egg into a dough. Form a ball with the dough in your hands, placing a crouton in the middle, and place in boiling water. (Keeping hands wet will prevent dough from sticking.) Reduce heat and simmer 2 minutes.

12 dumplings.

WILDFIRE RESTAURANT

Georgetown

The two buildings that now house the Wildfire Restaurant were originally constructed circa 1920 on the site where the City Hotel stood in the late 1890s. Their history is as varied as the history of American business itself. Over the past 80-plus years, these walls have housed a clothing store, a Piggly Wiggly Grocery, Peasley's Meat Market, Lawhon & Anderson Air Conditioning and Electrical, a Sears and Roebuck Catalog Store and then business offices. More recently, it was a ladies' apparel and gift shop until the current owners, Cynthia Behling and her brother, Bill Cox, opened the Wildfire Restaurant. Subsequently, they also opened the Lockett Banquet Facility in the nearby M. B. Lockett Building that was constructed circa 1890. Both locations offer private dining room accommodations for groups, while the Wildfire is a regular walk-in restaurant.

While it may seem unique to have two historic buildings still standing and in use in close proximity, in Georgetown it is the rule rather than the exception. Once home to roving bands of Tonkawa Indians and meeting site to Sam Houston and his governing peers, Georgetown's history is as interesting as it is varied. Situated on the Chisholm Trail along the edge of the gently rolling hill country just north of Austin, Georgetown was formally established more than 150 years ago. The year was 1848. Washington Anderson and a crew of men were charged with selecting the site for a new county seat. While relaxing under a large shade tree, Anderson's cousin and major landowner, George Washington Glasscock, Sr., rode up. Anderson volunteered a quick solution to his problem and said, "George, if you'll give us all the land between here and the San Gabriel River, we'll make this the county seat and name it after you." His cousin promptly agreed, donating 173 acres to create what is now Georgetown.

Known for its fastidiously preserved past, Georgetown is now a town of 30,000. Victorian-era downtown storefronts, antique streetlights and brick walks line its shaded downtown streets. More than 180 National Register Historic homes and buildings showcase its eclectic blend of past and present. Popular attractions, lively festivals and numerous waterside parks lend a special sense of adventure to Georgetown's charm. From the Historic Courthouse Square, to the Belford District full of turn-of-the-century homes, to the University district that encompasses Texas's oldest university,

Southwestern University, Georgetown offers a "Sunday buffet" every day to history buffs. Visit Georgetown in December for the "It's a Wonderful Life" Christmas Stroll, and you will discover "the way Christmas is supposed to be."

The Wildfire Restaurant, 812 South Austin Avenue, Georgetown, Texas 78626, (512) 869-3473, or visit www.wildfire.com. Open from 11 a.m. to 10 p.m. Monday through Saturday and 10 a.m. to 9 p.m. on Sundays. Reservations are accepted.

Red Poppy Raspberry Frozen Margarita

- 1 1/4 ounce gold tequila
- 1 ounce Chambourd liqueur
- 1/2 ounce Cointreau
- 1 cup raspberries
- 1 cup simple syrup (sugar water)
- 1 cup lime juice, freshly squeezed
- 2 cups ice

For sugar water: Bring 1 cup of water to a boil. Dissolve 1 cup of sugar in it, remove from heat and let cool. Combine all ingredients in a blender. Blend. Slowly add additional ice cubes until desired consistency is achieved.

This drink is especially popular during Georgetown's annual Red Poppy Festival in April.

YIELD

4 eight-ounce drinks.

Hill Country Peach Chutney

- 12 cups fresh peaches, sliced and peeled
- 4 1/2 cups dark brown sugar (2 pounds)
- 2 cups apple cider vinegar
- 5 cups Granny Smith apples, diced and peeled
- 2 cups raisins
- 1/2 cup red onion, minced
- 2 tablespoons lemon zest
- 1/3 cup lemon juice, freshly squeezed
- 1 tablespoon mustard seed
- 2 teaspoons ground ginger
- 2 teaspoons ground cumin
- 1 teaspoon paprika

Mix peaches, sugar and vinegar. Cook remaining ingredients, covered, over medium heat for 10 minutes. Stir frequently. Add peach mixture and bring to a boil. Boil gently, uncovered, 30 minutes or until slightly thickened.

Can be served hot or cold.

YIELD

Eight pints.

6

Panhandle Plains

The Plains. This area is comprised of big skies, great plains, rich canyons and sweeping sunsets. Ranches with flowing rivers often interrupt the mesas. The Palo Duro Canyon, second only to the Grand Canyon in size, is near Amarillo. In 1876 John Adair and Charles Goodnight founded the JA Ranch, and it is still a great place to see real cowboys at work. Many dude ranches abound and a thriving viticulture industry is evolving. Cities include Abilene, Lubbock, Amarillo, San Angelo and Wichita Falls.

MISS HATTIE'S CAFÉ & SALOON

San Angelo

Ken Gunter, owner and proprietor of Miss Hattie's Café & Saloon, was born and raised in San Angelo and is best known for his love of historic properties. Ken's Father, E. C. Gunter, owned and operated the Gunter Company from the early 1930s to the late 1970s in the building that currently is the Cox Cable office.

In 1977 Ken bought the building that today houses Miss Hattie's Café and Saloon. This building, one of the earliest permanent buildings in San Angelo, was built during the economic boom of the 1880s and was the original San Angelo National Bank building. It was restored and registered in 1981 on both the national and state level, as an historic landmark. The tin ceiling is the original one from the San Angelo Bank era. The brick walls in the restaurant are also from the original bank building, as are the rock walls in the bar and the room next to the bar. The original façade is still intact.

The room called the side room in the restaurant was built in 1885 and was run as a grocery store. The original building had a metal roof and is one of the few 1880s commercial structures designed by Oscar Fuffini. The cast-iron cornice with pediment was reproduced in fiberglass from historic photographic evidence. Ken also bought and restored the building that now houses J. Wilde's. Built in 1886, it was also designed by Oscar Fuffini and was originally a clothing and dry goods store.

Miss Hattie's original business was hospitality. Serving not only the thriving business community of San Angelo, but also the soldiers at Fort Concho, Miss Hattie found great pleasure in entertaining her clients. She believed that if she created a place that was intimate, private and romantic, no one could resist what she offered. Miss Hattie never pretended to be anything other than what she was—a great hostess. Miss Hattie's Bordello Museum is located nearby in downtown San Angelo.

Strategically located at the confluence of the North and Middle Concho Rivers in 1867, Fort Concho served for 22 years as home for U.S. Army forces involved in frontier peacekeeping. During its active life, cavalry and infantry units and all four regiments of black soldiers, known respectfully by their Indian enemies as Buffalo Soldiers, occupied Fort Concho. Today, it is recognized as the best preserved Indian Wars fort because of extensive restoration efforts during the last three decades. In its modern role, Fort Concho not only houses frontier-life exhibits, but also serves as the stage for special events throughout the year. Several of the 23 original and restored buildings are furnished with original antiques and exact replicas of items used when the fort was active.

Miss Hattie's Café and Saloon, 26 E. Concho Avenue, San Angelo, Texas 76903. Call (915) 653-0570. The restaurant is open Monday through Thursday from 11 a.m. until 9 p.m. Friday and Saturday it is open from 11 a.m. until 10 p.m.

Chicken and Corn Fritters

2 cups frozen corn, thawed

1/2 red pepper, diced

1/2 poblano pepper, diced

4 breasts cooked chicken, diced

2 tablespoons Cajun seasoning

1/2 yellow onion, diced

1 1/2 cups green chilies, chopped

1/2 quart beer batter (waffle mix with beer added as the liquid)

Roasted Red Pepper Sauce (recipe follows)

ROASTED RED PEPPER SAUCE:

3 red peppers, seeded and roasted

1 quart heavy cream

1/4 yellow onion, pureed

1 clove garlic

1 tablespoon chicken base

1/4 teaspoon cumin

roux to thicken

salt to taste

Put all ingredients except batter in a bowl and mix. Add the batter and mix everything together. Thicken with flour if needed. Cook like pancakes and serve over Roasted Red Pepper Sauce.

ROASTED RED PEPPER SAUCE:

When red peppers are roasted, the skin peels off nicely. Remove the seeds and puree. Place the onion, garlic, chicken base and cumin in a blender and puree. Place the heavy cream in a cooking pot on the stove and bring to a boil. As it starts to boil, add all the other ingredients. Use roux to thicken if necessary and salt to taste.

Serves 8.

Chicken del Rio

1 breast chicken (6 ounces)

1/2 cup seasoned flour

1 slice bacon, cooked, finely chopped

1/2 cup Cheddar cheese, grated

4 ounces tomatillo sauce

1/2 cup sour cream

Dredge chicken breast in seasoned flour. Grill to 170 degrees. Top chicken with bacon and cheese and place in an oven long enough to melt the cheese.

Lace tomatillo sauce on plate. Put chicken on sauce and paint with sour cream.

Serves 1.

NEON SPUR

Wichita Falls

Betty Young lived around the corner from the old Riverside Grocery and Meat Market building, at 200 North Burnett Street in Wichita Falls, Texas. She always passed the store on her way downtown, to tend to the bills. She could rarely afford the bus fare both ways and would walk back to her home at day's end. She always made sure to point out the staircase that flanked the left side of the old building that John Upton built in 1925. The wood staircase led to four boarding rooms with a single bathroom at the entry to the second floor. "Those boarding rooms up there," Betty Young would always say to her young nephew "are where Bonnie and Clyde used to stay when they would come to Wichita Falls."

She would also mention the arrangement that Bonnie Parker and Clyde Barrow were rumored to have with local lawmen. The local law would never cause the two criminals trouble while in town, if they promised to not cause any trouble while visiting this town. The only question seemed to be, when did they visit?

The most likely, or at least the most notable, may have been just prior to the violent death of the dangerous duo, in 1934. Bonnie and Clyde rescued a member of the gang from Huntsville Prison, named Raymond Hamilton. In the gun battle that ensued, Clyde took a bullet and would need a hideout, somewhere quiet to recover. Bonnie went home, for the last time, to see her mother.

Raymond Hamilton had a girlfriend in Wichita Falls named Mary O'Dare. The Bungalow Tourist Park almost surrounded the grocery store with campsites, mobile homes and cabins. It was known to be a hangout for the gang on occasion, but this time was different. Clyde would need somewhere quiet and being above a market would have made it easy to get the supplies needed to recover.

The boarding rooms above the store would have been the most likely answer to Clyde's dilemma. It is also rumored that these rooms at one time were available for rent by the hour and included a companion. It is said that lawmen and gangsters alike frequented the bordello located above the store.

Of course, we will never know exactly what decision Clyde made that day, because the hunted outlaw and the Alabama-born grocery store owner have both long since passed into history. So has Betty Young, but if you had asked her where Clyde decided to stay she would have pointed to the rooms above the old grocery store.

Although the old store/bordello has long since been closed, the signage painted on the building still shows. Many people still stop in what is now the Neon Spur and ask if groceries are available.

Today the building stands much as it did in the early 1900s, but now you can get some of the best barbecue in Texas. The Neon Spur is open Tuesday through Saturday from 11 a.m. until everyone goes home. They offer live music Wednesday through Saturday on an outdoor stage surrounded by a large, outdoor dining area, weather permitting. Ice cold drinks are served from a large, octagon-shaped bar with a huge oak tree growing in the middle. They also have an indoor dining area for those who would rather dine in.

The Neon Spur is located across from the Bridwell Agriculture Building, which is part of the large Multi-Purpose Event Center. They also provide event planning and host many family and class reunions and company parties.

The Neon Spur, 200 North Burnett, Wichita Falls, TX 76306. Call (940) 723-2720, or visit www.neonspur.com. They are open Tuesday through Saturday from 11 a.m. until 2 a.m. If everyone goes home early, they will too. They are closed Sunday and Monday.

Quesadillas

One of the favorites of regular customers.

- 8 flour tortillas
- 24 ounces cheddar cheese
- 24 ounces Monterey Jack cheese
- 2 pounds smoked brisket
- dash Mexican seasoning (the seasoning is shaken on)
- 24 ounces sour cream
- 24 ounces salsa or BBQ sauce

Load a flour tortilla with about 3 ounces each of cheddar and Monterey Jack cheese. Then add your favorite smoked brisket, shredding it over the cheese. Shake on a dash of our special Mexican seasoning. Fold tortilla in half and grill in a skillet or on a pancake griddle until it's crispy. Serve it with sour cream and salsa or barbecue sauce.

YIELD

Serves 8.

Neon Spur Chili Pie

This is served in wintertime only.

- 4 pounds chili meat, chopped
- 3 1/2 ounces chili powder
- 1 ounce paprika
- 1 ounce cumin
- 1/2 ounce black pepper
- 1 ounce chicken bouillon
- 4 cloves garlic, crushed
- 1 large onion, chopped
- 16 ounces tomato sauce
- 16 ounces water
- 8 servings corn chips
- grated cheese and onion, for garnish

Brown course-chopped chili meat, and then add all dry seasonings. Sauté for about ten minutes. Then stir in remaining liquid ingredients. Heat to slow simmer stirring often for about one hour or until meat is tender. Serve over a large bowl of corn chips. Add grated cheese and onion if desired.

Serves 8–10.

Texas Torpedoes

This is an item not served on our regular menu, but used for special occasions and parties. They are a bit labor intensive, but worth the effort. Everyone we have served them to loves them.

Start with fresh jalapenos and slice in half lengthwise, removing seeds and vein. Cut chicken into 12 large bite-size pieces. Cut bacon slices in half. Cross the bacon with a piece of chicken in center, half jalapeno on top filled with cream cheese and next a pineapple chunk. Wrap the bacon over the top of the stack and secure with a toothpick.

Smoke over a hickory fire at 225 degrees for about 1 hour, then finish off on the open grill brushing with BBQ sauce and serve. If you do not have a smoker you can simply cook until done over an open-flame grill. Do not apply sauce until they are done. Then simply baste the sauce on.

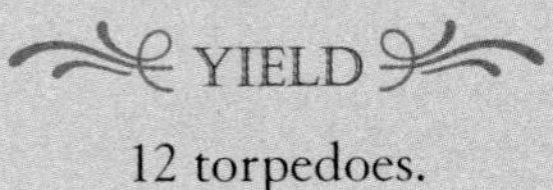

12 torpedoes.

- 6 fresh jalapenos
- 12 slices bacon, thick sliced
- 2 breasts chicken, boneless
- 14 ounces pineapple chunks
- 8 ounces cream cheese
- 12 ounces BBQ sauce

7

Big Bend Country

The Great Southwest. Various archaeological, geological, biological and ecological dimensions comprise this expansive land. Colorful mountains and an untamed paradise are part of the western region. The conquistadors wrote stories about the region and explained the rugged areas and courage of the inhabitants. Movies such as *Lonesome Dove*, *Texas* and *Dancer* have been filmed in the region. The native Apache, Comanche and Tigua tribes lived in Big Bend. Later, the Spanish and frontier cattle ranchers also chose to live here. Pancho Villa, Judge Roy Bean and Hallie Stillwell loved and tamed this wild country. El Paso, Del Rio, Alpine, Marathon, Odessa and Fort Davis are all part of Big Bend.

THE BARN DOOR STEAKHOUSE

Odessa

The Pecos Depot was built in 1892 in the town then called Pecos City. The depot was purchased from the Panhandle–Santa Fe Railway, which was closing the Pecos, Texas, station in 1972. The depot served as the terminal for an 89-mile short line from the Pecos Valley for Northeastern Railway Company. It ran north to Carlsbad, New Mexico, and from there to Clovis, New Mexico, where it connected with the Santa Fe. The railroad was built with private capital by two men who had extensive agriculture holdings in the rich Pecos Valley, James John Hagerman and Charles Bishop Eddy. A town in New Mexico bears Hagerman's name, and the county of which Carlsbad is the seat of government is named Eddy.

The Pecos Depot is filled with railroad relics gathered with painstaking care over a period of more than a year from antique dealers and collectors in Texas, New Mexico and Colorado. At center stage is the mahogany, maple and cherry wood bar. The entire 20-foot-long serving bar top is one solid piece of mahogany made from a single tree. The brass and bronze fixtures, doorknobs, hinges and side lamps on the back bar are the original ornaments.

According to early records the bar was delivered to the Garcia family in the hamlet of Mora in the ragged mountains of northern New Mexico territory in 1900. The manufacturer, The Brunswick Company, made the delivery over the steep and treacherous terrain using flatbed wagons pulled by mule teams. The bar was retired from active service about 1950 and consigned to a storage shed where it remained until resurrected in 1973 to grace The Pecos Depot.

The Barn Door Steakhouse was added to The Pecos Depot and opened its doors in May of 1963, under the ownership of Frank Green. Nancy and Bill Massey purchased it in April of 1994. They remodeled The Barn Door, giving it a more modern appearance but still keeping the original atmosphere. Now the Masseys, partnering with Roy Gillean, continue the fine tradition for which The Barn Door is known. The Barn Door, the downstairs of the Depot and the private rooms upstairs in the Depot that used to serve as their offices, now seat 338 diners. Their adjacent facility, known as the South Forty, serves special functions up to 500 people with the same great food served buffet style.

The Barn Door Steakhouse, 2140 Andrews Highway, Odessa, Texas 79761, (915) 337-4142, is open Monday through Thursday from 11 a.m. to 9:30 p.m., Friday 11 a.m. to 10:30 p.m., Saturday 4 p.m. to 10:30 p.m. and Sunday from 11 a.m. to 3 p.m.

*Exact proportions are guarded secrets, but you can try one at the bar and make your own educated guess.

YIELD

Serves 1.

Amaretto

Cointreu

Bacardi

Southern Comfort

strawberry juice

pineapple juice

THE GAGE HOTEL

Marathon

Alfred Gage left his native Vermont in 1878 and set out to make his fortune in the wide open spaces of far West Texas. Finding work as a cowhand, he and his brothers later founded the Alpine Cattle Company south of Marathon. By 1920 Gage was a prosperous banker and rancher. Needing headquarters for his extensive operations, he employed the acclaimed firm of Trost & Trost to design a hotel. He hired Ponfords and Sons of El Paso to build it.

Opening in 1927, the hotel became a gathering place for many ranchers and miners of the area. Gage, however, was unable to enjoy the success of his hotel. He passed away the year it opened.

After decades of neglect the hotel was purchased by J. P. and Mary Jon Bryan of Houston. Restoration was begun, as well as an expansion of the facilities. The Los Portales rooms were opened in 1992 and Café Cenizo opened in 1996.

The Gage Hotel, 101 Highway 90 West, Marathon, Texas 79842. Call (915) 386-4205 or (800) 884-GAGE or email: welcome@gagehotel.com; or visit www.gagehotel.com. The restaurant is open every morning for breakfast at 7 a.m. On Sunday through Thursday it closes at 10 a.m. and on Friday and Saturday it closes at 11 a.m. They are also open every evening for dinner at 6 p.m. Sunday through Thursday the last reservations are accepted for 8:45 p.m. and on Friday and Saturday the last reservations are accepted for 9:45 p.m.

Portobello Mushroom Enchiladas

SAUCE:

- 1 quart half-and-half
- 1 pound button mushrooms, cleaned
- 14 ounces chipotle chili
- 2–3 teaspoons cornstarch

ENCHILADA:

- 11 1/2 ounce package flour tortillas, regular size
- 4–5 portobello mushrooms
- 1/2 cup mild cheddar cheese, shredded

SAUCE:

Run the chipotle chili through a food processor to get it very finely chopped. Combine first 3 ingredients in a pan and bring to a boil, careful not to scorch the cream. After cooking for a few minutes remove from heat and thicken with cornstarch and set aside.

ENCHILADA:

Remove stems and gills from the mushrooms and slice into strips. Sauté the mushroom in a little bit of butter but not long enough to cook through. Take the sautéed mushroom strips and place them on a tortilla, about 3 per tortilla. Add desired amount of cheese and roll it up. Cut in half.

COOKING:

Take two enchiladas and place on an ovenproof plate with sauce and a little cheese and broil in the oven until heated through. Serve with wild rice, black beans and any steamed vegetable.

Serves 8.

Stuffed Bacon-Wrapped Quail

1 quail
1 serving wild rice
1 slice bacon
fajita seasoning

Take quail and stuff with wild rice (or any other rice that you prefer). Make a small cut in one thigh and slide the other leg through. This will keep the stuffing in the bird. Wrap with one slice of bacon. Next place on greased pan and season with fajita seasoning. Broil in the oven on high heat (500 degrees) turning once after about five minutes. Bird is ready when it is a nice, dark color all around. Serve with steamed vegetables and seasoned potato wedges.

YIELD

Serves 1.

Southwest Beef Tenderloin

5 ounce tenderloin
2 corn tortillas
2 teaspoons BBQ sauce
1 tablespoon Mango Mint Salsa
1 ounce black beans

Cut the tenderloin into a 5-ounce medallion. Cook on open mesquite grill until medium rare. Place on 2 quick-fried, corn tortillas. Next top with BBQ sauce and with Mango Mint Salsa (or any salsa or pico de gallo.) Top with black beans for garnish and serve with steamed vegetables and steak fries.

YIELD

Serves 1.

THE HOLLAND HOTEL

Alpine

The Holland Hotel was constructed in 1912 for John R. Holland, a successful area cattleman. Built in the Spanish colonial revival style, it is situated in downtown Alpine, in West Texas, in the midst of the scenic Davis Mountains of the Big Bend National Park area. Completed during the mercury mining boom days of Alpine, the hotel has been a cultural, social and historic center of the area for decades.

After Holland's death in 1922, the business was managed by his son Clay, who made several additions to the structure. In 1928 an extensive addition was added under the direction of the renowned architectural firm of Trost & Trost, the most famous regional architects of their time. They created the finest hotel between El Paso and San Antonio. The hotel showcases the beautiful Trost & Trost signature peach-colored ceramic tile and beamed ceiling lobby.

Vacant for several years, the building deteriorated badly. In 1973 it was purchased by Gene Hendryx, and extensive repairs were made, including restoration of Spanish architecture. Converted into an office building, The Holland Hotel building again became an asset to the area. In the 1980s the property again changed hands, with the McFarland family continuing the improvements begun in the previous decade. These improvements included renovating a portion of the first floor to accommodate the delightful Bistro Restaurant, the Club Holland and the Rio Grande Room—the most elegant private function room in the Big Bend area. Today, in addition to fine dining, the hotel offers distinctive overnight accommodations featuring marble wet bars and fine antiques.

The Bistro Restaurant features eclectic dining in the grand old lobby of the hotel. With a menu that changes daily, The Bistro offers such delights as fresh oysters on the half-shell, their renowned Hamburger Oscar, as well as homemade quiches and soups. Also offering a fine variety of freshly homemade entrées and the most decadent desserts in West Texas, The Bistro is a welcome respite from the day's labors.

The Holland Hotel has been so important to the town that they named the street after it. Alpine is a community of artists, boasting the best art of West Texas. Twice a year, the whole town opens its doors for the purpose of showcasing the talent of the local artists. People come from far and wide to stroll the streets of Alpine and soak up the creativity that thrives here.

There is much to see and do in the area. A scenic 108 miles south on Texas Highway 118 is the Big Bend National Park along the Rio Grande River. Twenty-six miles north resides historic Fort Davis, while forty miles north is one of the world's most modern telescopes at McDonald Observatory. Yes, there are mountains in Texas, but you have to be in the right part of Texas. And Alpine is. Remember all those scenic vistas from the cowboy movies? Many of them were set in this part of Texas, because that's where much of Western history was made. In fact quite a few westerns were shot right here in the Big Bend. When you drive around the area, you'll see why.

The mountains of the Big Bend have inspired many great Western artists and cowboy poets. They spurred them on to great works. They draw visitors and locals alike to return, time after time, to marvel at the pure gloriousness of the West Texas landscapes. One thing you can count on, the ranches around Alpine are real, working ranches, and when you see a cowboy, he's a real cowboy.

The Holland Hotel, 209 West Holland Avenue, Alpine, Texas 79830, (800) 535-8040, or visit www.hollandhotel.net. The restaurant is open daily from 11 a.m. to 10 p.m.

Fillet Oscar

8-ounce beef fillet, cooked to order
3 ounces hollandaise sauce
3 ounces fresh crabmeat
1 tablespoon butter
2 tablespoons white wine

Prepare beef fillet to customer-requested temperature. Sauté crabmeat in white wine and butter until it begins to fall apart. Heat hollandaise sauce and combine with crab mixture. Pour mixture on top of prepared beef fillet.

Serve with starch and vegetable choice.

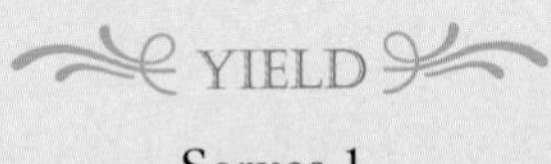

YIELD

Serves 1.

Bread Pudding
with Whiskey Sauce and Raisins

3 cups bread cubes
6 eggs
1 pint half-and-half
2 cups milk
1/4 cup raisins
1 1/2 tablespoons sugar
1 teaspoon vanilla
1 teaspoon cinnamon
1 teaspoon allspice

WHISKEY SAUCE:
1/2 pound butter
1 1/2 teaspoons vanilla
2 cups sugar
2 1/2 ounces bourbon

Place dried bread cubes in a pan sprayed with vegetable oil. Beat eggs. Add all other ingredients and beat well. Pour over bread cubes. If bread isn't completely moistened after 45 minutes, add more milk. Bake until brown and firm or about 1 hour at 375 degrees.

WHISKEY SAUCE:
Melt butter and add other ingredients. Whisk until mixed. Heat each serving with bread pudding.

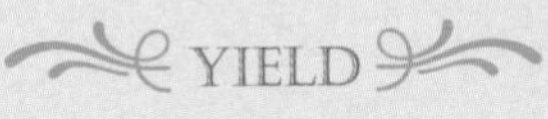

YIELD

Serves 8.

HOTEL LIMPIA

Fort Davis

The Hotel Limpia was named after Limpia Creek, which winds through the valleys of the Davis Mountains. The earliest Mexican settlers called the creek "limpia," meaning clean, referring to its clear water.

The Hotel Limpia was established in 1884 in a small, red brick building one mile north of downtown near the Overland Trail, across from the fort. In the early 1900s, East Texans found the beautiful Davis Mountain region of the state and its incomparable climate. The town became a summer destination.

When the owners of the local Union Trading Company saw a need for a larger, more modern hotel, the current structure was built and opened in 1913 on what would soon become the town square, near the courthouse, across from the bank, next to the Union Mercantile.

The building operated as a hotel until 1953 when a fire destroyed the lobby. Local rancher and civic leader J. C. Duncan purchased the hotel, reconfigured it and immediately leased the first floor to Harvard University for their local astronomy interests. The remainder of the building was remodeled into apartments. By 1978, Duncan felt it was time to convert the building back into a working hotel. Renovations were made and on July 2, 1978, it was rechristened the Hotel Limpia. Modern conveniences including private baths, central heat and air conditioning made rooms more comfortable than ever.

Today the Hotel Limpia is still much the same as it was when lawyers, judges, doctors, politicians and their families came to town to escape the sultry climate to the south and east. The rounded corners, high, metal ceilings and turn-of-the-century ambiance of the hotel remain the same.

J. C. Duncan's son and daughter-in-law, Joe and Lanna, now own and operate the Hotel Limpia. Since taking over in 1991 they have worked to improve the hotel and expand services for guests. In addition to the variety of standard rooms and spacious suites available at the Hotel Limpia complex downtown, guests may choose to stay at one of three guest houses in the older neighborhoods of Fort Davis.

The newly remodeled 1905 Mulhern House opened its doors to guests in 1997. This adobe house, that contains three suites, features a large front porch and a beautiful yard that is shaded by pecan and native fruit trees. From the hammock in the orchard, guests can listen for the white-wing dove in the peace and quiet.

The 1940s Etherige Cottage, a Sleeping Lion Mountain hideaway, is located on three acres that adjoin the Fort Davis National Historic Site property at the top of the mountain. From the patio, guests can enjoy the variety of wildlife and listen for the canyon wren singing from the cliffs. "The Cottage" has been a favorite guest site for years.

The 1903 Dr. Jones's House, the hotel's "Victorian Adobe," has three luxurious suites. It is also tucked up near the edge of Sleeping Lion Mountain on a two-acre property of cedars, junipers and pinion pines. From the fire pit on the back patio, guests can watch the nightly migration of the mule deer through the dry creek bed.

The Hotel Limpia offers Sutler's Club, Inc., a private club and the only watering hole in Jeff Davis County, if you would like to buy a drink. Due to their location in a dry precinct, the Texas Alcoholic Beverage Commission states that anyone who would like to purchase an alcoholic beverage must be a club member.

A one-day temporary membership for four persons is available for $2 while a three-day membership for four persons is $3. Annual memberships are $25 per household. A member may have up to three guests and must purchase all of their guests' beverages. Guests of the Hotel Limpia are complimentary members of "The Club" during their stay.

The Hotel Limpia, P.O. Box 1341, on Main Street on Town Square, Fort Davis, Texas 79734, (915) 426-3237, or (800) 662-5517 or visit www.hotellimpia.com or email diningroom@hotellimpia.com. The dining room is open for lunch Wednesday through Sunday from 11:30 a.m. until 2 p.m. and for dinner every night from 5:30 p.m. to 9:30 p.m. Reservations are necessary.

Creamy Cucumber Dressing

- 8 ounces cream cheese, softened
- 1 3/4 cups mayonnaise
- 2 cucumbers, peeled, shredded and drained
- 2 small green onions, chopped
- 1/2 teaspoon salt
- 1/8 teaspoon paprika
- 1/8 teaspoon pepper
- 4 teaspoons poppy seeds
- 1 teaspoon granulated garlic
- 1 drop green food coloring

Combine cream cheese and mayonnaise in a medium mixing bowl. Add cucumbers and green onion. Mix well. Add seasonings and food coloring. Mix well and chill. Serve as a salad dressing or as a dip with fresh vegetables.

YIELD

1 pint.

Burgundy Marinated Roast Beef

- 2–3 pounds rump roast (or roast of your choice)
- 3 carrots, peeled and sliced in bite-sized pieces
- 1 cup onions, sliced or quartered and separated
- 1 bay leaf
- 1 teaspoon thyme
- 1 teaspoon Lawry's Salt or other seasoned salt
- 2 teaspoons black pepper
- 2 cloves garlic, peeled and chopped
- 1/4 cup Worcestershire sauce
- 1/2 cup red wine
- 4 cups beef broth or bouillon

Place roast in large roasting pan. Add onions and carrots to roast. Cover roast with bay leaf, thyme, Lawry's, pepper and garlic. Add remaining ingredients to roasting pan. Cover. Bake in a 225-degree oven for 5–6 hours or until tender and falls apart with a fork.

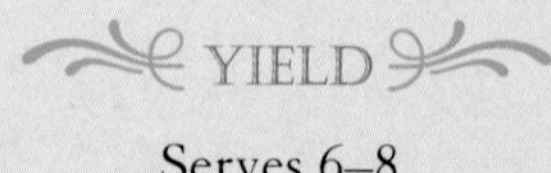
YIELD

Serves 6–8.

INDEX TO RESTAURANTS

INDEX OF RECIPES

APPETIZERS

SALADS AND SALAD DRESSINGS

SOUPS AND STEWS

SIDE DISHES

BREADS AND SPREADS

CAKES AND COOKIES

PIES AND DESSERTS

POTPOURRI

We are working on a second edition of *Recipes from Historic Texas*. For any suggestions to include a favorite historic restaurant, or if you would like to have the authors speak at an event or you want to purchase autographed quantities of this book, contact us at (281) 292-6526 or email bauerandbauer@hotmail.com.